SCHOOL COUNSELING PRINCIPLES

FOUNDATIONS AND BASICS

AMERICAN
SCHOOL
COUNSELOR
ASSOCIATION

MT

1101 King St., Suite 625, Alexandria, VA 22314
(703) 683-ASCA, (800) 306-4722, fax: (703) 683-1619
www.schoolcounselor.org

ISBN 1-929289-06-5

4/24/06

Table of Contents

School Counseling Principles: Foundations and Basics

INTRODUCTION

Parents, teachers, administrators, students, and even school counselors themselves have many different questions that pertain to the nature of school counseling. This is particularly true because the school counseling profession is relatively young and rapidly evolving. Even now, the way that school counseling students are trained and the way in which school counseling is practiced can vary a great deal, even among schools in the same district. Such inconsistency, sometimes caused by simple philosophical disagreements about how school counseling should be practiced, has stifled the way in which we can more effectively and efficiently carry out our primary goal: to help students and families best achieve.

Hence, the primary purpose of this book – to further assist in helping school counselors, school counseling students, educators, administrators and other school counseling stakeholders best converge on the most highly agreed upon responses to common professional questions. A valuable help file, if you will, that can help our stakeholders and us "point all of our arrows in the same direction" to best "meet our mark."

Think about the importance of school counselor training and professional practice being more uniform. When we reduce confusion regarding who school counselors are, who they work with, what they do and how they do it, we stand to benefit in many ways, including:

- School counseling professionals will have more quality information with which to make important decisions (such as resolving ethical dilemmas or deciphering one's duties).

- Researchers will have greater opportunity to design studies, especially comparing school counseling programs across the country, without serious threats of validity and reliability.
- School counselor education programs can provide more uniform training that produces professionals who speak the same language, have similar expectations, and thus can contribute to more fruitful collaborations.
- Professional development, tools and resources can be more easily developed when the target audience (i.e., school counselors) is better understood.
- Administrators and school counseling directors can more accurately evaluate a school counselor's performance and, relatedly, more reliably audit the quality of a comprehensive program.
- Parents, community members and other stakeholders may better support comprehensive school counseling programs when the value of such programs is clarified.
- Parents and teachers can more confidently and appropriately refer children for developmental and other guidance and counseling-related issues.
- Professionals in related disciplines such as school psychologists, social workers, mental heath therapists and family therapists can learn how they may more effectively team with school counselors as part of a comprehensive guidance and counseling program.
- School counselors can be more accountable when they follow more standardized ways of operating.

This book also endeavors to supplement "The ASCA National Model: A Framework for School Counseling Programs" (2005), a landmark document which has helped to create one vision and one voice for school counseling programs. The ASCA National Model® reflects a comprehensive approach to program foundation, delivery, management and accountability. The ASCA National Model provides the mechanism with which school counselors and school counseling teams will design, coordinate, implement, manage and evaluate their programs for students' success. It provides a framework for the program components, the school counselor's role in implementation and the underlying philosophies of leadership, advocacy and systemic change. (Visit www.schoolcounselor.org to access an executive summary).

HOW THE BOOK WAS DEVELOPED

How exactly does one determine the most frequently asked questions (FAQs) about a profession such as school counseling? The answer is simple – just ask. For approximately three years (2002-2004), we surveyed thousands of school counselors, parents, administrators and teachers. We asked them, "What questions do you have about the practice and profession of school counseling?" We posed this question in a variety of places using the following procedures:

- Created a Web page that visitors could use to submit their school counseling-related questions
- E-mailed a request for school counseling FAQs on counseling listservs such as:
  - International Counselor Network (ICN, *listserv.utk.edu/archives/icn.html*)
  - Counselor Education and Supervision Network List (CESNET-L, *listserv.kent.edu/archives/cesnet-l.html*)
- Posted a request on appropriate Internet newsgroups including:
  - Sci.med
  - sci.psychology.psychotherapy
  - sci.psychology.theory
  - sci.psychology.personality
  - sci.psychology.misc
  - pdaxs.services.counseling
  - sci.psychology.psychotherapy
  - soc.org.nonprofit
  - alt.education.distance
  - ucsc.baskin.grad
- Solicited questions at counseling conferences throughout the country (by either attending or sending flyers to the conference coordinator)
- E-mailed a request for FAQs to the accredited programs listed on the Council for Accreditation of Counseling and Related Educational Programs Web site (*www.cacrep.org/directory.html*), including a request to forward the notice to others such as school counseling students
- Included questions posed about school counseling in the relevant professional literature, including professional journals and other publications

The resulting number of questions from which to choose was approximately 450. We collated, sorted, selected based on frequency and then categorized the questions. The resulting 11 categories were: school counseling as a career, collaboration, credentials, ethical and legal issues, guidance and counseling issues, counseling related legislation, school counselor performance, research, school counselor roles and responsibilities, counseling technology, and school counselor training.

Next, it was time to identify expert responders from a variety of backgrounds, including professional school counselors, school counseling students, district level directors, parents, school counselor educators (professors), professionals from related professions, state and national association leaders, state consultants, and even a lobbyist. We identified responders as professionals having appropriate expertise through topical searches of professional literature, the World Wide Web, school counseling conference programs throughout the country and my own contact list. We developed a database of experts and invited their participation in this endeavor.

Finally, as the responses came in, it was time to assemble them into the compilation you see today. The goal of this book is to serve as a ready reference for advancing our common understanding of prevalent school counseling inquiries. The hope is that, as we speak more with one vision and one voice, people within the profession and throughout the public will better know school counseling and more effectively become part of comprehensive school counseling programs.

We hope that you enjoy reading this unique compilation of wisdom as much as we did putting it together. Let's agree to continue sharing our vision of school counseling at professional meetings, conferences, presentations and online (such as via e-mail, listservs, blogs or other media). And, in the process, our rapidly evolving profession is certain will discover more questions to tackle by future generations of experts.

REFERENCES AND RESOURCES

American School Counselor Association. (2005). *The ASCA national model: A framework for school counseling programs, second edition.* Alexandria, VA: Author.

School Counseling as a Career

The profession of school counseling is growing, changing and will continue to be a viable prospect for those interested in helping children and their families. According to the "Occupational Outlook Handbook" published by the U.S. Department of Labor Bureau of Labor Statistics, overall employment of counselors is expected to grow faster than the average for all occupations through 2012, and job opportunities should be very good because there are usually more job openings than graduates of counseling programs. In addition, numerous job openings will occur as many counselors retire or leave the profession.

This chapter addresses common questions about school counselor preparation, the difference between a school counselor and mental health counselor, and predictions for how the profession will change in the upcoming years. In addition, one contributor clarifies several myths about school counseling. Finally, this chapter provides answers to questions about various aspects of professional school counseling as a career and characteristics of effective school counselors.

ASCA has developed role statements for each of the levels of school counseling (elementary, middle and secondary), which include the rationale excerpted here:

Elementary school years set the tone for developing the knowledge, attitudes and skill necessary for children to become healthy, competent and confident learners. Through a comprehensive developmental school counseling program, counselors work as a team with the school staff, parents and the community to create a caring climate and atmosphere. By providing education, prevention, early identification and intervention, school counselors can help all children can achieve academic success. The professional elementary school counselor holds a master's degree and required state certification in school counseling. Maintaining certification includes on-going professional development to stay current with education reform and challenges facing today's students. Professional association membership enhances the school counselor's knowledge and effectiveness.

Middle school students are characterized by rapid physical growth, curiosity about their world and an emerging self-identity. Through a comprehensive developmental school counseling program, counselors work as a team member with school staff, parents and the community to create a caring, supportive climate and atmosphere whereby young adolescents can achieve academic success. Middle school counselors enhance the learning process and promote academic achievement. School counseling programs are essential for students to achieve optimal personal growth, acquire positive social skills and values, set appropriate career goals and realize full academic potential to become productive, contributing members of the world community. The professional middle school counselor holds a master's degree and required state certification in school counseling. Maintaining certification includes on-going professional development to stay current with education reform and challenges facing today's students. Professional association membership is encouraged as it enhances the school counselor's knowledge and effectiveness.

High school years are full of growth, promise, excitement, frustration, disappointment and hope. It is the time when students begin to discover what the future holds for them. Secondary school counselors enhance the learning process and promote academic achievement. School counseling programs are essential for students to achieve optimal personal growth, acquire positive social skills and values, set appropriate career goals and realize full academic potential to become productive, contributing members of the world community. The professional high school counselor holds a master's degree and required state certification in school counseling. Maintaining certification includes ongoing professional development to stay current with educational reform and challenges facing today's students. Professional association membership is encouraged as it enhances the school counselor's knowledge and effectiveness.

REFERENCES AND RESOURCES

American School Counselor Association
  www.schoolcounselor.org

Department of Labor Bureau of Labor Statistics Occupational Outlook Handbook, "Counselors" entry bls.gov/oco/ocos067.htm

How long does it take to become a school counselor?

Reid Stevens, Counselor Educator
University of Southern Maine in Gorham
Gorham, Maine
stevens@usm.maine.edu

It typically takes students about two to three years of full-time graduate study to become eligible for entry into the field at the master's level. Different states have different requirements, but a master's degree is a definite preference.

Typically most of one's credit hours are completed in traditional classroom settings; however, about a third of training should be conducted via practica and internship experiences (work with real clients in school settings).

The U.S. has many school counselor training programs. To find a quality program, however, look for one that is accredited by the Council on the Accreditation of Counseling and Related Educational Programs.

REFERENCES AND RESOURCES

American Counseling Association
www.counseling.org

American School Counselor Association
www.schoolcounselor.org

Council on the Accreditation of Counseling
and Related Educational Programs
www.counseling.org/cacrep

How might the role of the school counselor change in the next 20 years?

Reese House, Program Specialist
The Education Trust
Washington, D.C.
rhouse@edtrust.org

In the next 20 years, school counselors will transform their work to become key players in the success of all students in schools. They will do this by connecting their work to the mission of schools – academic achievement – and design their work in schools to support all students in successfully achieving high academic standards. School counselors will provide proactive, focused assistance to get students into rigorous curricula and support them in overcoming the barriers to success facing all students.

More specifically, counselors who work in schools as advocates and change agents ensure educational equity for all their students. They can do this by practicing in collaborative ways with other professionals in the school building to influence system-wide changes. These changes affect whole schools as well as individual students and can have a profound effect on student achievement. Working in this way, school counselors will:

- Influence attitudes and beliefs regarding all groups of students' abilities to achieve high standards
- Improve access and success in rigorous academic courses for under-represented students
- Provide attention to equity, access, instructional programs and support services
- Manage resources designed to improve the learning success for students experiencing difficulty with rigorous academic programs
- Develop high aspirations in students rather than just attending to aspirations as they emerge
- Influence systemic change so that practices and procedures support student achievement for all groups of students
- Function in schools as social justice advocates and system change agents

With this model, school counselors' work will be driven by a vision of access and equity for all students. No students will be denied the opportunity to be successful in school because school counselors are constantly working as members of the leadership team of the school and advocating for opportunities that enhance success. This means not working for the status quo and not defending practices that are not working for students. Instead, school counselors will be voicing their concerns about policies that prevent some students from access and opportunity.

In 2024, school counselors working in this model will design data-driven programs in schools that show results for all students. Accountability will be a cornerstone of the program, and the advocacy, leadership, teaming and collaboration skills will drive the work. Underlying principles also include a commitment to diversity and inclusiveness of all students.

Implications for school counselors working as key players in school success are widespread:

- Since school counselors 20 years from now will be integrally involved in creating strategies for success for all students, they will no longer be assigned inappropriate duties in schools.
- Students will benefit from the high expectations for all students that are now evident in every school.
- The entire school community will benefit from the technological competence that school counselors use to access and use data to show results and communicate the effectiveness of their work to all stakeholders.
- When school counselors aggressively perform actions that support a quality education for all groups of students, they create a school climate where access and support for rigorous preparation is expected.
- Students not served well in the past will have a chance to acquire the skills necessary to participate unconditionally in the 21st century economy.

These efforts move school counseling from the periphery of school business to a position front and center in constructing student success.

Clarence Johnson, Consultant
San Juan Capistrano, Calif.
cdjohnson2@cox.net

In an attempt to draw a picture of what school counselors might be doing in 2025, it is helpful to identify a few of the current trends that affect our lives and schools. Many of the trends are precursors of what is to come:

- Technology will continue to impact classroom instruction, home-school communication, parental involvement in their students' learning and career decisions, and life in general. The current way to keep student records and classroom placement will change.
- The number of virtual high schools and colleges and universities will continue to increase, bringing both positive and negative results, and affecting counselors' expected results.
- The current national and local push to move school counseling programs from services to results will help lead the school management and leadership to new ways of employing resources.
- A national effort exists to shift school counselor education from the focus on a mental health model to a results-based model advocating individual and program accountability.
- Medical research continues on the brain and body development that affects learning.
- The demographics of our communities are changing, with public schools playing an important role in the establishment of community and becoming the pivotal center for community communication.
- It is also projected by some educators that making career decisions will be moved from the current practice in grades 11 and 12 to grades seven and eight.

Based on these trends, the following is a proposed outline of how 2025 school counseling programs might look.

EDUCATION AND ASSIGNMENT

In 2025, the current structure of how school counselors are educated and assigned will undergo a shift to a more comprehensive student support program approach, which will coordinate the efforts of school counselors, nurses, social workers and psychologists to reach each student. The configuration will use a career ladder or lattice with master counselors who will administer the program and will manage all student support staff in cooperatively planning, implementing and evaluating program efforts.

Based on the trends and research, school counselors will be assigned differently. For example, they might be assigned families rather than specific students, or they may be assigned by grade levels. One condition that seems certain is that there will be a change in school counselors' contributions, which may bring a change of title.

MASTER COUNSELOR

The master counselor will be the administrator of the student support program and will be equal in position to what is currently an assistant principal. The master counselor will have a degree in school counseling and will have specific leadership competencies including personnel performance evaluation. In addition, this leader will have gone through the other counselor levels described below.

COUNSELOR SPECIALISTS

A set of counselor specialists will address specific results and populations. These might include counselor specialists who focus on the following:

- Virtual schools
- Learning skills to ensure that each child has learned how to learn
- Career development to ensure that each student will develop specific skills in career planning and preparation by ninth grade
- Personal development to ensure that each student has basic communication, decision-making and problem-solving skills
- Interpersonal relationships
- School/home/community partnerships

APPRENTICESHIPS

There will a two-year apprenticeship for counselor interns to develop and practice the competencies needed to become specialists.

OUTSOURCING

If the current counseling force does not embrace change to match the changing societal progress, someone other than school counselors will define the new world of school counseling. The world is changing dramatically and rapidly; preparing students to enter that world necessitates a new way of doing business.

As a result, there is the possibility that school counseling will be outsourced (i.e., a company will supply all school counseling for a specific fee). For example, maybe the College Entrance Examination Board will contract to handle all college/university bound students. Or, a computer company will take a contract to do all school and parent career planning. There are numerous options to be examined.

Schools, teaching and administration are all changing; student support programs must become part of and a leader in those changes.

REFERENCES AND RESOURCES

Dimmitt, D. (2003). Transforming school counseling practice through collaboration and the use of data: A study of academic failure in high school. *Professional School Counseling, 6*(5), 340–349.

Fullan, M. (2001). *Leading in a culture of change.* San Francisco: Jossey-Bass.

Hesselbein, F., & Cohen, P. (1999). *Leader to leader.* San Francisco: Jossey-Bass.

Hesselbein, F., Goldsmith, M., & Beckhard, R. (1997). *The organization of the future.* San Francisco: Jossey-Bass.

House, R., & Hayes, R. L. (2002). School counselors: Becoming key players in school reform. *Professional School Counseling, 5,* 249–256.

Johnson, C., Johnson, S., & Hays, D. (2002). *Building stronger school programs: Bringing futuristic approaches into the present.* Greensboro, NC: University of North Carolina. (ERIC Document Reproduction Service No. ED464268)

Paisley, P. O., & McMahon, H. G. (2001). School counseling for the 21st century: Challenges and opportunities. *Professional School Counseling, 5,* 106–115.

Pérusse, R., & Goodnough, G. E. (2004). *Leadership, advocacy, and direct service strategies for professional school counselors.* Belmont, CA: Wadsworth.

Reynolds, S. E., & Hines, P. L. (2001). *Vision-to-action: A step-by-step activity guide for systemic educational reform* (6th ed.). Bloomington, IN: American Student Achievement Institute. Available online at asai.indstate.edu/

What are five myths surrounding school counseling? What is the truth?

Bob Bowman, Consultant
Developmental Resources Inc. and Lighthouse Inc.
Chapin, S.C.
bbowman@sc.rr.com

Myth #1: School counselors provide therapy for students.

The Reality: Some principals, teachers and parents believe that it is inappropriate for counselors to provide individual or small-group therapy with students within the school. Unfortunately, their use of the term "therapy" reflects a basic misunderstanding of what services school counselors actually provide students.

School counselors do not provide therapy or psychotherapy. They do, however, provide several services for students that are therapeutic in nature. For example, counselors meet directly with students individually, in small groups and in classrooms. In these sessions, counselors work with the students on their personal beliefs, perceptions and decisions about social, emotional and academic issues.

Like in psychotherapy, counselors work to establish a therapeutic relationship with students marked with perceptions of caring, acceptance, understanding and trustworthiness. However, unlike psychotherapy, the primary goal of counseling sessions is not to work toward major personality adjustment. Instead, the therapeutic nature of school counseling is intended to help students become more aware of themselves and others, learn coping skills, establish goals and plans of action, and ultimately assist them in becoming more effective and efficient learners. School counselors also use their mental health and educational training to help identify students needing responsive services to help them meet their immediate needs.

Myth #2: School counselors primarily advise and lecture troubled students in an attempt to help "straighten them out."

The Reality: This myth is difficult to dispel. Most helping professionals in western cultures provide quick-fix assistance. For example, many of us grow up with our primary perception of how professional help works, based upon our experiences with medical doctors. Doctors typically work to collect information, diagnose and then prescribe a solution. In fact, most patients would not happily leave an office with their physician without some kind of prescription or advice.

Likewise, many of us have sought guidance from financial counselors and from counselors at law. Unfortunately, the use of the term "counselor" with these professions has resulted in an assumption in the public that school counselors provide a similar approach to helping students.

School counselors can and do sometimes respond to students with specific information and advice. However, this type of help is not always the best way to assist students. Without an adequate exploration of sometimes unseen, underlying factors related to a student's problem, some quick-fix solutions can actually aggravate recurring problems the student may be experiencing.

Counselors are trained in the fact that it sometimes takes patience and time to help students become aware of underlying issues that need to be understood and addressed before long-lasting solutions should be sought and formulated. This patience must also be solicited, at times, from teachers, parents and others who may wonder why the counselor can't help to quickly "straighten the problem out."

Myth #3: Counselors can be called upon to assist in the performance of disciplinary actions with students.

The Reality: School counselors are not disciplinarians. They should never be placed in a position in which they are involved in administering or witnessing the punishment of students. They can, however, be directly involved in working with a student before and/or after a disciplinary action is taken.

For example, school counselors can help to deter student behavior that will lead to disciplinary action through the delivery of the developmental guidance curriculum. They can also work with individual or small groups of students on issues that can help prevent them from behavior that would lead to disciplinary action.

Counselors can also work with students after they have experienced disciplinary action in the school. The effects of discipline without such follow-up can be short-lived. School counselors can help students take personal responsibility for their actions, explore issues and develop a plan to help prevent a recurrence of the situation that led to the disciplinary actions. In this way, school counselors can provide a valuable component to the discipline system in a school, without becoming directly involved in the punitive action.

Myth #4: Counselors should spend most of their time responding to the needs of high achievers or high-risk students.

The Reality: School counselors ensure that their guidance programs reach out to all students, not just to the needs of those that others may identify as needing special support or assistance. Counselors do provide special targeted assistance to students identified as needing specific types of help. However, they also deliver services to every student in the school.

Through classroom guidance, for example, counselors deliver a curriculum for every student in the school. When counselors come to their classrooms, students also gain the opportunity to become familiar with their professional roles. In addition, the various topics counselors address in classroom guidance often lead to an increased number of students' self-referrals to them on issues that might not have been otherwise addressed.

Myth #5: School counselors have more free time than teachers.

The Reality: This perception is familiar, in particular to many school counselors in the first years of their work in a school. Teachers and school administrators are currently feeling more pressure than at any other time in their careers to ensure increased academic gains in students. Their work is often full of pressure to follow a strict time schedule and to maximize every learning moment in their students' school day. As a result, they typically do not feel they have much flexibility to choose how they will spend their time.

On the other hand, teachers see a school counselor who seems to be able to make and follow his or her own schedule each day. It is not surprising that a few teachers become envious of the school counselor's role.

While a school counselor's schedule is more flexible in some ways than that of a teacher, counselors do need to keep some times available daily to allow them to provide a quick response to crises that may occur.

Although flexible, a school counselor's schedule can sometimes feels chaotic. When counselors who were former classroom teachers enter their first practicum in a school, they discover quickly how difficult a counselor's schedule can become. School counselors sometimes have five or more tasks that call for immediate attention. For example, the counselor may be listening to a crying student when a teacher suddenly knocks at the office door, the phone rings, a classroom meeting is forthcoming, and the intercom interrupts with a question from the school secretary.

To be successful, school counselors must learn how to manage these potentially chaotic events they face daily. They must learn to prioritize their tasks and work to develop an understanding from their stakeholders about the many challenges of their actual roles and functions.

REFERENCES AND RESOURCES

American School Counselor Association. (2005). *The ASCA national model: A framework for school counseling programs, second edition*. Alexandria, VA: Author.

Gysbers, N., & Henderson, P. (2000). *Developing and managing your school guidance program* (3rd ed.) Alexandria, VA: American Counseling Association.

Muller-Ackerman, B. (Ed.) (2002). *Public relations toolbox: A practical hands-on approach to promoting a K-12 counseling program*. Chapin, SC: YouthLight.

Myrick, R. D. (2004). *Developmental guidance in schools: A practical approach* (4th ed.). Minneapolis, MN: Educational Media.

Schmidt, J. (2004) *A survival guide for the elementary/middle school counselor* (2nd ed.). San Francisco: Jossey-Bass.

What is the best way to learn more about the amount that different schools/districts pay beginning school counselors?

Dawn Kay, Counseling Coordinator
Utah State Office of Education
Salt Lake City, Utah
dkay@usoe.k12.ut.us

Generally, a professional school counselor will be employed by a school district and assigned to a specific school. Pay for professional school counselors can vary widely from district to district, so beginning school counselor will have to consult each local district where he or she is seeking employment to find out what the base pay might be.

Pay scales for public education vary from district to district because revenues to support the local schools are often tied to property tax values – thus the common belief that "good neighborhoods have good schools." However, even that practice may vary from state to state, so a little comparison survey within any state may be wise.

Many districts do not have a pay scale just for professional school counselors; often they use a teacher pay scale at a master's degree level. Some districts pay counselors for an extended contract, beyond the teacher contract, to allow counselors time for planning before and after the school year. Again, the beginning counselor will need to inquire about these policies to find the district that best suits them.

What is the difference between a school counselor and mental health counselor?

Bill Weikel, Counselor Educator
Florida Gulf Coast University
Fort Myers, Fla.
billweikel@aol.com

School counselors and mental health counselors share a basic philosophy that includes a growth orientation, as well as a belief in the client and power of the relationship, that can be traced back to the work and influence of Carl Rogers. As Palmo (1996) wrote, "The birth of the field of counseling as a separate entity from guidance, psychology and psychiatry can be traced directly to the work of Rogers." In the last 50 years or so, the profession has evolved so that we now have "counselors" whose function can be further defined by describing their work setting such as school, mental health or rehabilitation. The central point is that school counselors and mental health counselors have more in common than may be readily apparent.

SCHOOL COUNSELORS

School counselors traditionally engage in the "three C's" of counseling, consulting and coordinating; however, as the job has evolved, so has the profession. In the school counseling arena, school counselors are more likely these days to be involved in brief interventions and use methods such as brief solution focused therapy, reality therapy or choice theory due to the constraints of time and setting. School counselors manage their limited time (with student loads frequently exceeding 500 students per counselor) while providing guidance, testing and other services mandated by their employers.

MENTAL HEALTH COUNSELORS

Mental health counseling as a profession is a relative newcomer, tracing its roots to the 1960s and its professional identity to 1976 (Brooks and Weikel, 1996). Many of these early counselors were in fact trained to be school counselors and migrated to the newly opened community mental health centers that evolved from the 1963 Community Mental Health Centers Act (Brooks and Weikel, 1996).

Thus, a new profession was born. As much as ASCA nurtured the development of the profession of school counseling, the American Mental Health Counselors (AMHCA) promoted and defined the profession of mental health counseling. These days, thanks in a large part to AMHCA, mental health counselors are well prepared and fully licensed by most states. They are also eligible for national certification and reimbursement by many third-party health programs.

Generally speaking, mental health counselors have the time to engage in more in-depth interventions and tackle problems that the school counselor would be likely to refer due to time constraints. Mental health counselors frequently work with groups, couples and families, helping them adapt to personal concerns, overcome environmental barriers and facilitate self-understanding and personal growth (Palmo, 1996). In addition, mental health counselors, depending on their particular work setting, are more likely than school counselors to be part on an interdisciplinary mental health care team.

The school counselor, on the other hand, may have 100 seniors needing financial aid forms, 100 juniors preparing for the PSATs, 20 students needing an interest inventory, 10 parents in the front office waiting to discuss their child's grades and a dozen kids in serious trouble whom they are doing their best to see every week for counseling intervention.

As those numbers swell and more students need long-term intervention for serious problems that would overextend the time available for any school counselor, the mental health counselor, whether in public or private practice, is a viable referral source and one who speaks the same core language as a school counselor.

REFERENCES AND RESOURCES

Brooks, D. K., & Weikel, W. J. (1996). Mental health counseling: The first twenty years. In W. J. Weikel & A. J. Palmo (Eds.), *Foundations of mental health counseling* (pp. 5–29). Springfield, IL: Charles C Thomas.

Palmo, A. J. (1996). Professional identity of the mental health counselor. In W. J. Weikel & A. J. Palmo (Eds.), *Foundations of mental health counseling* (pp. 51–69). Springfield, IL: Charles C Thomas.

What's the difference between a school counselor and guidance counselor?

Pam Paisley, Counselor Educator
University of Georgia
Athens, Ga.
ppaisley@coe.uga.edu

The difference in the two terms reflects the evolution of this specialty of the counseling profession. The histories of both the profession and the specialty are well-grounded in the concept of guidance. As the specialty has evolved, however, distinctions in terminology have been drawn at both the macro and micro levels.

GUIDANCE COUNSELORS

Gysbers and Henderson (2000) defined guidance as a program that is comprehensive, developmental and collaborative, and the professionally certified school counselor as a central member of the collaborative team involved in delivering the program. From this perspective, the distinctions in terminology support the conceptual move from a focus on person or position delivering a set of services to a program promoting development across domains in a systematic manner.

In addition, guidance is also often thought of as a process of leading or directing another or of providing information. Counseling tends to be associated with a set of professional activities and processes using a variety of approaches. While guidance defines one part of the set of activities that might be a part of a comprehensive program, the term guidance counselor is considered somewhat dated and limited in describing the current role and function of a school counselor. It has been associated with more directive and stereotypical notions of services usually focused on educational and career planning.

SCHOOL COUNSELORS

Professional school counselors, on the other hand, are typically master's level practitioners who are actively involved in developing and managing a program to enhance academic success and promote career preparedness and social/emotional development for students in K-12 schools. They function as both counselors and educators within the school setting. In addition to the traditional roles of counseling and coordination, today's professional school counselors serve as educational leaders, advocates and team builders. They also use data to determine program priorities and evaluate outcomes.

ASCA uses the term professional school counselor to identify the person who plans, manages and evaluates the school counseling program; participates in site-based planning and implementation; and builds partnerships with other stakeholders. ASCA sees professional school counselors as indispensable partners with other educators to assist in the development of the next generation of contributing members of society.

REFERENCES AND RESOURCES

American School Counselor Association
    www.schoolcounselor.org

Erford, B. T. (2003). *Transforming the school counseling profession.* Upper Saddle River, NJ: Merrill Prentice Hall.

Gysbers, N. C., & Henderson, N. C. (2000). *Developing and managing your school guidance program.* Alexandria, VA: American Counseling Association.

Myrick, R. D. (2003). *Developmental guidance and counseling: A practical approach* (4th ed.). Minneapolis, MN: Educational Media.

Collaboration

Collaboration is a process in which a human service professional assists a consultee with a work- or care taking-related problem with a client or client system, with the goal of helping both the consultee and the client or client system in some specified way (Dougherty, 2000).

School counselors collaborate with all stakeholders, both inside and outside the school system, to develop and implement responsive educational programs that support the achievement of the identified goals for every student. School counselors build effective teams by encouraging genuine collaboration among all school staff to work toward the common goals of equity, access and academic success for every student. This may include collecting and analyzing data to identify needed changes in the educational program.

Further, school counselors create effective working relationships among students, professional and support staff, parents or guardians and community members. By understanding and appreciating the contributions others make in educating all children, school counselors build a sense of community within the school, which serves as a platform from which to advocate for every student.

In addition, school counselors are a vital resource to parents or guardians, educators and the community agencies. Offering parent or guardian education, information and training in the community, school counselors are essential partners who enhance the educational opportunities of students and their families (ASCA, 2004).

This chapter addresses questions on how school counselors collaborate with important others such as administrators, community members, counselor educators, school nurses, parents and teachers.

REFERENCES AND RESOURCES

American School Counselor Association. (2004). *Ethical standards for school counselors*. Alexandria, VA: Author. Available online at www.schoolcounselor.org/

Dougherty, A. M. (2000). *Psychological consultation and collaboration in school and community settings* (3rd ed). Pacific Grove, CA: Brooks/Cole.

How can school counselors and administrators best collaborate?

Tom Valesky, Counselor Educator
Florida Gulf Coast University
Fort Myers, Fla.
tvalesky@fgcu.edu

Effective administrators work collaboratively with school counselors, and they understand the importance of using counselors as key school leaders.

LEADERSHIP ROLE OF SCHOOL COUNSELORS

School leadership teams take many forms, but most often they are only composed of principals and assistant principals who meet to analyze data (from anecdotal incidents to specific quantitative and qualitative data) and identify ways to implement school-wide goals and objectives. Hopefully, these goals and objectives were determined by input and decision-making structures that involved all stakeholders. Regardless or these overall organizational patterns, counselors should be considered key members of the leadership team (as should key teacher leaders).

Why should school counselors be on the school's leadership team? Counselors work from many perspectives with students (personal/social, academic, career), thus providing the leadership team with a unique, broad view of student needs. The resulting collaboration has tremendous potential.

Unfortunately, administrators often have limited knowledge, or perhaps a biased view, of the roles and function of school counselors, and they don't see school counselors as vital to school effectiveness. Therefore, they do not integrate counselors into effective school-wide decision-making teams.

Similarly, school counselors do not always understand the entire gestalt of school leadership; that is, they do not have a system's perspective of the organization. In order to make this collaborative relationship work, the school counselor and the principal need to understand each other's roles and responsibilities.

ADMINISTRATOR RESPONSIBILITIES

So, what should school administrators know and do to ensure effective collaborative teamwork? First and foremost, administrators must educate themselves about the job responsibilities of school counselors. The best sources of information that contains current best practices and research-based information are ASCA and the American Counseling Association.

The ASCA National Standards indicate that counselors facilitate student development in three broad domains:

- Academic development
- Career development
- Personal/social development

School administrators need to familiarize themselves with these standards and discuss them with the counselors. In addition to the ASCA standards, school administrators should become familiar with their own state standards and requirements for school counselors. The first place to start might be the national and state Web sites for these organizations.

Once administrators understand the counseling curriculum, they can collaborate on how to hold counselors accountable for implementing a counseling curriculum that helps meet overall school objectives. They should also work together to determine the specific data that will show how counselors implement the counseling curriculum, including how they contribute to improved school climate and student achievement.

SCHOOL COUNSELOR RESPONSIBILITIES

At the same time, school counselors need to educate themselves about the roles and responsibilities of school administrators. A good place to start would be to become familiar with school administrator national standards.

Initially developed by the Interstate School Leaders Licensure Consortium (ISLLC), the national standards for school administrators are being integrated into national accreditation of university programs by the National Policy Board on Educational Administration (NPBEA) and the Educational Leadership Constituent Council (ELCC). Referred to as either ISLLC or ELCC standards, these national standards have been adopted by many states or integrated into existing state standards.

Example areas in which school counselors can collaborate with school administrators are the following, as identified by ASCA:

- School climate
- Academic support interventions
- Behavioral management plans
- School-wide needs assessments
- Data sharing and results
- Student assistance
- Team development

When including counselors on the leadership team, administrators must respect the school counselor's time to implement the counseling curriculum by using counselors to assist in team decision-making, rather than key implementers of decisions, unless appropriate to the counseling curriculum.

Working together and developing strong relationships, administrators and counselors can learn about, respect and support each others' roles and responsibilities. Together, they can identify those tasks that will provide the students with the best chances for success.

REFERENCES AND RESOURCES

American School Counselor Association
    www.schoolcounselor.org

The Interstate Consortium of School Leadership
    www.ccsso.org/projects/Interstate_Consortium_on_School_Leadership/

National Policy Board for Educational Administration. (2002). *Standards for advanced programs in educational leadership for principals, superintendents, curriculum directors, and supervisors.* Alexandria, VA: Author. Available online at www.npbea.org/ELCC/ ELCCStandards%20_5-02.pdf

Owens, R. (2004). *Organizational behavior in education: Adaptive leadership and school reform* (8th ed.). Boston: Allyn & Bacon.

How can school counselors and counselor educators best collaborate?

Toni Tollerud, Counselor Educator
Northern Illinois University
Dekalb, Ill.
tollerud@niu.edu

School counselors enter the field leaving their training program where most of them have been inundated by ideas, perceptions, teachings and views from the counselor educators who have taught them. However, for many school counselors there is a radical shift that occurs when they enter the school counselor world and realize that their teachers and mentors did not prepare them as well as they had thought. The new school counselor's lofty expectations are burdened by the daily surge of school counseling issues, such as:

- Role confusion among professionals in the school
- Lack of advocacy from administrators and teachers for school counselors
- Overwhelmingly high student to counselor ratios
- High demand for noncounseling-related activities
- Students who also do not buy into the role of school counselor as developmental specialist

Collaboration between counselors and counselor educators would go a long way in helping counselors address these issues.

RECONNECT POST-GRADUATION

As our graduates enter the field, I believe it is up to the counselor educator to reconnect after graduation to establish a different relationship, not as mentors or teachers, but as collaborators around the most pressing word for the field today ... advocacy. I often talk about how much I despised the word "political" and that no one ever taught me to be political in my training programs. And yet, that is exactly where I believe my most important calling lies if I am to assist in the promotion and emulation of the professional school counselor.

The model that I was trained in during the 1980s is not the model I teach today. So I must not only revise what I teach, but listen to those I have trained and sent into the field about the best ways to reach the goal that every child deserves to have a professional and effective school counselor in his or her life.

ADVOCATE FOR THE PROFESSION

So the theme I believe as essential in collaboration is to join together as advocates for our profession. By doing so, both are forced to realistically address the role of the school counselor in the school and to address what needs to change in order to effectively reach children. From my experience this includes time management, strategies that help students grow and change, readjusting attitudes of administrators, teachers, parents and students themselves, and the integration of school counseling outcomes into the core of the school program.

As partners in this collaboration of advocacy certain obstacles can be overcome and change instituted. Here are some specific suggestions. The key is working together and having the counselor educator go into the school as an expert and advocate for change on behalf of the school counselors.

School Advocacy
At the school level, school counselors and counselor educators can collaborate on program development and improvement. The school counselor can identify a need for consultation and request that counselor educators be hired to work with the counseling program. Because of their neutral position, the counselor educator is able to enter the school as the outside expert, take the pressure off school counselors who are enthusiastic about change in the current program but who may have not power, and substantiate the need for program redesign based on state and national standards as well as best practices.

Once money is earmarked for program development, more attention is given to the task from administrators and even the counselors themselves. At the school level, counselor educators help school counselors to:

- Assess current programs
- Identify strengths and gaps
- Provide ideas collaboratively that result in program change and redesign, including the development of a needs assessment.

Counselor educators, as the outside professionals, then herald the work of the school counselors for the change they are making and bridge that work with administrators and teachers. This might involve leading an in-service or assisting in a presentation to the school board.

Minimally, it results in a written document that parallels the components of the ASCA National Model® including curriculum development, needs assessment, evaluation tools, mission statement, and student and program written goals.

State and Regional Advocacy
Counselor educators can also collaborate around advocacy at the regional and state level on behalf of the school counselors. Administrators want their school counselors in their buildings serving the needs of students. Therefore, few school counselor professionals are able to be in strategic positions to write legislation, speak to administrators and state leaders, write newsletters, serve on important committees, or do professional development.

Counselor educators can and must provide the leadership that will result in new laws, mandates, grants, and state and national programs. When school counselors are able to step up and become involved, they need to know that the counselor educators will stand at their sides and take up the slack when they must stay in their school buildings. University professionals may also be seen as experts in speaking to state legislative committees and persuading legislators to vote for bills that advocate for school counselors and their programs.

BE AN ONGOING RESOURCE

Finally, I believe that school counselors must know that the counselor educators are a resource available to them when they become discouraged or are faced with issues in their schools that may seem unfair or insurmountable. Counselors may believe they have little power to make things different, but our counsel and support may assist the school counselor to act and advocate for the changes sought in their school district. With collaboration, this change can occur.

Teesue Fields, Counselor Educator
Indiana University Southeast
New Albany, Ind.
thfields@ius.edu

School counselors and counselor educators have a great deal to offer each other, and their collaboration can make the profession of school counseling stronger. Myrick (1997) proposes that school counselors who deal with the everyday problems of schools have the opportunity to offer a dose of realism to the counselor educator, while the counselor educator through observations and insights can help the school counselor gain some perspective and a new way to approach entrenched problems.

Using the lenses of reality and perspective, there are a number of ways in which school counselors and counselor educators can establish effective partnerships, both in the schools and at the university. These partnerships can include such activities as research and grants, consultation, program planning and fieldwork experiences.

RESEARCH AND GRANTS

By working together to identify areas that need to be researched and providing the real world laboratory to conduct the research, school counselors and counselor educators can better ensure that the techniques and approaches that school counselors use and counselor educators teach are proven to be effective.

For instance, counselors at a Minneapolis middle school teamed up with counselor educators and graduate students at the University of Minnesota to develop a practical approach to violence prevention by interviewing middle school students and using them at the intervention experts (Skovholt, Cognetta, Ye, & King, 1997). The resulting program was one that was tailored to a specific school environment and student population.

Increasingly, state departments of education like to see partnerships between K-12 schools and the university when they award grants to investigate or evaluate new educational approaches. This is a win-win situation for both partners because the grant money allows school counselors to have materials and resources they could not otherwise afford, and the grant allows counselor educators to have support for their own research or for that of their graduate students.

CONSULTATION

School counselors often do not have time to research the latest counseling techniques or new program approaches to problems. This can mean being stuck in what is familiar even when the old approach no longer works. Counselor educators often have more access to library resources and are expected to spend time keeping up with journals in the field.

By using local counselor educators as consultants, the practicing school counselor can gain some new insight into problems and receive training in new techniques. Counselor educators often collaborate with local school systems to provide training to groups of counselors or may be available by e-mail or phone for consultation. Such consultation also forces the counselor educator to stay current and be aware new problems that emerge in the field.

PROGRAM PLANNING

School counselors are often trained in individual and group counseling approaches to interventions. However, the ASCA National Model asks school counselors to examine the disaggregated data for their school and identify those groups who are not achieving to high standards (ASCA, 2003). This requires a program approach to school-based prevention and intervention programs. Often such large group approaches take an extensive effort, and the school counselor can use the expertise of counselor educators in designing appropriate interventions. Counselor educators are valuable people to be on the advisory council for a school counseling program or even on the school improvement committee.

In a similar way, school counselors can be valuable members of the advisory councils for university counseling programs or for the advisory groups of schools of education. By participating in the program planning for each group, the programs enrich each other's programs with their expertise.

FIELDWORK EXPERIENCES

Although fieldwork is supposed to help the counseling student bridge the gap between the ideal world of the university and the real world of the school, often school counseling fieldwork experiences have remained clinic-based and not closely related to the world of the K-12 school. Even when the fieldwork has been in the school, sometimes the student is only practicing individual and group counseling based on a clinic model, rather than the multitude of skills required of the school counselor.

The Transforming School Counseling Initiative of The Education Trust advocates the collaboration between practicing school counselors and counselor educators in designing fieldwork experiences so that they can be truly representative of the training needs of school counselors (The Education Trust, 1997). For example, the school counseling program at the University of Nevada at Las Vegas transformed its clinic-based practicum into a school-based practicum with the help of local school counselors (Coker & Schrader, 2004) that resulted in fieldwork with a "richness of experience not previously seen."

School counselors and counselor educators can collaborate in variety of ways to better serve their constituents and to provide high quality educational services. When both parties recognize the gifts of the other, then a true partnership can develop to their mutual benefit.

REFERENCES AND RESOURCES

American School Counselor Association. (2005). *The ASCA national model: A framework for school counseling programs, second edition.* Alexandria, VA: Author.

Coker, K., & Schrader, S. (2004). Conducting a school-based practicum: A collaborative model. *Professional School Counseling, 7*(4), 263–267.

The Education Trust. (1997). *The national transforming school counseling initiative.* Washington, DC: Author.

Gysbers, N. C. (2001). School guidance and counseling in the 21st century: Remember the past into the future. *Professional School Counseling, 5*(2), 96–105.

Lapan, R. T., Gysbers, N. C, & Sun, Y. (1997) The impact of more fully implemented guidance programs on the school experiences of high school students: A statewide *evaluation study. Journal of Counseling and Development, 75*, 292–302.

Paisley, P. O., & McMahon, G. (2001). School counseling for the 21st century: Challenges and opportunities. *Professional School Counseling, 5*(2), 106–114.

Myrick, R. D. (1997). Traveling together on the road ahead. *Professional School Counseling, 1*(1), 4–8.

Skovholt, T., Cognetta, P., Ye, G., & King, L. (2004) Violence prevention strategies of inner-city student experts. *Professional School Counseling, 1*(1), 35–38.

How can school counselors and school nurses best collaborate?

Donna Mazyck, School Nurse
Maryland State Department of Education
Baltimore, Md.
dmazyck@msde.state.md.us

and

Marcia Lathroum, School Guidance and Counseling Specialist
Maryland State Department of Education
Baltimore, Md.
mlathroum@msde.state.us

School counselors and school nurses are part of student support services, which facilitate the emotional, personal, social health and well-being of students to ensure optimal conditions for academic success. School counselors and school nurses share a common purpose: promote a safe and supportive environment for all students and remove barriers to learning.

Overlapping areas in which school counselors and school nurses work with students, staff and parents include the following:

- Attendance
- Attention deficit hyperactivity disorder
- Chronic illness
- Eating disorders
- Home and hospital teaching
- Physical abuse
- Psychosomatic and secondary symptoms
- Sexual abuse
- Teenage pregnancy/parenting
- Victims of harassment

School counselors and school nurses can best collaborate by joining forces to provide support in these areas, rather than debating who owns what area. To the extent that school counselors and nurses operate from the guiding principle of promoting a safe and supportive environment for all students, turf battles are minimized.

PARENT AND COMMUNITY PROGRAMS

The synergistic effect of these two professions collaborating can often reach more students, staff and families than one profession working alone can accomplish. For example, in addressing the issue of eating disorders, school counselors and school nurses can work in partnership to provide parent and community education programs that promote healthy body images (U.S. Department of Health and Human Services, 2000). They can meet with groups of students who want information about health eating and physical activity. Together they can offer teacher workshops or individual sessions on the topic of eating disorders.

PREVENTION PROGRAMS

School counselors and school nurses are an ideal team to plan school-wide and specific group prevention and intervention activities on the topic of bullying and harassment. "Dealing with bullying and harassment in schools requires a team effort involving teachers, administrators, school nurses, students and parents, to create a positive and safe learning environment vital for each student's academic and social growth" (Cavendish & Salomone, 2001, p. 31). As they present educational programs together, school counselors and school nurses offer a unified message to all staff, students and parents. This teamwork helps promote a school culture that does not tolerate harassment and bullying.

SMALL GROUP PROGRAMS

Students experiencing challenging concerns can sometimes benefit from meeting in small groups with students going through similar issues. School counselors and school nurses form an effective partnership when they co-lead topical small groups. In a small group setting, school counselors and school nurses offer a safe place for learning practical skills (such as social skills or decision-making) or working through tough issues (such as grieving losses or parenting).

The benefits of school counselors and school nurses working together are many. As they continue to promote a safe, learning environment by addressing barriers and developing an integrated approach to student support, opportunities for effective outcomes abound. These two professionals can lead the way in mapping available resources for students, staff and families and how best to use them (Center for Mental Health in Schools, 1997).

REFERENCES AND RESOURCES

Cavendish, R., & Salomone, C. (2001). Bullying and sexual harassment in the school setting. *The Journal of School Nursing, 17,* 25–31.

Center for Mental Health in Schools at UCLA. (1997). *Continuing education modules on mental health in schools: New roles for school nurses.* Los Angeles: Author. Available online at smhp.psych.ucla.edu/

U.S. Department of Health and Human Services, Office on Women's Health. (2000). *Bodywise: Eating disorder information for middle school personnel.* Washington, DC: Author. Available online at *www.4woman.gov/BodyImage/Bodywise/bp/nurses.pdf*

How can school counselors and school psychologists best collaborate?

Renee Staton, Counselor Educator
James Madison University
Harrisonburg, Va.
statonar@jmu.edu

The realities of the school day include busy counselors, overextended psychologists and little time for systematic planning. Frequently, collaborative projects between school counselors and school psychologists, if they are offered at all, are planned hurriedly in the hallways as the counselor and psychologist rush to student study meetings. Although the interventions that result from these efforts are often helpful, they usually overlook the dynamic and systemic factors that influence schools, and they fail to acknowledge the unique strengths of both groups of professionals. Therefore, the best way for school counselors and school psychologists to collaborate is to conceptualize collaboration as multi-staged process.

IDENTIFY FEELINGS ABOUT COLLABORATION

The first stage requires the collaborators to identify how they genuinely feel about collaborating. The effectiveness of collaborative intervention is dependent, to some degree, on how committed the professionals are to the collaboration process. The collaborators may be tempted to skip this first stage, believing that expediency or pragmatism demands that they jump to quick solutions. However, building collaborative interventions requires building effective relationships. Taking time to give thoughtful consideration to each person's attitude toward a potential partnership is likely to result in a more honest, effective working relationship.

ARTICULATE NEEDS

The second stage of the process is to articulate specific needs at the student, staff, system and community levels. As the counselor and psychologist identify these needs, they are encouraged to keep in mind the overall mission and annual goals of the school and school system. For instance, the counselor and psychologist may determine that they want to educate parents regarding the benefits of parental involvement in schools. The administration, teachers and community members may be primarily concerned about school violence. The collaborators will likely receive a more welcoming response if their efforts at parental outreach directly address school violence.

PRIORITIZE NEEDS

Keeping an eye on the mission and goals will facilitate the next stage, which is to prioritize needs. One of the benefits of taking a reflective, multi-stage approach to collaboration is that the school counselor and psychologist can look at all levels within the system as potential entry points for their interventions. Then, when they begin to prioritize, the counselor and psychologist can identify issues that affect not only students, but teachers, staff and the overall functioning of the school.

The process of identifying priorities is most effective when the collaborators identify:

- Acute needs, such as responding to specific crises
- Chronic needs, such as school climate concerns or inclusive classroom management
- Existing systemic opportunities for collaboration, such as student study and/or IEP meetings
- Unique skills and interests of the counselor and psychologist

These priorities should suggest the most efficient and viable goals for collaboration.

GAIN SYSTEM SUPPORT

As needs are prioritized, the counselor and psychologist move to the next stage, which is to gain system support. The authority and autonomy of school counselors and psychologists vary depending on their school system and setting, so at this stage the two professionals must work together to model collaborative and systemic thinking and demonstrate the potential effectiveness of multidisciplinary collaboration. The counselor and psychologist at this stage become salespeople, "pitching" the idea that providing time and support for collaborative interventions is worthwhile.

IMPLEMENT THE PROJECT

Finally, the collaborative project is implemented, with both professionals undertaking formative and summative evaluation procedures throughout the process.

In an ideal world school counselors and psychologists would have time at the beginning of each academic year to thoroughly discuss and plan their potential work together. Even in the real world, however, counselors and psychologists can follow the general procedure above by dedicating an occasional hour dedicated to their collaborative ventures. More comprehensive and efficient interventions are likely to result.

REFERENCES AND RESOURCES

American School Counselor Association
www.schoolcounselor.org/

Brown, D., Pryzwansky, W., & Schulte, A. (2001). *Psychological consultation: Introduction to theory and practice* (5th ed.). Boston: Allyn & Bacon.

Dougherty, A. M. (2000). *Psychological consultation and collaboration in school and community settings* (3rd ed.). Belmont, CA: Brooks/Cole.

Gutkin, T. B., & Curtis, M. J. (1998). School-based consultation theory and practice: The art and science of indirect service delivery. In T. B. Gutkin and C. R. Reynolds (Eds.), *The handbook of school psychology* (3rd ed., pp. 598–637). New York: Wiley.

Idol, L., Nevin, A., & Paolucci-Whitcomb, P. (1995). The collaborative consultation model. *Journal of Educational and Psychological Consultation, 6,* 347–361.

National Association of School Psychologists
www.nasponline.org/

How can school counselors and teachers best collaborate?

Nancy Beale, Doctoral Student
Walden University
Colonial Heights, Va.
nancybeale@hotmail.com

Teachers and school counselors work hand-in-hand, sometimes with one dragging the other one along. The relationship you have with your teachers is imperative to the success of your school counseling program. The most effective way to reach and help students is through their teachers. You can work smart and reach more students by nurturing good relationships with all the teachers in your school, through empathy, communication, visibility and flexibility.

UNDERSTAND TEACHERS

To work effectively with your teachers, you must first understand them – what they face, expectations placed on them and what they are balancing (e.g., testing, individual evaluation plans, standards, achievement, discipline, technology, administration and violence in the classroom). Understand your teachers and empathize with them. Take a few minutes each day, if possible, to stop and greet each teacher. By sowing these seeds, you build a sense of security with your teachers. Establish this security further by not emphasizing failure or placing blame when an intervention or plan does not succeed.

FIND TEACHERS' STRENGTHS

Find the individual strengths of your teachers. You achieve results by combining your skills and knowledge with theirs. If you are an organizer-goddess but the teacher's centers look like a war zone, offer to assist with setting up an organized system that the teacher can use. If your teacher creates incredible lesson plans and IEP goals, turn her talents towards a fellow teacher that is struggling with an IEP or daily plans. Capitalize on individual resourcefulness by using your facilitator skills.

ENVISION GOALS

Envision with your teachers an improved student, a well-oiled classroom, an orderly day. Take that picture and brainstorm ideas, solutions and plans that could make that vision happen. Make it a team effort and support each other. It is easy to come up with a list of 10 interventions for a teacher to enact, but it is another thing to support that teacher with manpower, materials and moral support to assist her in making it happen. Don't get discouraged if your first attempts do not work. Reevaluate and reassemble the troops for another attack at the problem.

BUILD COLLABORATION

Counselors are natural communicators and can use these skills to build collaboration in teachers through consistent and effective communication. First, let the staff know what you are doing through a published and posted schedule of your comprehensive counseling program. Post it weekly or monthly in a common area. Add a blurb to the school newsletter and give a brief update at faculty meetings. Teachers like schedules and can use your schedule to find times to collaborate with you and know what services you are providing to their students. It is essential that you communicate, either orally or written, with your teachers on referrals they have made and of your ethical boundaries. Give them the information they need to assist the student, but also give them the understanding of your ethical limits.

BE FLEXIBLE

Be Gumby. Remember the little green guy that was extremely bendable and flexible? That is what counselors need to be. Classroom teachers do not have the schedule flexibility that counselors do, so you may be the one that has to reschedule things so that you can meet with a teacher and/or parent. Teachers have very defined roles and it seems that each minute of their day has a required task to do. The counselor should be the one to make the effort to stop by each teacher for a courtesy hello and to touch base. You may find that the more flexible you are with a teacher in scheduling classroom guidance or group counseling, the more positive and collaborative the relationship. Teachers appreciate when a staff member tries very hard to work with them and for them.

REFERENCES AND RESOURCES

American School Counselor Association Resource Center. Available online at *www.schoolcounselor.org/*

Bender, J. (2003). *Ready...set...go: A practical resource for elementary counselors.* Chaplin, SC: YouthLight.

Brickman, R., & Kirschner, R. (1994). *Dealing with people you can't stand.* New York: McGraw-Hill.

Eby, L., & Schlachter, J. (2003). Get yourself noticed. *ASCA School Counselor,* January/February, 19–21.

Johnson, M., & Semrau, S. (2003). Three sides to a common goal. *ASCA School Counselor,* January/February, 25–29.

Credentials

State-accredited school counselors ensure equitable access to the school counseling program for all students (ASCA, 2004). So, what are the credentials that distinguish the professional school counselor? How can parents be confident in knowing that school counselors are qualified to work with their children? How can school counselors learn more about obtaining multiple certifications or licensure, say in mental health counseling? These questions, and others, are addressed in this chapter.

REFERENCES AND RESOURCES

American School Counselor Association. (2004). *Ethical standards for school counselors.* Alexandria, VA: Author. Available online at www.schoolcounselor.org/

As a parent I wonder, how are school counselors qualified to work with my child?

Lynne Miller, Counselor Educator
Kent State University
Kent, Ohio
lguillot@kent.edu

Parents can take comfort in knowing that school counselors are qualified professionals who are prepared and equipped with the skills necessary to:

- Address students' needs in personal/social, academic and career domains of development
- Meet the unique needs of students at their particular level: elementary, middle or high school

- Collaborate with parents, teachers, school administrators and community leaders to meet the needs of students

To achieve these qualifications, school counselors meet rigorous educational, legislative, credentialing and continuing education standards.

EDUCATIONAL STANDARDS

The vast majority of states and public school systems require that school counselors have a master's degree or a certain number of graduate courses taken in counseling and guidance or a related field. Teaching experience or related experience may also be a requirement for entry-level school counselors.

In addition, counselor preparation commonly includes some form of internship experience that allows school counseling students to practice under the supervision of experienced counselors. These internships may range from 200 to 700 hours of supervised practice in a school setting.

In preparing for the profession, school counselors study many areas relevant to the optimal development of the students that they serve, such as:

- Counseling techniques
- Counseling theories
- Human growth and development
- Group counseling
- Career development
- Crisis intervention
- Coordination of services
- Legal and ethical issues
- Advocacy

LEGISLATIVE STANDARDS

For more than 30 years, all states have had some method to verify that school counselors qualify as professional counselors able to work in a school setting. Criteria standards have been set forth by the state legislatures or other governmental agencies such as the state's department of education (Bradley, 1991). These standards help verify that school counselors have received adequate preparation and training.

CREDENTIALING STANDARDS

All states offer some type of entry-level credentials for school counselors. These credentials have various labels and each label carries with it distinct requirements. Common labels include certification, licensure and endorsement (Lum, 2003). The categories that help establish the credentialing requirements in states include:

- Post-baccalaureate education
- Experience
- Examinations
- Background checks

School counselors may also be required to take an examination prior to entering the profession. The examination may be developed by the university the school counselor attended, the state educational agency, or an outside educational or counseling testing service. National examinations commonly required for school counselors are:

- Praxis I: Pre-Professional Skills Tests
- Praxis II: Specialty Area Exam in School Guidance and Counseling

The information covered on these exams and the exams developed by the university or state educational agency usually includes the skills necessary to be effective school counselors and, in some cases, an evaluation of the testee's skills.

CONTINUING EDUCATION STANDARDS

In addition to meeting educational, legislative and credentialing standards, school counselors may be required to complete continuing education units to renew their certifications or licenses. To gain or increase knowledge in areas that will allow them to meet the diverse and evolving needs of the students, school counselors may:

- Complete additional coursework
- Attend professional development activities
- Attend workshops

To obtain specific information regarding their state's qualifications for school counselors, it would be helpful for parents to contact their school counselor, school district, local university or state's department of education.

REFERENCES AND RESOURCES

American Counseling Association
www.counseling.org

American School Counselor Association
www.schoolcounselor.org

Bradley, F. O. (Ed.). (1991). *Credentialing in counseling.* Alexandria, VA:
American Association for Counseling and Development.

Lum, C. (2003). *A guide to state laws and regulations on professional
school counseling.* Alexandria, VA: American Counseling
Association Office of Public Policy & Legislation. (ERIC Document
Reproduction Service No. ED4741133)

What does a practicing school counselor typically have to do to obtain an additional license in mental health or marriage and family counseling?

Suzan Nolan, Retired School Counselor
Rapid City, S.D.
kensuz5@rap.midco.net

This is a question school counselors often explore, especially in rural areas where the demand for expanded counseling services is great. Many school counselors do get additional licenses, such as the licensed professional counselor (LPC) or licensed professional counselor-mental health (LPC-MH), to expand their services to clients.

While the specific process varies from state to state, the overall process to obtain additional licensing is as follows (based on South Dakota's process):

STEP ONE: GET A MASTER'S DEGREE

To obtain the LPC license, a school counselor would first need to have a master's degree in counseling from a 48-hour master's degree program that is accredited by the Council for Accreditation of Counseling and Related Educational Programs or contains coursework in these specific areas:

- Counseling theory
- Counseling techniques

- Counseling internship
- Human growth and development
- Social and cultural foundations
- Helping relationships
- Group counseling
- Lifestyle and career development
- Individual appraisal
- Research and evaluation
- Professional orientation

STEP TWO: COMPLETE POST-GRADUATE SUPERVISION

The LPC applicant must then receive 2,000 hours of post-graduate supervision from a qualified supervisor. To be qualified to supervise post-graduate work, the supervisor must be one of the following:

- LPC or LPC-MH
- Licensed marriage and family therapist (LMFT)
- Clinical social worker-private independent practice (CSW-PIP)
- Licensed psychologist or psychiatrist

In addition, supervisors must:

- Have had their license for at least three years prior to supervision
- Comply with the ACA Code of Ethics and Standards of Practice

If the candidate is seeking the LMFT license, the only person who can supervise the candidate's work is another LMFT counselor. In addition, the LMFT candidate must have a 48-hour master's degree in marriage and family therapy.

It takes approximately two years for the LPC candidate to get the required 2,000 hours of supervision, which must be clinical experience in the following areas:

- 800 hours of direct client contact
- 1,200 hours of counselor-related activity (anything done directly to address the client's needs, ranging from taking case notes to consulting with another professional)

STEP THREE: OBTAIN NATIONAL CERTIFICATION

The applicant must take and pass the National Counselor Exam, which was written by the National Board of Certified Counselors. The fee for taking the National Counselor Exam is $125.

STEP FOUR: APPLY FOR LICENSURE AND KEEP IT CURRENT

The counselor must apply for licensure and pay the $100 application fee. After that, the counselor must renew the license annually. The yearly renewal fee is $100.

REFERENCES AND RESOURCES

American Association for Marriage and Family Therapy
www.aamft.org

American Counseling Association
www.counseling.org

American School Counselor Association
www.schoolcounselor.org

South Dakota Board of Counselor Examiners
www.state.sd.us/dhs/Boards/counselor/lmft.htm

Why do some states require teaching credentials as a prerequisite for becoming a school counselor and others do not? What are the advantages and disadvantages of such a requirement?

John Schmidt, Counselor Educator
East Carolina University
Greenville, N.C.
schmidtj@mail.ecu.edu

TRADITION AND MYTH

Approximately 16 states continue to require teaching experience to be a school counselor, due to the combination of tradition and myth:

- The tradition is that "guidance counselors" in the early years of the school counseling profession often came from classrooms or other educational positions within the schools.

- The myth perpetuated by this tradition is that teaching experience better prepares one to be an effective school counselor.

Over the years, however, researchers have failed to support this assertion that teaching experience better prepares counselors (Randolph & Masker, 1997; Baker, 1994; Olson & Allen, 1993). On one hand, some research of professional perceptions has confirmed the perpetuation of this myth among classroom teachers (Quarto, 1999). On the other hand, principals' perceptions did not find a relationship between counselor effectiveness and teaching experience. Similarly, research of counselor educators' views showed a significant majority (75 percent) saw no relationship between teaching experience and school counselor effectiveness (Smith, 2001).

Unfortunately, no definitive studies in recent years have examined school counselor effectiveness with and without teaching experience, mostly likely due to the methodological challenges of performing such studies, not the least of which is defining school counselor effectiveness.

ADVANTAGES OF REQUIRING TEACHING EXPERIENCE

With the lack of research to support the notion of teaching experience as a requirement for school counselor licensure, it is difficult to find clear advantages for having such a regulation. Appeasing teachers who perceive a relationship between counselor effectiveness and teaching experience seems to be the only advantage, but I believe that is unfounded.

Successful school counselors in the majority of states not requiring teaching experience (Randolph & Masker, 1997) show that effective school counseling is based on many factors other than teaching experience. While empathic understanding of the challenges of classroom teaching may play a role in successful counseling, teaching experience in and of itself has not been shown to elicit such empathy.

DISADVANTAGES OF REQUIRING TEACHING EXPERIENCE

The disadvantages of requiring teaching experience for licensure in school counseling outweigh any assumed advantages. The restriction:

- Limits the pool of eligible people who might enter the profession
- Creates a narrow view of how professional counselors might best serve students, parents and teachers in school settings

Therefore, continuing to close the profession to nonteaching personnel might stifle innovative ideas and strategies to move school counseling forward in providing effective and comprehensive services.

REFERENCES AND RESOURCES

Baker, S. B. (1994). Mandatory teaching experience for school counselors: An impediment to uniform certification standards for school counselors. *Counselor Education and Supervision, 33,* 314–326.

Baker, S. B., & Herr, E. L. (1976). Can we bury the myth? Teaching experience for school counselors. *Bulletin of the National Association of Secondary School Principals, 60,* 114–118.

Olson, M. J., & Allen, D. N. (1993). Principals' perceptions of the effectiveness of school counselors with and without teaching experience. *Counselor Education and Supervision, 33,* 10–21.

Quarto, C. J. (1999). Teachers' perceptions of school counselors with and without teaching experience. *Professional School Counseling, 2,* 378–383.

Randolph, D. L., & Masker, T. (1997). Teacher certification and the counselor: A follow-up survey of school counselor certification requirements. *ACES Spectrum, 57*(4), 6–8.

Smith, S. L. (2001). Teaching experience for school counselors: Counselor educators' perceptions. *Professional School Counseling, 4,* 216–225.

Ethics/Law

Ethical and legal standards are developed and published by a profession to help its members aspire to and practice in an ideal manner. In contrast, laws are standards set by a society that communicate the minimal level of tolerance that is acceptable for a professional's behavior or practice. Whereas ethical standards are derived from ethical codes, laws are found in federal and state constitutions, statutes, regulations and common law actions. Still, ethical decisions are usually not clear-cut and can vary even across similar situations. As society changes, the issues change; and, indeed, as counselors change, their perspectives change.

If we understand and accept that ultimately counselors will have to struggle to determine the appropriate action in each situation, then we realize the importance of ethical and legal awareness and sensitivity. We also understand the need for periodic re-examination of the issues throughout our professional lives (Remley, Hermann & Huey, 2003).

The universe of knowledge concerning ethical and legal issues in any profession is significant and continually developing. This chapter brings into focus several of the most pervasive ethical issues that professional school counselors inevitably face. These ethical issues include recording and using information such as notes and files, maintaining confidentiality and practicing within the scope of one's competency.

REFERENCES AND RESOURCES

Remley, T. P., Jr, Herrmann, M., & Huey W. C. (2003). *Ethical and legal issues in school counseling.* Alexandria, VA: American School Counselor Association.

Are a school counselor's notes considered confidential and therefore not available to the court, even with a subpoena?

Carolyn Stone, Counselor Educator
University of North Florida
Jacksonville, Fla.
cstone@unf.edu

All educational records are governed by the federal legislation entitled Family Education Rights and Privacy Act (FERPA). This legislation also affects school counselor's case notes. For the protection of the student and the student's family, FERPA dictates how all written information on a student will be handled.

COUNSELOR NOTES EXEMPT IF SPECIFIC CRITERIA ARE MET

Not all of the information collected and maintained by schools and school employees about students is subject to the access and disclosure requirements (FERPA, 1973). One of the five categories exempt from the definition of "education records" under FERPA is records made by teachers, supervisors, counselors, administrators and other school personnel that "are kept in the sole possession of the maker of the record and are not accessible or revealed to any other person except a temporary substitute for the maker of the record."

FERPA means that school counselors' case notes are "sole possession records" and not educational records (which parents are entitled to see) if the notes meet four specific criteria. The notes must be:

- A memory aid
- Not accessible or shared in either verbal or written form
- Private, created solely by the individual possessing them
- Observations and professional opinions only

Since parents have rights to educational records, if case notes do not meet the above criteria, counselors are legally required to respect the spirit and intent of FERPA and provide these case notes/educational records to the requesting parent. In other words, the general belief that unless shared and accessible, case notes remain sole possession records is inaccurate. Counselor's case notes must meet all four conditions to be exempt from FERPA access and disclosure requirements.

HOW TO MEET EXEMPTION CRITERIA

School counselors do not usually keep prolific notes; rather, they typically record the date, the student's name and a few details to jog their memory. However, when detailed notes are required (for example, in situations such as child abuse, self-mutilation, or potential suicide), school counselors should write with the understanding that case notes can be:

- Subpoenaed (in most states)
- Accessed by parents if they record other than observations and professional opinion

WHAT TO DO IF SUBPOENAED

Even when school counselors manage to meet the criteria of sole possession records, in most states these records can still be subpoenaed. Generally speaking, counselors do not want their records or testimony in court. Counselors' loyalty is to their students and the confidentiality owed them. If subpoenaed, the school counselor should:

Be careful not to purge or rewrite notes
Seek advice from the school district's legal counsel, the attorney who issued the subpoena or the opposing attorney and ask for a motion to quash, a procedure that voids the counselor's obligation to respond to a subpoena

If a counselor is unsuccessful in getting the motion to quash, they can advocate for the privacy of their students in other ways such as:

- Ask the judge to excuse their testimony or take their notes into chambers to determine if the notes are really needed
- Advocate to protect their case notes and be excused from testifying

REFERENCES AND RESOURCES

American Counseling Association. (1999). *Professional counselors' guide to federal law on student records.* Alexandria, VA: Author.

Fischer, G. P., & Sorenson, L. (1996). *School law for counselors, psychologists and social workers* (3rd ed.). White Plains, NY: Longman.

Stone, C. (2003). Case notes, subpoenas, and educational records. *ASCA School Counselor*, September/October. Alexandria, VA: American School Counselor Association.

U.S. Department of Education, Family Policy Compliance Office. A guide titled *Information on Family Educational Rights Privacy Act* (FERPA) is available by calling (202) 260-3887 or online at www.ed.gov/policy/gen/guid/fpco/ferpa/index.html

---

How long should I have to keep student counseling files? For instance, is there a minimum number of years that we need to keep counseling records on file?

Rhonda Williams, Counselor Educator
University of Colorado at Colorado Springs
Colorado Springs, Colo.
rwilliam@uccs.edu

While there is much written about the school counseling role regarding confidentiality of records, there is little written about the length of time a school counselor should legally or ethically keep school counseling case notes. Typically, the three basic types of records that concern school counselors are: counseling case notes, documentation of action taken to protect the school counselor and the cumulative academic records of individual students (Remley, Hermann, & Huey, 2003).

DIFFERENCE BETWEEN CUMULATIVE
RECORDS AND CASE NOTES

It is important to differentiate between students' cumulative records and the individual counseling case notes that are kept by the school counselor to record counseling interaction with students. The cumulative records might include: identifying data; scores on the standardized intelligence, aptitude and psychological tests; interest inventories; health data; family background information; or observations (Shannon, as cited in Huey & Remley, 1998).

However, the personal counseling case notes kept by the school counselor might include: personal counseling sessions, students' journaling, teacher's comments or concerns of a student, or case notes about a particular counseling situation.

LENGTH OF TIME NOT ADDRESSED
IN FEDERAL REGULATIONS

FERPA clearly documents the requirements for maintaining the confidentiality of school records. Briefly put, this act authorizes parental inspection of a child's school records, giving parents the right not only to receive information contained in the student records, but also the right to deny others access to that information. The Health Insurance Portability and Accountability Act (HIPAA, 1996) also supports the rights of parents to access student records.

However, these laws do not specifically speak to the personal counseling case notes of the school counselor nor to the number of years these records should be maintained.

ASCA Ethical Standards A.2.e. stipulates that the school counselor "protects the confidentiality of student's records and releases personal data in accordance with prescribed laws and school policies." However, length of storage for those records is not specified. Section A.8. clearly states that school counselors should "maintain and secure records necessary for rendering professional services to the student as required by laws, regulations, institutional procedures and confidentiality guidelines" (ASCA, 2004).

STATE REGULATORY LICENSURE RULES
AND SCHOOL POLICIES

In considering legal and ethical issues in any counseling setting, it is always imperative to follow an ethical decision-making model. Knowing the federal and state laws regarding confidential records of a minor and consulting with other professionals should be the first steps taken. Since FERPA and HIPAA do not speak directly to the length of time school counselors should keep their personal counseling notes, it then becomes important to consider state regulatory licensure rules and specific school district policies.

Because state regulations vary, as do school district policies, it might be helpful to consider state licensure regulations even though not all school counselors are licensed professional counselors. For example, the licensure board for Colorado mandates keeping the files for five years unless the client is under the age of 18. It is then stipulated that the records be kept till the age of majority (Colorado DORA, 2002, Section 19). Remley et al. (2003) suggest purging records periodically for the sake of space or to avoid the notes falling into the wrong hands. However, it is also suggested by these authors that it may be helpful to maintain personal counseling records indefinitely.

CONCLUSION

Since neither FERPA nor HIPAA clearly indicates a timeframe, it might be wise to consult the following resources when considering the length of time to hold onto school counseling case notes:

- ASCA code of ethics
- State department of education policies
- State department of regulatory services
- Individual school district policies

If none of these resources provides clear time stipulations, it may be best to follow the suggestion to maintain these records indefinitely—just to be on the safe side.

REFERENCES AND RESOURCES

American School Counselor Association. (2004). *ASCA ethical standards for school counselors.* Alexandria, VA: Author. Available online at www.schoolcounselor.org/

Colorado Department of Regulatory Agencies. (2002) *Colorado state board of licensed professional counselors.* Available online at *www.dora.state.co.us/mental-health/lpcrules.pdf*

Huey, W., & Remley, T. P. (1998). *Ethical and legal issues in school counseling.* Alexandria, VA: American School Counselor Association.

Remley, T. P., Hermann, M. A., & Huey, W. C. (Eds.). (2003). *Ethical & legal issues in school counseling.* Alexandria, VA: American School Counselor Association.

How much information can I share with my administrator and/or staff about my counseling sessions with students? What if, for instance, a principal makes the case that he or she should be informed of counseling issues because of school safety and violence prevention concerns?

Jackie Hoagland, School Counselor
St. James High School
Murrells Inlet, S.C.
jackieandwalt@hotmail.com

As a high school counselor, I see students for a wide range of problems. Most of those problems do not warrant sharing with others. In counseling sessions that involve serious issues, however, I begin by telling students that I am required to report any information they share with me that involves possible danger to themselves or others. This established requirement eliminates the need for the principal to have to "make the case that he or she should be informed of counseling issues because of school safety and violence." The principal knows he or she would be informed immediately.

Other types of information remain confidential. If I feel there are other issues that would be in the best interest of the student for me to share with administrators and teachers, I would get permission from the student and/or, in some cases, the parent. After evaluating the situation, I would take measures that I felt would best help the student.

For example, a student may have health problems or may be dealing with the death or critical health problem of a loved one. This may affect his or her attendance or performance in class. If teachers and administrators know this, they are generally understanding and will go the extra mile to help the student.

According to ASCA's Ethical Standards, counselors "will consult with other professionals when in doubt as to the validity of an exception." So, if you are not sure whether you should break a student's right to confidentiality, check with another professional. I am fortunate to work in a school that has a full-time mental health counselor; therefore, I can consult my fellow school counselors as well as a mental health counselor.

At counseling conferences, I have attended several informative workshops that dealt with confidentiality, ethics and legal issues. A particularly helpful class, "What Do I Do Now? Ethical and Legal Issues in School Counseling," is sponsored by the South Carolina Department of Education and taught by Dr. Ron Miles.

REFERENCES AND RESOURCES

American Counseling Association
www.counseling.org

American School Counselor Association
www.schoolcounselor.org

American School Counselor Association. (2004). *Ethical standards for school counselors.* Alexandria, VA: Author.

I am battling a divorce case and would like for my child to see the school counselor. However, I'm very afraid that my husband will take what the counselor says and hold it against me. What is a school counselor allowed to say?

Mary Hermann, Counselor Educator
Mississippi State University
Mississippi State, Miss.
mhermann@colled.msstate.edu

There are both legal and ethical dimensions to what a school counselor is allowed to say about information obtained in counseling sessions. Two relevant ethics documents are:

- Code of Ethics and Standards of Practice (ACA, 2005)
- Ethical Standards for School Counselors (ASCA, 2004)

Both codes stress that the counselors' primary obligation is to their clients (ACA, §A.1.a.; ASCA, §A.1.a.) and that counselors are obligated to respect their clients' privacy (ACA, §B.1.a.; ASCA, §A.2.f.). Ethical standards clarify that even if clients are minors, counselors are to act in their clients' best interests and take measures to protect confidentiality (ACA, §B.3.).

However, though school counselors are required to protect confidential information, ethical standards direct school counselors to respect parents' rights and, when appropriate, establish a collaborative relationship with parents (ASCA, §B.1.a.). Thus, though minor clients have an ethical right to privacy, this right is somewhat ambiguous considering potential school counselor/parent collaboration.

A minor client's ethical right to privacy is further complicated by legal mandates. ASCA's Ethical Standards (ASCA, 2004) addresses legal considerations related to confidentiality by explaining that when making decisions related to confidentiality, school counselors need to consider federal and state laws (§A.2.f.). From a legal perspective, in most states parents probably have a right to the information provided in counseling sessions.

Thus, in the situation described above, the school counselor cannot guarantee the mother that information about counseling sessions will be completely confidential because the father may have a legal right to the information.

If the mother is concerned about how information about counseling sessions would affect her divorce case, it is important to note that even if the father was able to gain information about counseling sessions from the school counselor, he may not be able to use the information in court. Whether he would be able to utilize this information in court depends on the relevant state privileged communication law.

Privileged communication statutes protect individuals from disclosing information in court proceedings if the information was gained through special relationships (for example, the counselor/client relationship). Though in most states licensed professional counselors are included in privileged communication statutes, most state statutes do not extend privilege to school counselor/student relationships.

However, even if the school counselor is not covered by a privileged communication statute, ethical standards direct school counselors who have been asked for confidential information by a court to request that the disclosure not be required if the information could harm the counselee (ASCA, 2004, §A.2.d.).

As this discussion of confidentiality indicates, school counselors often have no clear answers to the challenging legal and ethical issues related to confidentiality. Yet, it is wise for school counselors to remain cognizant of their primary ethical responsibility to promote the welfare of their students. A student whose parents are going through a difficult divorce is likely to benefit from the services of a school counselor.

Thus, in this situation, the school counselor could inform the mother that the child would probably benefit from talking to the school counselor. The school counselor could address the mother's concerns about her divorce by stating that though the school counselor could not guarantee confidentiality, school counselors are ethically required to maintain confidentiality in most instances and do their best to avoid disclosure of confidential information.

REFERENCES AND RESOURCES

American School Counselor Association
www.schoolcounselor.org/

Glosoff, H. L., & Pate, R. H., Jr. (2002). Privacy and confidentiality in school counseling. *Professional School Counseling, 6,* 20–27.

Isaacs, M. L., & Stone, C. (1999). School counselors and confidentiality: Factors affecting professional choices. *Professional School Counseling, 2,* 258–266.

Remley, T. P., Jr., Hermann, M. A., & Huey, W. C. (Eds.). (2003). *Ethical and legal issues in school counseling* (2nd ed.). Alexandria, VA: American School Counselor Association.

Sealander, K. A., Schwiebert, V. L., & Weekley, J. L. (1999). Confidentiality and the law. *Professional School Counseling, 3,* 122–127.

Other than a lack of training, how might a school counselor mistakenly practice beyond his or her competence?

Warren Throckmorton, Counselor Educator
Grove City College
Grove City, Pa.
ewthrockmorton@GCC.EDU

There are several ways a school counselor can practice outside of competence, including the following.

DIAGNOSING MENTAL HEALTH DISORDERS

School counselors who are not also trained in diagnosing mental health disorders and conditions should not render a diagnosis for a child to parents, children or fellow school staff. Sometimes parents and/or teachers want a school counselor to function as a diagnostician. If the school counselor has coursework and experience in diagnosis, and is permitted by state scope of practice to render diagnoses, it may be appropriate. However, if these factors are not true, then the counselor should refer to someone trained to diagnose mental health disorders.

TREATING MENTAL HEALTH CONCERNS

Students bring very difficult mental health problems to school. School counselors may be tempted to treat clinical concerns even if the counselor does not have sufficient training or experience to do so. Providing such treatment is an ethical violation in that competence to treat must be substantiated by coursework, supervised experience and appropriate legal scope of practice.

IMPOSING SOLUTIONS TO PERSONAL HEALTH ISSUES

Other health concerns may also tax a counselor's competence. For example, many students have social or personal concerns surrounding sexuality, reproduction and medical issues such as sexually transmitted diseases. While most counselors have some level of training in these areas, a culturally competent counselor does not impose solutions on children or families, but rather attempts to frame interventions within the value framework of the family and community.

In highly conservative areas, more personally progressive counselors may need to learn more about the prevailing views. In more progressive or politically liberal areas, conservative counselors may need to work toward an increased awareness of other views.

What advice and exact direction could you provide school counselors about documentation requirements for counseling sessions? For instance, how long should the records be retained on students? What are the rights for parents to have access to their student's records?

Carolyn Stone, Counselor Educator
University of North Florida
Jacksonville, Fla.
cstone@unf.edu

School counselors are not required to document counseling sessions in the form of case notes except in those rare incidences where there is a school board policy requiring this practice. Because of the varied nature of a comprehensive school counseling program (where counseling is but one of a multitude of roles delivered) and the short-term nature of counseling (the standard in a school setting), detailed case notes are not a reality or a necessity for the school counselor.

Best practices dictate that school counselors try to capture pertinent information such as the name, date and a few general descriptors to help as a memory aid in their future work with a student. However, for certain cases such as child abuse, suicidal ideation or self-mutilation, it is important to capture every word, nuance and nonverbal expression.

Any time a school counselor has reason to believe that recollections will be needed to protect a child, give testimony or document actions on a child's behalf, it will be important to record as much detail as possible. Accuracy and professionalism are critical because what is written in case notes must always be filtered through the lens that these notes can be subpoenaed and/or requested by parents.

Do parents have a right to see what a school counselor has written about their child? It is very difficult to meet the criteria for sole possession records and avoid having case notes cross over to become educational records. (See previous question concerning case notes.) Because parents have rights to view educational records, the answer most authors give is that if parents push to review case notes, they probably have a right to them even if the counselor has managed to meet the criteria of sole possession records (Fischer & Sorenson, 1996; Loewenberg & Dolgoff, 1996).

The best defense against having to give out case notes and, therefore, breach confidentiality, is to try to set up parameters with parents in advance and use good communication and collaboration skills with parents at all junctures of the counseling work. Again, best practice is to write with care with the full knowledge that case notes can be read by parents or subpoenaed.

Suggested guidelines for purging case notes are the following:

- Establish a reasonable timeline for purging sole possession records or case notes
- Shred the sole possession records on a student when he or she transitions to the next level (for example, elementary to middle or middle to high school), transfers to another school or graduates
- Apply careful discretion and deliberation before destroying sole possession records that may be needed by the legal system (such as notes on child abuse, suicide, sexual harassment or violence)

These guidelines should serve as suggestions only; counselors must establish for themselves a pattern of purging case notes that is appropriate for their situation.

REFERENCES AND RESOURCES

American School Counselor Association. (2004). *Ethical standards for school counselors*. Alexandria, VA: Author.

Fischer, L., & Sorenson, P. (1996). *School law for counselors, psychologists, and social workers*. White Plains, NY: Longman.

Loewenberg, F. M., & Dolgoff, R. (1996). *Ethical decisions for social work practice*. Itasca, IL: F. E. Peacock.

Stone, C. (2003). Case notes, subpoenas, and educational records. *ASCA School Counselor*, September/October. Alexandria, VA: American School Counselor Association.

How does a school counselor know when or when not to breach confidentiality when a legally minor student has engaged in some form of sexual activity?

Nadene A. L'Amoreaux and Rachel Campbell
Counselor Educator and Graduate Student
Indiana University of Pennsylvania
nlamoro@iup.edu

When determining whether to breach confidentiality, school counselors have several resources available to them to assist with decision making: ethical codes, state/federal law, school district policy and consultation with other colleagues. Additionally, school counselors need to also be mindful of parental rights and expectations related to their children's health, safety and well-being (Mitchell, 2002).

One of the first questions to be asked in a situation in which a legally minor student has engaged in some form of sexual activity is whether this sexual activity presents a danger to the child's health or safety. Some more specific questions to be asked include: Where did the activity take place? How did the counselor learn of this information? Who is involved? Was the child a consenting participant or was this an unwanted experience? What is the age of the child/other participant(s)? Who else knows of the incident/occurrence? What are the child's thoughts about the incident and how likely is this to be repeated? How high risk is the behavior in terms of jeopardizing the child's health and welfare or the health and welfare of others? What is the purpose or intent of breaching confidentiality in this type of situation?

In consulting ethical standards, almost all codes of ethics address the importance of confidentiality in the counseling relationship and provide protection to the client against unwarranted and illegal disclosures of private information, unless there is clear and imminent danger to the client or others (Remley & Herlihy, 2005). In this situation, the counselor must determine if participation in sexual activity constitutes clear and imminent danger to the student or others. ASCA's Ethical Standards for School Counselors further specify the conditions under which such a disclosure should be made. Additionally, the counselor must balance his/her obligation to maintain confidentiality with the legal rights that parents have to be informed of and to make decisions about their children's lives.

Furthermore, counselors must be cognizant of any state or federal laws relating to this issue. For instance, if a student is in harm's way and is being threatened by some sort of violence or abuse, the counselor must respond. Most notably with minors, sexual and physical abuse must be reported by law in most states (Koocher & Keith-Spiegel 1990). Failure to report this type of abuse is illegal. Each state will have its own laws and cases related to the topic and these should be used to inform the counselor's decision. Most states require that counselors violate confidentiality if there is a reason to believe a client poses a clear threat to self or others (Orton 1997). Counselors who fail to predict potential danger make themselves potentially liable for legal action (Corey, Corey & Callanan, 2003).

School district policy is another source of information for the school counselor. Some districts place no restrictions on what is disclosed during counseling sessions, whereas others place restrictions on certain topics including drugs, weapons, sexual activity and pregnancy. If a client is a minor and his/her parents want to know what the client has been disclosed in confidence, they may have legal rights to this information, and the school district policy may compel a counselor to disclose this information.

In short, if the counselor has reason to believe the student is in danger from engaging in sexual activity or is endangering others by engaging in sexual activity, the counselor may be warranted in breaching confidentiality. On the other hand, if there is no evidence that laws have been broken and the counselor feels that no one has been harmed or will be harmed, then there is little basis to make such a breach.

REFERENCES AND RESOURCES

Corey, G., Corey, M.S., & Callahan, P. (2003). *Issues & ethics in the helping professions.* Portland: Wadsworth Group.

Herlihy, B., & Remley, T. P. (2005). *Ethical, legal, and professional issues in counseling.* New Jersey: Prentice-Hall, Inc.

Koocher, G. P., Keith-Spiegel, P.C. (1990). *Children, ethics, & the Law.* Lincoln, NE. The University of Nebraska Press.

Mitchell, Clifton W. (2002). When parents want to know: Responding to parental demands for confidential information. *Professional School Counseling, 6,* p.156-161.

Orton, G. L. (1997). *Strategies for counseling with children and their parents.* New York: Brooks/Cole.

Counseling and Guidance Issues

This category focuses on a sundry of common professional school counseling issues that all school counselors, at one time or another, will experience. Practical responses in this chapter include the following:

- Staying motivated and focused during trying times
- Working within a school district in which the school counselor grew up
- Classifying school counselors among districts
- Advocating for the profession
- Understanding the conditions under which a school counselor may need permission from parents to work with students
- Differentiating the different methods used for school counselor-student assignments
- Understanding the most pervasive academic, career and social/personal issues among K-12 students that school counselors address
- Identifying special issues that school counselors need to consider when implementing comprehensive school counseling programs in urban and rural schools
- Maintaining school counselor notes

How does a school counselor stay motivated and focused in trying times?

Mark Boggie, School Counselor
Buena High School
Sierra Vista, Ariz.
mpboggie@theriver.com

You have a caseload that is well above the recommended levels. You have a parent on the phone and one waiting on you in the front office; the secretary has two messages for you; five students are waiting to see you; you have an individual education plan (IEP) meeting to attend; and you have to get the report done for the principal.

Sound like a typical day in the counselor's office? If so, you know the meaning of workplace stress. Your job demands that you multitask daily. The tasks thrown at you are hard to deal with even when you are "on top of your game." What happens if you also have to deal with just as much stress in other aspects of your life? How can you stay motivated to provide the necessary services your students need? How can you stay focused and motivated in times that are not ideal? In one word: balance.

To stay focused and motivated in trying times, seek balance in these four areas: physical, mental, professional and personal.

PHYSICAL BALANCE

To deal with the demands of a being a counseling professional, a little physical conditioning goes a long way. You will deal with setbacks and obstacles much better if you have taken care of your body by eating right, getting some physical conditioning and making sure you have the proper amount of sleep. While this may sound like common sense, physical balance is usually the first thing to be ignored when we do not have time to tend to it. Making time for yourself is the best investment you can make.

MENTAL BALANCE

The brain needs exercise just as the body does. Mental balance includes conferring with others about your ideas, stretching yourself mentally and, of course, letting your mind rest when appropriate. Taking care of the mental aspect of life can be the most difficult because of the abundance of information we process daily. Take a mental break by doing something you enjoy, such as reading, gardening, games or other hobbies.

PROFESSIONAL BALANCE

Take care of yourself professionally by seeking renewal through exploration of new ideas, information and ways of doing business. You can accomplish this by attending workshops and conferences, or just conferring with colleagues. A fresh approach to the same old tasks can spark action.

PERSONAL BALANCE

Personal balance comes from within, through being at peace with who you are and with whatever higher power you believe in. Through personal balance, you can derive the strength needed to get through difficult times. Being satisfied with who you are and your place in the world can give you a sense of peace and the knowledge that whatever life throws at you, you can deal with it.

REFERENCES AND RESOURCES

American Institute of Stress
www.stress.org

Stress Assess
wellness.uwsp.edu/Other/stress/

What are the pros and cons of working as a counselor within a school district in which I currently live? (I have been born and raised in this community and know many people.)

Cheryl Holcomb-McCoy, Counselor Educator
University of Maryland
College Park, Md.
ch193@umail.umd.edu

I believe there are many benefits to working as a counselor within a school district in which you were raised and now live.

COMMUNITY RELATIONSHIPS

First, you will be at an advantage when developing partnerships and relationships with families and community representatives. With the increased attention being paid to the school counselor's role in developing school, family and community partnerships (Colbert, 1996; Bryan & Holcomb-McCoy, 2004), your connection to the community will only enhance your ability to build these connections. You will have a unique understanding of the people in the community, which will only contribute to your school's positive climate.

Because of your familiarity with the history of the community and its culture, you will better understand the needs and worldview of community members. This is beneficial because research indicates that school person-nel who are knowledgeable of the community and are willing to reach out to the community are more likely to build successful and lucrative rela-tionships with community stakeholders (Henderson & Mapp, 2002). We also know from research that as parent involvement increases, so does student achievement (Epstein, 1994; Davies, 1996).

COMMITMENT TO COMMUNITY AND SCHOOL

Second, I believe you are at an advantage because of your commitment to the community and the school. School personnel who are detached and unfamiliar with the school community have more difficulty connecting to students and their families. Oftentimes, school counselors spend an enor-mous amount of time building trusting relationships with community members, key community stakeholders and parents. This might not be the case if you know or are familiar with these key people.

PERSONAL CONNECTION

A final benefit of your working as a counselor in your community is your own personal connection. Because the community in which you work is your home community, you will likely be more invested in the school's success and its mission because it is your family's community.

The only possible problem that I can foresee of working as a counselor in a school district where you currently reside is the phenomenon of being "too connected." As is the case when trying to determine whether an internal or external expert is better, there are some scenarios where being an internal person can be problematic because of one's loss of objectivity.

Being a member of the community could mean that you have biases or beliefs that reflect the community's biased perceptions. Your beliefs could be faulty or misperceived, which might be more difficult for you to see. For instance, if there is a negative community perception of newly arrived immigrants living in a housing development, it might be more difficult for you to see another perspective. Clearly, this lack of objectivity and neu-trality could hinder the process of change within a school community.

REFERENCES AND RESOURCES

Bryan, J., & Holcomb-McCoy, C. (2004). School counselors' perceptions of their involvement in school-family-community partnerships. *Professional School Counseling, 7*, 162–171.

Center on School, Family, and Community Partnerships
www.csos.jhu.edu/p2000/center.htm

Colbert, R. (1996). The counselor's role in advancing school and family partnerships. *The School Counselor, 44,* 100–104.

Epstein, J. (1994). Theory to practice: School and family partnerships lead to school improvement and student success. In C. Fagnano & B. Werber (Eds.), *School, family, and community interactions: A view from the firing lines.* Boulder, CO: Westview Press.

Henderson, A. T., & Mapp, K. L. (Eds.). (2002). *A new wave of evidence: The impact of school, family, community connections on student achievement* [Electronic version]. Austin, TX: National Center for Family and Community Connections with Schools, Southwest Educational Development Laboratory.

National Coalition for Parent Involvement in Education (NCPIE)
www.ncpie.org

Under what conditions might a school counselor need permission from parents to work with students?

Ercell Somerville, School Counselor
Toledo Public Schools
Toledo, Ohio
e.somerville@juno.com

I do not think school counselors need permission from parents for individual counseling of students. In the past, I have always asked students if it was okay if I mailed a letter to their parents to inform them that I am seeing the student. No other information is given in the letter. I then show the student the form letter that her parent will receive. If the student agrees, then I send the letter. (In the past, many have agreed.)

However, if students don't want a letter mailed home, I don't send one. Student objections send up red flags to me. Therefore, I try to explore the reasons (with the student) why he or she does not want home (parents, guardians) to know. However, I've never been pushy about this matter, nor have I sent a letter without a student's consent.

I do, however, think that school counselors should get parental consent for group counseling. In most cases, group counseling takes more class time during the day, and groups usually meet anywhere from six to eight weeks. Student can elect not to participate in the group if parental consent is a problem for them. However (once again), this would send up a red flag, and I would pursue the reason(s) why the student does not want his or her parent to know.

In conclusion, I strongly believe in parental involvement in all facets of education, including counseling. However, it is a student's right to receive counseling, with or without parental consent.

What are the advantages and disadvantages of school counselor assignments based on the alphabet or student's last name versus their grade level?

Kevin D. Quinn, School Counselor
South Kingstown High School
Wakefield, R.I.
kevindquinn@verizon.net

Assigning school counselor caseloads is an emotionally charged issue for school counselors. Because they become personally responsible for their students, school counselors exhibit a sort of territorial protection on how students are assigned to them.

High school districts use various methods of assigning counselor case-loads. The most frequently applied systems are distribution based on the alphabet or separation by grade level. With the alphabetical method, the school counselor remains with the same students throughout their high school years, based on the student's last name. With the grade-level method, the school counselor remains stationary and provides school counseling curriculum to one particular grade level each year (for example, the 10th grade school counselor).

High school counselors have weighed in and shared the advantages and challenges of each. Implementing the ASCA National Model® has solidified the delivery and management of school counseling curriculum through both the alphabetical and grade-level approach. It is important to understand that whatever system works within your particular school or district is the most valuable application.

ALPHABETICAL APPROACH – ADVANTAGES AND CHALLENGES

The alphabetical approach of assigning students has many advantages and certain challenges affecting the implementation of school counseling programs, especially in the areas of student rapport, family continuity, networking and accountability.

Student Rapport
Understanding the growth and development of each student is a major advantage with the alphabetical division. Working with the student for all four years allows the school counselor to fully understand the individual. The personalization of knowing the student helps with the academic, career and social/personal domains.

However, in working with larger ratios, it is more appropriate to deliver your school counselor program through collaborative efforts and working through classroom lessons. Even with the alphabetical designation and four years of assignment, the school counselor is hard pressed to know each individual student well.

Family Continuity
School counselors using the alphabetical method are privy to family history, and parents gain a comfort zone in working with the same school counselor.

The challenge, however, is understanding the family dynamics and building a trust and rapport with the new school counselor. When the need arises for an intervention, the school counselor must gather feedback, build rapport and develop family strategies.

Networking
School counselors consistently build partnerships and network with professionals in post-secondary settings. Remaining in the loop year after year allows the counselor to foster continued connections (for example, college admissions officers and chambers of commerce).

The challenge is that school counselors need to establish partners for post-secondary options, establishing connections, and collaborating and implementing guidance curriculum per grade level.

Accountability
In the area of accountability, the advantage of the alphabetical method is that the school counselor is solely responsible for overseeing the student's permanent records.

The challenge is making a clear distinction when clarifying student management of records such as graduation requirements.

GRADE-LEVEL METHOD – ADVANTAGES AND DISADVANTAGES

The grade level method of assigning students also has many advantages and certain challenges affecting the implementation of school counseling programs, especially in the areas of specialization, team approach, collaboration and communication.

Specialization
Using the grade-level method allows for smooth implementation of a school counseling program. When the school counselor "owns" an entire grade level, the counselor becomes more knowledgeable and skilled in the delivery of certain lessons. The focus on one particular group of students helps in the overall planning.

The challenge is keeping the big picture in perspective and not allowing the school counselor to become stagnant and complacent. Changing the stimuli and keeping up with professional development is a must.

Team Approach
Planning events and activities runs smoothly for counselors using the grade level approach because each school counselor knows their role and has rehearsed it over and over. The challenge is that students and school counselors must annually reacquaint themselves with one another.

Collaboration
Another advantage of the grade level approach is that it improves faculty rapport and interactions, since faculty members know which counselor is assigned a particular student. The challenge is the lack of student history in sharing with teachers and administrators.

Communication
Designation by grade level allows for clearly defined communication with administration, faculty and staff. The communication challenge, however,

is that writing numerous letters of recommendation for the seniors is a monumental task for school counselors, especially without a complete understanding of the student's history. This can be overwhelming and exhausting to a senior counselor. One must consider time constraints while working with college information and searches.

CONCLUSION

Because each district is unique and student needs vary from school to school, it is essential that a strategic plan help differentiate the most appropriate assignment of school counselor caseloads. Which is the best way to effectively reach all students and provide a quality school counseling program? Some schools and districts use a combination and other districts loop their counselors. Still others use transitional counselors, academies and specialized counselors to meet the needs of students and the program. In the end, each district must look at the needs of the students and families to determine the most effective way to deliver the comprehensive school counseling program.

What are the most pervasive (perhaps five) social issues among K-12 students that school counselors address?

Stuart Chen-Hayes, Counselor Educator
Lehman College, The City University of New York
Bronx, N.Y.
stuart.chen-hayes@lehman.cuny.edu

The most pervasive social issues among K-12 students that school counselors address are the gaps that develop among students in the areas of achievement, opportunity and attainment.

BRIDGING ACHIEVEMENT, OPPORTUNITY AND ATTAINMENT GAPS

Achievement gaps illustrate student educational performance differences at the local school, district, city, state and national levels based on cultural variables such as ethnicity, race, gender, socioeconomic status, language status and disability status.

Opportunity gaps occur as certain students of privileged dominant cultural groups and statuses receive advanced placement courses, college preparation curriculum, and high expectations and certified teachers for all of their K-12 coursework. At the same time, many students from nondominant or oppressed groups are more likely not to be enrolled in advanced placement courses (if they are at all available) or college preparation curriculum. In addition, these students often have teachers with low expectations or who are not certified; therefore, they never receive the chance to obtain quality educational and college preparatory skills.

Attainment gaps are the percentage of students who enroll in college versus the percentage of students who graduate with a college degree. Members of privileged dominant cultural groups consistently graduate at higher levels from college than members of nondominant cultural groups.

The Education Trust and the National Center for Education Statistics Web sites both contain volumes of data specific to these three gaps, including who is succeeding and who needs more work in closing these gaps. School counselors can use these national databases uncover the disparities by race, gender, disability and language background in terms of student academic achievement, access and enrollment in college preparation curriculum and advanced placement classes, and graduation rates from colleges state by state and often by district or even individual school.

All of this information helps school counselors create data-driven school counseling programs that are accountable for assisting in closing achievement, opportunity and attainment gaps K-12. The following activities help close these gaps: affirming cultural diversity, building family strengths for successful learners, providing accurate sexuality information and interventions and creating safety.

AFFIRMING NONDOMINANT CULTURES

The U.S. has always been a culturally diverse society, but the dominant cultural identities and voices in education, media and government have often ignored, denied and denigrated persons of nondominant cultural identities. School counselors in most major urban areas now work with primarily students of color from poor and working class families of immigrants who speak multiple languages. Suburban and rural counselors also work with multiple cultural identities in schools.

The challenge is for school counselors to take leadership roles in affirming cultural diversity in the school through involvement in curriculum decisions, creating school counseling curriculum on affirming diversity and responding to bias-related incidents by ensuring that policies are in place so all students are given a place of respect for successful learning in school. Key multicultural competencies for all school counselors include self-knowledge of one's own biases and issues of oppression, ethnic/racial identity development and worldview models.

School counselors need to apply these models in daily situations to challenge incidents of racism, classism, heterosexism, ageism, ableism, sexism, linguicism, beautyism and other forms of oppression that inhibit successful learning for all students. The tourist approach to multiculturalism (foods, clothing, music) is not enough. The real issue is creating group counseling sessions and developmental school counseling curriculum lessons that allow students to explore and affirm the deep values, beliefs and ways that learning is enhanced when students' multiple cultural identities are acknowledge and affirmed in the school environment.

Culturally affirming school counselors helps break down barriers that keep students of nondominant cultural identities from achieving high levels of success in school, including working with students and faculty of privileged, dominant cultural backgrounds to be allies in stopping oppressive practices in schools.

BUILDING FAMILY STRENGTHS FOR SUCCESSFUL LEARNERS

The stereotypical school counselor is the person parents and guardians only hear from when there is a problem at school. School counselors who have basic knowledge of the family life cycle, successful parenting skills and how to engage families in the learning process, however, have specific tools that can successfully unite students and families in learning strategies and techniques to affirm the presence of families in schools.

School counselors who promote family strengths in the learning process do so through engaging parents and guardians early and often by providing workshops on subjects that are vital to the success of families in schools: academic development skills for parents and guardians, career and college development skills for parents and guardians, and personal/social workshop skills such as parenting, communication skills, violence intervention skills, challenging peer pressure skills, how to talk to children and adolescents about sexuality effectively and understanding ways to assist families deal with the developmental tasks that occur during the family life cycle.

By creating workshops for parents and guardians and developmental school counseling curricula for K-12 students on issues related to academic, career/college and personal/social success for students from a family perspective, school counselors enhance family and student participation and successful academic outcomes in schools.

PROVIDING ACCURATE SEXUALITY INFORMATION AND INTERVENTIONS

The U.S. is the only country where the government is spending money on abstinence-only education programs with no research base proving their effectiveness in keeping teens from getting pregnant. A research-based approach, including guidelines for comprehensive sexuality education, is something all school counselors can access to provide accurate information and assistance to children, youth, educators, and parents and guardians in co-creating appropriate sexuality education and counseling curriculum in K-12 schools.

The Sex Information and Education Council of the United States guidelines cover six basic areas of curriculum suggestions for early elementary, late elementary, middle and high school students that all school counselors need to know: human development, relationships, personal skills, sexual behavior, sexual health, and society and culture.

Professional school counselors can create developmental school counseling curriculum addressing these core areas of sexuality education and counseling, and can facilitate administrator, educator, parent and guardian, and student discussions related to how to address these areas in the school curriculum and in the home.

CREATING SAFETY

Although crime in the U.S. is not as high as it was in the 1990s, the media continue to create fear of crime. At the same time, many schools continue to struggle to provide safe environments for learning, with students of nondominant cultural identities often targeted for harassment and violence.

Adults, especially school counselors, need to take the leadership role to ensure that students are not bullied, harassed or violated in physical, emotional or sexual ways in their school experiences, and that they have the skills to challenge and prevent emotional, physical and sexual violence.

Students in nondominant cultural groups are most likely to be targeted for bullying and violence that if left unchecked only creates greater violence and the desire for revenge due to repeated humiliation. Examples of nondominant cultural groups include:

- Girls and women
- Lesbian, bisexual, gay, transgendered and intersex students
- Poor and working class students
- Students of color
- Students with disabilities
- Students who speak English as a second language or with an accent
- Students with nondominant religious or spiritual beliefs
- Students whose appearance is less than the current standards of attractiveness

Multiple curricula exist to challenge violence and create safe schools. Professional school counselors can develop K-12 anti-violence curricula and workshops and run large-group counseling for students with behavioral concerns to assist in reducing violence in schools. Most importantly, school counselors can model for other adults in the school the importance of being preventive and creating a zero-tolerance policy for name-calling, insults and harassment in K-12 schools and creating peer and adult-led conflict resolution and mediation teams.

Ann Vernon, Counselor Educator
University of Northern Iowa
Cedar Falls, Iowa
ann.vernon@uni.edu

I think the most pervasive social issues that school counselors address include all aspects of relationships, ranging from normal developmental friendship issues (such as making and keeping friends, fights with friends and being rejected or teased) to more serious relationship issues (such as intimacy and sexual experimentation, abusive dating relationships, termination of significant romantic relationships and betrayal).

Since relationships involve connections with people of all ages, I think this adds yet another layer to what children and adolescents have to deal with. All children have to learn to negotiate relationships with peers, parents and siblings, but increasing numbers of children have to learn to relate to stepparents and siblings, and extended family members. And, increasingly, they may have two or three different stepparents and families. All of these dynamics present challenges for youth.

I tend to look at these social development issues along a continuum: at one end are the normal developmental problems that all children experience and at the other end are the more significant, serious relationship issues that increasing numbers of youth encounter. Bullying is a good example. It is normal for children to have to learn to deal with teasing, but when children are afraid to go to school because they are being threatened and bullied, this is a far more serious matter. Likewise, it is normal for adolescents to have fights with someone they are dating, but it is not normal to be abused physically, emotionally or verbally in that relationship.

Another social development issue that I think is far too prevalent is experimenting with social roles before children are developmentally ready to do so. What will be left for them to try when they are older? I think to some extent this is a result of lack of boundaries within families and the lack of good role modeling. Examples of this issue include:

- Adolescents thinking nothing of spending the night in a motel with their boyfriend or girlfriend
- Parents inviting the boyfriend or girlfriend on family vacations and allowing them to sleep in the same room
- Adolescents becoming so intimately involved with the family of the person they are dating that it is very difficult to break up because of all the connections, just as it is in a divorce among adults

I recently had an 18-year-old in my private practice say that she and her boyfriend were bored with their sexual relationship – it had gotten too routine and they needed to experiment more. In years past, this might have been what a person twice her age would have shared.

The same holds true for other things that may or may not be related to social development issues, but force the "growing up" issue all the same:

- Renting a limo for a sixth grade birthday party
- A mother allowing her seventh grader to dress up in a fancy formal and drink champagne on a cruise, but then getting angry when her daughter dresses provocatively and starts drinking with her friends the next year

- A father inviting his 16-year-old daughter and her boyfriend to "double date" with him and his girlfriend, dad showing significant affection to his girlfriend on the date, but then getting angry at his daughter when later that night he catches her making out in front of the house

In addition, I think the media influences social development because children and adolescents see things but may not comprehend their significance. Or, what they see then becomes their norm, and they are most likely not developmentally ready to handle all of the ramifications. In some ways, I think youth are almost numb to some things and because of their sense of invulnerability, they may not realize that things can happen to them that have serious long-term consequences.

What comes to mind is the 16-year-old I am presently working with who just gave her baby up for adoption and is now regretting the decision. Her decision to become intimately involved with her boyfriend has had a domino effect on other social relationships (her parents who are now grandparents to a baby they will never see, her boyfriend who is a father but had little say in her decision and so forth). The pain she is going through is incredible, and too much for a 16-year-old to have to deal with.

Social development encompasses so many issues and areas – these are the things that come to mind as I work in my private practice with youth and their families.

REFERENCES AND RESOURCES

Adams, M., Bell, L. A., & Griffin, P. (1997). *Teaching for diversity and social justice: A sourcebook*. New York: Routledge.

American School Counselor Association. (2005). *The ASCA national model: A framework for school counseling programs, second edition*. Alexandria, VA: Author.

Arredondo, P., Toporek, R., Brown, S. P., Jones, J., Locke, D. C., & Sanchez, H. (1996). Operationalization of the multicultural counseling competencies. *Journal of Multicultural Counseling and Development, 24*, 42–78.

Bailey, D. F., Getch, Y. Q., & Chen-Hayes, S. (2003). In B. T. Erford (Ed.). *Transforming the school counseling profession* (pp. 317–330). Upper Saddle River, NJ: Merrill Prentice Hall.

Bemak, F., & Chung, R. C. (2003). Multicultural counseling with immigrant students in schools. In P. B. Pedersen & J. C. Carey (Eds.). *Multicultural counseling in schools* (2nd ed, pp. 84–104). Boston: Pearson Allyn & Bacon.

Carter, B., & McGoldrick, M. (Eds.). (1999). *The expanded family life cycle: Individual, family, and social perspectives* (3rd ed.). Boston: Allyn & Bacon.

Counselors for Social Justice
www.counselorsforsocialjustice.org/

Creighton, A., & Kivel, P. (1992). Helping teens stop violence: A practical guide for counselors, educators, and parents. Alameda, CA: Hunter House.

The Education Trust's National Center for Transforming School Counseling
www2.edtrust.org

Elkind, D. (1988). *The hurried child*. Reading, MA: Addison-Wesley.

Fontes, L. A. (2003). Reducing violence in multicultural schools. In P. B. Pedersen & J. C. Carey (Eds.). *Multicultural counseling in schools* (2nd ed., pp. 211–233). Boston: Pearson Allyn & Bacon.

Holcomb-McCoy, C. (2003). Multicultural competence. In B. T. Erford (Ed.). *Transforming the school counseling profession* (pp. 317-330). Upper Saddle River, NJ: Merrill Prentice Hall.

Johnson, R. S. (2002). *Using data to close the achievement gap: How to measure equity in our schools*. Thousand Oaks, CA: Corwin.

Kivel, P., Creighton, A., & The Oakland Men's Project. (2002). *Making the peace: A 15-session violence prevention curriculum for young people*. Alameda, CA: Hunter House.

Lee, C. C., & Walz, G. R. (Eds.). (1998). *Social action: A mandate for counselors. Alexandria, VA: American Counseling Association*. (ERIC Document Reproduction Service No. ED417372)

Lewis, J. & Bradley, L. (Eds.). (2000). *Advocacy in counseling: Counselors, clients, & community*. Greensboro, NC: University of North Carolina at Greensboro. (ERIC Document Reproduction Service No. ED435904).

National Center for Education Statistics
nces.ed.gov/nationsreportcard/

Nieto, S. (2004). *Affirming diversity: The sociopolitical context of multicultural education* (4th ed.). Boston: Pearson Allyn & Bacon.

Perusse, R., & Goodnough, G. E. (Eds.). (2004). *Leadership, advocacy, and direct service strategies for professional school counselors.* Pacific Grove, CA: Brooks/Cole-Thomson Learning.

Ripley, V. V. (2003). Conflict resolution and peer mediation in schools. In B. T. Erford (Ed.), *Transforming the school counseling profession* (pp. 297–316). Upper Saddle River, NJ: Merrill Prentice Hall.

Sandhu, D. S., & Aspy, C. B. (2000). *Violence in American schools: A practical guide for counselors.* Alexandria, VA: American Counseling Association.

Sex Information and Education Council of the United States (SIECUS) *www.siecus.org*

Steinberg, L. (1996). *Adolescence* (4th ed.). New York: McGraw-Hill.

Stone, C. B., & Dahir, C. A. (2004). *School counselor accountability: A MEASURE of student success.* Upper Saddle River, NJ: Pearson Merrill Prentice Hall

Vernon, A., & Clemente, R. (2005). *Assessment and intervention with children and adolescents: Developmental and multicultural approaches.* Alexandria, VA: American Counseling Association.

Walsh, F. (Ed.). (2003). *Normal family processes: Growing diversity and complexity* (3rd ed.). New York: Guilford.

What are the most pervasive academic issues among K-12 students that school counselors address?

Sharon Johnson, Consultant
San Juan Capistrano, Calif.
sjohnso4@cox.net

The most pervasive academic issue for students today is the lack of opportunities within schools for all students to experience a comprehensive approach to learning that provides knowledge, attitudes and skills in developing a balanced life.

The inordinate emphasis on standardized tests at the expense of learning appropriate personal and social life skills such as how to lead a balanced life including good nutrition, exercise, sports, friendship and communication implies that the only success that matters is the ability to do well on specific standardized tests.

Without the emotional, values and decision-making components of education, students cannot compete. They are unaware of their own aptitudes, interests and identity, and there is little opportunity to develop personal excellence in a variety of areas. The only recognized success for many students is academic achievement, and if they don't achieve it, they feel worthless and unappreciated.

Perhaps the most devastating result of this situation is that students have no feeling of belonging to the school, a social group or a family. Nor do they understand their own strengths and value to others. Such alienation is seen in many of the symptoms that counselors address, including suicide attempts, self-mutilation, gangs, bullying, drop-outs, sexual abuse, vandalism, drugs and the many other self-destructive behaviors that plague our children. Unfortunately, these concerns are often not seen as important academic issues and yet they dramatically affect the success or lack thereof of most students.

Patricia Neufeld, Counselor Educator
Emporia State University
Emporia, Kan.
neufeldp@emporia.edu

and

Judith Sasser, Counselor Educator
Emporia State University
Emporia, Kan.
sasserj@emporia.edu

Recently, one of our school counseling interns stated, "Our future as an accredited school lies in the hand of students and the tests they are taking. As school counselors we not only need to be sure our students accomplish their state standard learning objectives; we need to be there for them emotionally as they rise to meet these challenges."

Every activity school counselors engage in is designed to enhance the learning of all students. School counselors act as an integral part of the school environment by being engaged in promoting the developmental growth and learning of all students as opposed to working only with special needs students.

School counselors meet the needs of students through the delivery of a comprehensive school counseling program that encompasses three distinct domains in counseling:

- Academic
- Career
- Personal/social

These domains are broad developmental areas that promote behaviors that enhance learning for all students. School counselors work to increase academic achievement through assisting students in the growth and resolution of personal and social matters and the development of personal/social knowledge. Attitudes and skills are addressed that assist students to be more focused on learning. Working with students in the career domain helps to provide motivation for learning as well. Academic achievement becomes much more relevant to students as they develop a vision for their own future through career exploration and planning.

The result of this work in the personal/social and career domains serves to clarify and influence student work in the academic domain. Thus, the work of the school counselor in the three domains becomes inextricably related and influential to the successful academic achievement of the students as well as their ability to become life-long learners.

Designing a comprehensive school counseling program that can support the mission statement of the school to produce life-long learners is essential to making the counseling program part of the school community. Program delivery is achieved through individual and group counseling, school-wide programs and classroom guidance, consultation with teaching staff and alignment of the overall program with the school's goals for educational excellence. Individual and small group counseling is used to provide assistance for personal/social issues that may interfere with the learning process.

Guidance activities promoting the character traits of always doing your best, striving for excellence and reaching high goals can and should be developed. Consultation that motivates the staff to challenge students by providing support, information and research creates an environment that helps to increase student achievement.

School counselors are trained to work with many of the barriers that keep students from achieving academic success. Many of these barriers are included in Ruby Payne's definition of poverty, "the extent to which an individual does without resources." The ability to leave poverty is less dependent upon financial resources than on other types of resources. These would include emotional, mental, spiritual, physical, support systems, relationships/role models and knowledge of hidden rules. School counselors have endless opportunities to influence some of the nonfinancial resources that can and do make a different in students' lives.

The No Child Left Behind legislation was enacted to attempt to meet the needs of students who are academically disadvantaged and experience a lack of resources. For many of these students, much more is needed than an enhanced academic curriculum. Without comprehensive counseling programs in schools, there may be little or no impact on the students who most need to improve their academic success, set goals for their future and become lifelong learners. School counselors by the very nature of their professional training can and do play a vital role in supporting, advocating and investing in the developmental growth and learning of all students.

REFERENCES AND RESOURCES

American School Counselor Association. (2005). *The ASCA national model: A framework for school counseling programs, second edition.* Alexandria, VA: Author.

Payne, R. K. (1996). *A framework for understanding poverty.* Highlands, TX: aha! Process.

What are the most pervasive career issues among K-12 students that school counselors address?

Kay Brawley, Consultant
Ponce Inlet, Fla.
kbrawley@mindspring.com

The career issues of students that U.S. school counselors address are similar to the same challenges found globally in this profession. Let me answer by drawing upon some research from A.G. Watts of the National Institute for Careers Education and Counseling, Cambridge, UK (Watts, 2004).

Public policy is not of interest to most school counselors. What draws counselors to career development work with students, and what inspires and motivates them, are not policy goals, but a concern for helping young people. They are interested in students as individuals, rather than in political ideas, and that is as it should be.

However, public policy is crucial to school counseling, particularly since national, regional or local governments usually pay for career services. In the U.S., knowledge of legislation such as the Elementary and Secondary School Counseling Program, Individuals with Disabilities Education Act, and Perkins Vocational and Technical Education Act, is important in finding resources to be successful as a counselor (ACA, 2004).

Another way to make the right connections is through specific training in programs that integrate career development public policies into the curriculum. For example the following three programs offer fresh perspectives on career exploration and lifelong learning keys to success for students of all ages:

- Working Ahead: Global Career Development Facilitator training
- America's Career Resource Network's Real Game career management programs
- America's Career Resource Network's Smart Options programs

The Organisation for Economic Co-operation and Development, an intergovernmental organization with 30 member countries, including the U.S., recently conducted a study to enable countries to see how they compare with regards to career development and to share good practices. The review concentrated on career counseling issues, and the findings are useful to those in this country responsible for career development and school counseling.

General findings of this study include the following:

- All countries are seeking to re-examine their career guidance systems in the context of encouraging lifelong learning and sustained employability for all.

- Career guidance services are still predominantly concerned with two groups: young people and the unemployed. The needs of adults, young and older, outside the labor market altogether, or who are employed but seeking to change or develop their career, are relatively neglected.
- A need exists for career guidance services that go beyond the provision of career information. For career information to be of value, individuals need to be able to find it, understand it, relate it to their needs and convert it into personal action. Strategies for providing this service from professionals are therefore essential.
- No country has yet developed a universal lifelong guidance system capable of supporting a lifelong learning strategy. However, if the strengths of each of the countries could be brought together, a powerful model would emerge.

Specific findings of this study include the following:

- A growing recognition of the importance of career development and counseling in schools, including lifelong learning and career development
- A risk of career development and counseling in schools being subsumed and marginalized by the counselor's holistic role covering personal and social as well as educational and vocational guidance
- A need for career development and counseling within the school to partner with specialized career guidance available outside the school, offering closer links with the labor market, clearer professional career guidance and stronger impartiality
- A growing concern for young people who have dropped out of formal education and training with few or no qualifications, requiring a highly individualized counseling approach
- A need to integrate public employment services more closely into lifelong learning, including lifelong access to guidance
- A need for stronger measures to coordinate the envisioning and development of strategies for delivering lifelong access to career services, particularly in government, where guidance services policy is often fragmented across numerous branches
- A need for strategic instruments that are useful across the whole range of career development, including organizational quality standards and competency frameworks
- A need for better coordination between governments and professional associations on establishing standards

Strengthening the connections between public policy and professional counseling is crucial if lifelong access to career guidance, in support of lifelong career development for all, is to become a reality. All school counselors could greatly benefit by embracing public policy focus on lifelong learning needs of students in making informed decisions.

REFERENCES AND RESOURCES

American Counseling Association Public Policy & Legislation, Resources for Counselors
www.counseling.org/public

America's Career Resource Network Association, Real Game Series career management programs
www.acrna.net
acrna.net/realgame.htm

America's Career Resource Network Association, Smart Options Assessment for career exploration
acrna.net/smart.html

John J. Heldrich Center for Workforce Development, Rutgers University. Working Ahead: The National Workforce and Career Development Instructor Program – Global Career Development Facilitator Training
www.heldrich.rutgers.edu/WorkingAhead/working11.asp

Organisation for Economic Co-operation and Development: Global Issues Review. A Career Guidance Policy Review
www.oecd.org/

Van Horn, C., Pierson-Balik, D., & Schaffner, H. (2004). *The 70 percent solution: Five principles for helping young people make better choices during and after high school.* New Brunswick, NJ: John J. Heldrich Center for Workforce Development, Rutgers University.

Watts, A. G. & Fretwell, D. H. (2004). *Public policies for career development: Case studies and emerging issues for designing career information and guidance systems in developing and transition economies.* Washington, DC: World Bank.

What special issues do school counselors need to consider when implementing comprehensive school counseling programs in rural schools?

Angie Stansell, School Counselor
Hatton High School
Town Creek, Ala.
akounsel@yahoo.com

A school counselor should always first seek the counselor's state plan and guidelines for public schools before establishing a guidance program. (Hopefully each state plan is modeled after the ASCA National Model.)

The rural school is in a culture all its own. The residents usually are there because they were born and grew up there. They are the descendants of many generations in their farming family and usually reside on at least a parcel of the family land. Generally, the income is low and many rural schools qualify for Title I monetary support. Many students have grown up with work assignments either before or after school hours such as feeding the cows or chickens. With farming constantly changing, most farmers now are also blue-collar workers and, as with most families in our country, both parents work. While there are few professionals, the parents are generally more involved and supportive of the children and school than their city counterparts.

Often multiculturalism and diversity are missing unless it is an area with many transitional/migrant families who have come to the area as seasonal workers. This in itself has created the need for changes to be made in the counseling program, such as introducing English as a second language programs and language translators.

To help students achieve, the application of the ASCA National Standards in the domains of academic, career and personal/social development is crucial. Implementation of the personal/social development standard will not vary much from a guidance program in a city school because there will be some of the same needs. However, the areas of academic and career development will be different in the rural school program. In addition, resources will also be different.

ACADEMIC DEVELOPMENT

Many rural schools have kindergarten through 12th grade at one site in one school. Elementary classrooms are on one wing of the building, and secondary is on the other wing. Thus, there is usually one school counselor covering all grades. Often in the high school, students will not be able to take as many electives or AP courses (if any) since classes are limited or prohibited due to the size of the faculty. Inclusion of cultural events, such as theater and the arts, may mean transporting the students to a nearby town or city. Extracurricular activities often center on athletics, band and agriculture-related activities/clubs. After-school activities are limited due to transportation problems since many of these students ride school buses to and from school daily.

CAREER DEVELOPMENT

The counselor will have to emphasize this standard and show students how to find their own strengths for the world of work, acquire skills to investigate their job possibilities jobs and learn how to achieve future career goals. Many may not have thought of "life beyond" or acquiring a trade/skill, much less attending college. Even if they have, they will not go off very far and certainly will plan to come back to their home or farm, even though they may never plan to be involved in farming as an adult. Students must be able to see how academics relate to work and life outside their rural culture if they do choose to move. The rural school counselor should be careful not to put down the rural lifestyle while providing career development opportunities.

RESOURCES

Resources will be limited and different from those in city schools. The school counselor will rely on many agencies in the closest town to serve the student/family population in the personal/social domain. Examples include:

- Human services departments
- Health and mental health departments
- Abuse prevention agencies
- Big Brother/Sister organizations
- Civic clubs (such as Lions Club who can help with money for eye exams)

The school system may have grant and federally/state funded programs that can serve as resources. Examples include:

- Migrant/outreach for the homeless
- 21st Century (tutors)
- Teen pregnancy
- Agriculture programs (farming-home extension)
- Technology centers, which may offer technical classes (such as welding, electronics, cosmetology)

It would be wise to make a personal directory or resources with contact names and phone numbers so that referrals may be made.

The rural school counselor will find the school counseling role expanded to include registrar, clerk, nurse, social worker, club sponsor and many more jobs not related to counseling.

REFERENCES AND RESOURCES

American School Counselor Association. (2005). *The ASCA national model: A framework for school counseling programs, second edition.* Alexandria, VA: Author.

Gysbers, N. C., & Henderson, P. (2000). *Developing and managing your school guidance program* (3rd ed.). Alexandria, VA: American Counseling Association.

State plan or model in the school counselor's state

What types of notes do school counselors need to maintain in the course of their work? What is the most efficient and effective way to do this?

Janice Tkaczyk, School Counselor
Cape Cod Regional High School
Harwich, Mass.
jtkaczyk@capetech.us

School counselors need to keep the following:

- Personal notes on individual counseling sessions
- Legal forms

- Meeting notes
- Organizational notes such as to-do lists, appointments and weekly plans
- Individual student success plans
- Correspondence
- Presentation notes

I have moved all of my "notes" to my computer with the exception of the personal notes I maintain on my individual sessions with students. The latter are maintained in a locked cabinet next to my desk and are accessible only to me. In my absence, the school counselor in charge is given a key should a situation occur with one of my students and there is a need for him/her to refer to these notes in order to provide support or intervention.

Right now all forms such as 622, Title IX and 51 A are hard copy. We do not receive these from the Office for Civil Rights or the Department of Social Services in downloadable format. I expect to see that soon. Therefore, these are done by hand and secured in the same locked cabinet.

I have a laptop that I use at all meetings for taking notes. Whether it is a 504 meeting, parent conference or staff meeting, taking down my thoughts this way is a real time saver. I put my weekly appointments and classroom presentations in my weekly calendar in Microsoft Office. My next move will be to a Palm Pilot, which will be even easier.

I have folders on my computer for correspondence with colleagues, parents and staff. I keep my workshop presentations both on my computer and on disk. I usually save important e-mails for the full school year in case I need to either refer to one of them or document communication. I regularly e-mail about 10 percent of my parents, and that number increases by one or two parents a month.

Joe Rotter, Counselor Educator
University of South Carolina
Columbia, South Carolina
jrotter@gwm.sc.edu

Note taking in schools has a history that predates school counseling as a profession; schools have been keeping records on students since the beginning of time. What to keep notes of and what not to keep has been a perennial question. It has been known for some time that the child who has had the most difficulty in school is also the child with the thickest file folder in the school office.

Although legislation in the past several decades has reduced the volume of hearsay notes in student files, there is an ongoing battle over what to put on file. More specifically, what counselors should make formal note of regarding their interactions with students is a point of contention.

A clear distinction should be made between student academic files and student counseling and disciplinary notes and records. Clearly the grades, test scores and teacher anecdotal notes regarding a students' academic progress are routinely kept and accessible to those authorized to see them. The dilemma for school counselors is how much of the personal counseling that they engage in with students should be noted.

Counselors must become familiar with federal, state and local laws, regulations, and policies governing record keeping and access to such records. Although federal laws such as the Family Educational Rights and Privacy Act (FERPA) and now the Health Insurance Portability and Accountability Act (HIPAA) apply universally, state laws and local policy may provide additional constraints on record keeping practice. Schmidt (2003), indicates that, "Private notes kept by counselors … are not addressed by FERPA, and, therefore, may be held in confidence if in the judgment of the counselor it is best to do so" (p. 290). According to James and DeVaney (1995), "Careful records can prevent lawsuits against the counselor or the school when, for example, they record the onset and nature of the problem, consultation and treatment strategies, and referral or problem resolution." They go on to say however, that, "Personal notes as distinguished from school records, are intended only for the counselor's eyes, but nonetheless should be written using factual, concrete, and behaviorally oriented language" (p. 99). In more general terms, Piazza and Baruth state that "The client record should contain all information about the client necessary for his or her treatment" (1990, p. 313).

One might assume that only applies to counselors in private practice or those working for mental health agencies. Perhaps this was true at one point; however, as more and more school counselors acquire credentials above and beyond school counselor certification (such as, NCC, LPC, play therapy registry, and marriage and family licensure), they become bound by the standards of practice established by these respective groups. With this in mind and increasing legislation at both the state and federal levels, most recently in reference to HIPAA, making counselors more vulnerable to litigation, it behooves school counselors to keep detailed and accurate records of their counseling sessions.

In fact, there are documented cases where, although the counselor's practice might be questioned, the fact that they kept specific notes detailing the interaction and actions taken saved them from prosecution. In one recent case involving a student who allegedly missed the deadline for a college scholarship, if it hadn't been for good record keeping on the part of the counselor documenting that proper procedures were followed by the school, the counselor and the school could have been held liable for what was actually an error on the part of the college.

The bottom line is that everything you do as a school counselor must be in the best interest of your client. The most important concept and subsequent practice are based upon nonmalfeasance, that is, do no harm. When in doubt, consult with another professional and document your discussion. The time has long gone when it was policy to keep few notes for fear that they could be misused or misinterpreted. In today's world, it behooves the school counselor to be prolific in their note taking, albeit limited to objective statements of fact.

Although state laws and local policy may differ, generally the counselor would maintain the following on file:

- Signed copy of the informed consent
- Artifacts such as poetry, drawings, journal entries and photos of sand tray
- Detailed notes including verbatim statements from client and counselor when necessary
- Statement of the problem(s)
- Counseling plans
- Discussions with other professionals
- Referral to other professionals
- Consultation with parents or guardians
- Evaluation of procedures and effects
- Statement of termination
- Other items as deemed appropriate or required by law or policy

For an example of case notes, see Accountability Strategies for School Counselors: a Baker's Dozen by Fairchild and Seeley (1995).

It is now considered a matter of malpractice by professional associations not to maintain appropriate records of counseling. Good records are in the best interest of both the counselor and the client.

REFERENCES AND RESOURCES

American Counseling Association. (2005). *Code of ethics and standards of practice*. Alexandria, VA: Author. Available online at www.counseling.org

American School Counselor Association. (2002). *The professional school counselor and confidentiality*. Alexandria, VA: Author. Available online at www.schoolcounselor.org

American School Counselor Association. (2004). *Ethical standards for school counselors*. Alexandria, VA: Author. Available online at www.schoolcounselor.org

Fairchild, T. N., & Seeley, T. J. (1995). Accountability strategies for school counselors: A baker's dozen. *The School Counselor, 42*(5), 377–392.

Family Educational Rights and Privacy Act, 20 U.S.C. § 1232g (1974). Available online at *www.ed.gov/offices/om/fpco/ferpa*

Fischer, L., & Sorensen, G. P. (1996). *School law for counselors, psychologists, and social workers*. New York: Longman.

Health Insurance Portability and Accountability Act of 1996, 45 C.F.R. parts 160 and 164. Available online at *www.hhs.gov/ocr/hipaa*

James, S. H., & DeVaney, S. B. (1995). Preparing to testify: The school counselor as court witness. *The School Counselor, 43*(2), 97–102.

Peterson's
www.petersons.com

Piazza, N. J., & Baruth, N. E. (1990). Client record guidelines. *Journal of counseling and Development, 68*(3), 313–316.

Schmidt, J. J. (2003). *Counseling in schools: Essential services and comprehensive programs*. New York: Allyn & Bacon.

SOS, Depressions Screening and Suicide Prevention
www.mentalhealthscreening.org

Counseling-Related Legislation

Not surprisingly, those who submitted legislation-related questions for this project focused on two areas specific areas. First, the No Child Left Behind (NCLB) Act of 2001 attempts to improve the performance of America's primary and secondary schools by increasing the standards of accountability for states, school districts and schools, as well as providing parents more flexibility in choosing which schools their children will attend. Additionally, it promotes an increased focus on reading and re-authorizes the Elementary and Secondary Education Act (EDEA) of 1965.

Second, the Family Educational Rights and Privacy Act (FERPA) is a federal law that protects the privacy of student education records. The law applies to all schools that receive funds under an applicable program of the U.S. Department of Education. FERPA gives parents certain rights with respect to their children's education records. These rights transfer to the student when he or she reaches the age of 18 or attends a school beyond the high school level.

This chapter tackles the counseling-related issues surrounding both NCLB and FERPA legislation.

REFERENCES AND RESOURCES

No Child Left Behind Act of 2001, 20 U.S.C. § 6301 (2002). Available online at *www.ed.gov/nclb/*

Family Educational Rights and Privacy Act, 20 U.S.C. § 1232g (1974). Available online at *www.ed.gov/offices/om/fpco/ferpa*

What are the top three most pressing implications of NCLB for school counselors?

Cynthia Floyd, Consultant
North Carolina Department of Public Instruction
Raleigh, N.C.
cfloyd@dpi.state.nc.us

The top three most pressing implications of NCLB for school counselors are: showing accountability, affecting a positive school climate and providing prevention and intervention programs for children who are at-risk.

SHOWING ACCOUNTABILITY

In this age of accountability, school counselors are asking how they can show the significance of what they do. They understand that today's school counselors need to be able to convince decision makers that their positions and roles are critical to student success.

To do this, school counselors should maintain performance data on the services they provide that indicates how their services affected the students. For example, a counselor providing anger management services would want to collect participant data before and after counseling in areas such as discipline referrals and academic achievement to demonstrate a student's improvement in those areas.

AFFECTING A POSITIVE SCHOOL CLIMATE

A safe, orderly and caring school environment is essential to student success. School counselors can affect a school's climate by getting students, staff and parents involved in programs and activities that promote a positive school environment. For example, students can join clubs and participate in activities that send the message that bullying is not allowed and fights are unacceptable. Peer pressure can be a wonderful influence if properly directed. In addition, school counselors can help students take ownership of their school and their choices.

PROVIDING PREVENTION AND INTERVENTION PROGRAMS FOR CHILDREN WHO ARE AT-RISK

Many students who lag behind academically are the same students that come to our schools abused, hungry, neglected or at-risk in many other ways. While closing this academic gap is a primary focus in education, a child who is hungry or afraid of a situation at home or school is not ready to learn. School counselors are the primary service providers trained to assist these students through counseling, community service referrals and multiple support efforts that promote coping skills and resiliency.

REFERENCES AND RESOURCES

American School Counselor Association. (2005). *The ASCA national model: A framework for school counseling programs, second edition.* Alexandria, VA: Author. Available online at www.schoolcounselor.org

Center for School Counseling Outcome Research, University of Massachusetts at Amherst *www.umass.edu/schoolcounseling/index.htm*

Dahir, C., & Stone, C. (2003). Accountability: A MEASURE of the impact school counselors have on student achievement. *Professional School Counseling, 6,* p. 214–221.

Diverse topics related to teens and mental health *www.athealth.com/Practitioner/newsletter/FPN_7_8.html*

Educational Resources Information Center *www.eric.ed.gov/*

Guidance Channel *www.guidancechannel.com*

Multiple School Counselor Resources at Jefferson County School (Tennessee) *classroom.jc-schools.net/guidance/*

National Association of School Psychologists document specifying portions of No Child Left Behind Act that specifically relate to counseling and mental health *www.nasponline.org/pdf/SchoolMentalHealthProvisions.pdf*

North Carolina's Guidance Curriculum for the Comprehensive School Counseling Program; aligned with ASCA's National Model *www.ncpublicschools.org/curriculum/guidance/*

Part D of the No Child Left Behind Act *www.ed.gov/policy/elsec/leg/esea02/pg9.html*

Questia: The World's Largest Online Library, Students At Risk *www.questia.com/Index.jsp?CRID=students_at_risk&OFFID=se1&KEY=at_risk_students*

What are the top three or four challenges or issues for school counselors when complying with FERPA? What are practical suggestions?

Amy Milsom, Counselor Educator
University of Iowa
Iowa City, Iowa
amy-milsom@uiowa.edu

Complying with FERPA requires school counselors to consider best practices in record keeping. While school counselors should not be solely responsible for monitoring student records, as student advocates they can contribute by sharing with administrators their knowledge of privacy and confidentiality issues.

DETERMINING WHETHER TO KEEP CASE NOTES

One challenge in complying with FERPA is determining whether to keep case notes. Best practice guidelines encourage school counselors to keep case notes in order to:

- Monitor student progress
- Protect themselves in the event of future lawsuits
- Comply with administrators who request that counseling progress notes be included in student files

At the same time, ethical guidelines emphasize the importance of client confidentiality, with exceptions made for potential harm or abuse. According to FERPA, any records kept by school personnel and available to or shared with others are considered part of a student's educational record, and therefore accessible to parents. Case notes kept by school counselors would be included under this guideline, unless those notes are kept secure and private; no one else must know they exist.

So how do school counselors protect student confidentiality when keeping case notes? Here are a few suggestions:

- Assume that all counseling records might at some point be seen
- For records that must be shared with school personnel, be succinct and summarize themes only

- For personal notes (i.e., private, not shared), write the notes in such a manner that no harm would be done to the student if anyone happened to gain access
- Be succinct and report only important details and facts
- Secure your personal notes in a locked drawer or file cabinet rather than storing them on a computer where someone could more easily gain access

DEVELOPING AND ENFORCING STRICT ACCESS POLICIES

Another challenge in complying with FERPA is developing and enforcing strict access policies. Whether student records are kept in the school counseling office or in the main office, school counselors should be involved in ensuring policies exist to control access to those records. Access policies are necessary because:

School personnel who maintain or frequently access student records often have no formal training in or understanding of FERPA.
School personnel may not understand why they have limited or no access to student files.

To ensure appropriate access to student records, school counselors should work with administrators to develop access policies that:

- Enforce strict monitoring of student records
- Identify who is responsible for maintaining student records
- Designate the location and content of student records
- Include lists of who has access to student records, and at what access level
- Formalize sign-out procedures
- Identify procedures for releasing information to outside personnel
- Provide yearly reminder activities for all school personnel to ensure their understanding of access policies

DEALING WITH PARENTAL REQUESTS TO RESTRICT ACCESS

A third challenge in complying with FERPA is dealing with parental requests to restrict a noncustodial parent's access to student records. According to FERPA, unless the school district is provided a copy of a court order specifically prohibiting them from sharing information with one parent, schools should continue to allow all legal guardians access to records.

Court cases where the custodial parent filed a complaint against a school district for sharing records with a noncustodial parent have consistently upheld the rights of both parents, emphasizing how fortunate a student is to have more than one parent interested in his or her education.

Robert Pate, Counselor Educator
University of Virginia
Charlottesville, Virginia
rhp9m@virginia.edu

The greatest challenges facing school counselors as they attempt to comply with the letter and spirit of FERPA are the following:

- Determining who has parental rights
- Determining what material should be the counselor's personal notes (not subject to FERP) and what material should be in official school records (subject to FERPA)
- Confusing rights to educational records with rights to counselors' opinions
- Providing frank references for colleges and universities without creating conflict with parents

DETERMINING WHO HAS PARENTAL RIGHTS

FERPA defines a parent of a student as "a natural parent, a guardian, or an individual acting as a parent in the absence of a parent or a guardian" (Authority: 20 U.S.C. 1232g). While this definition of a parent seems clear, determining who is "acting as a parent" is not defined in the statute.

School systems typically define parents as people who have responsibility for making educational decisions. FERPA policy interpretation separates rights to records from custody. That means that a noncustodial parent has FERPA rights pertaining to educational records unless such rights have been removed by a judicial proceeding.

DETERMINING WHAT MATERIAL SHOULD BE THE COUNSELOR'S PERSONAL NOTES

Counselors are often confused by what records should be considered accessible as the result of FERPA and the fact that any document that is relevant to a legal proceeding can be subpoenaed.

According to FERPA, counselors can keep personal counseling notes or memory aids. The FERPA statute exempts "records of instructional, supervisory and administrative personnel and educational personnel ancillary thereto which are in the sole possession of the maker thereof and which are not accessible or revealed to any other person except a substitute (Authority: 20 U.S.C. 1232g(a)(4)).

It's important to note that a subpoena can be challenged; however, a counselor should seek legal assistance before doing so. Like most in the field, I suggest that counseling notes be private and not available even to a substitute unless the responsibility is being permanently transferred.

CONFUSING RIGHTS TO EDUCATIONAL RECORDS WITH RIGHTS TO COUNSELORS' OPINIONS

Related to the challenge of separating counseling notes from the records covered by FERPA is the requirement for the counselor who is subpoenaed to testify in domestic disputes on matters of opinion that are not part of the record subject to FERPA.

In such a case, a counselor can present reasons to the presiding judge why he or she should not be required to testify about the content of counseling sessions. The rationale behind this is based on Wigmore's conditions for privileged communication:

- Privacy of the original communication
- Necessity of privacy for the relationship between the counselor and student
- Notion that society wants to foster the counselor-student relationship
- Belief that justice can be served without forcing the counselor to break a confidence

PROVIDING FRANK REFERENCES WITHOUT CREATING CONFLICT

Counselors in secondary schools are often troubled about being chastised, or even worse, sued, by parents who believe that a counselor's letter of recommendation, required by many post-secondary institutions, has harmed their child.

The school system should shield counselors from aggressive or abusive parents and provide clear guidelines about the availability of recommendation letters to parents. FERPA policy interpretation separates rights to records from custody.

Counselors should remember that parents are probably not reacting to a bad recommendation per se, but rather to a truthful recommendation that contains information they wish withheld. Or, they're reacting to a good recommendation they don't consider good enough. A counselor who has provided a recommendation in good faith based on facts and opinions drawn from these facts has little to fear from a defamation suit.

REFERENCES AND RESOURCES

American Counseling Association, Office of Public Policy & Legislation. (2000). *Professional counselor's guide to federal law on student records*. Alexandria, VA: Author.

Family Educational Rights and Privacy Act, 20 U.S.C. § 1232g (1974). Available online at *www.ed.gov/offices/om/fpco/ferpa*

Guillot-Miller, L., & Partin, L. (2003). Web-based resources for legal and ethical issues in school counseling. *Professional School Counseling, 7,* 52–57.

Policy Studies Associates, Inc. (1997). Protecting the privacy of student education records. *Journal of School Health, 67,* 139–140.

Remley, T. P., Hermann, M. A., & Huey (Eds.). (2003). *Ethical and legal issues in school counseling* (2nd ed.). Alexandria, VA: American School Counselor Association.

U.S. Department of Education FERPA Summary *www.ed.gov/policy/gen/guid/fpco/ferpa/index.html*

U.S. Department of Education Links and FAQS *www.ed.gov/policy/gen/guid/fpco/index.html*

Walker, P. A., & Steinberg, S. J. (1997). Confidentiality of educational records: Serious risks for parents and school districts. *Journal of Law and Education, 26,* 11–27.

Wigmore, J. H. (1940). *Evidence in trials at common law.* Boston: Little, Brown.

School Counselor Performance

This chapter includes questions and answers related to how counselors most effectively and efficiently perform their jobs. However, a particular focus of this chapter would fit under two different quadrants of the ASCA National Model®, the delivery and management systems.

Based on the core beliefs, philosophies and missions identified in the foundation, the delivery system describes the activities, interactions and methods to deliver the program.

Intertwined with the delivery system is the management system, which incorporates organizational processes and tools to ensure the program is organized, concrete, clearly delineated and reflective of the school's needs. This is a relatively new concept for administrators and school counselors who traditionally have not viewed counselors as "managers."

In the pages ahead, you will read expert opinions on a range of questions related to understanding advisory programs, meeting the needs of diverse students, managing your time, dealing with discipline, picking a counseling approach, communicating the role of the counselor to students and stake holders, working with difficult parents, developing peer helper programs and much more.

Advisory programs are one possible delivery system for school counseling intervention. What are the advantages, disadvantages and tips for success?

Colette Dollarhide, Counselor Educator
University of South Carolina
Columbia, S.C.
ctdollarhi@aol.com

OVERVIEW OF ADVISORY PROGRAMS

Advisory programs arose from discussions about developmentally appropriate education for middle school students, and are now found in high schools and middle schools alike. They are generally defined as a group of one adult and 12 to 15 students who meet for at least 20 minutes a day in the school setting (formerly known as homeroom). The adult, usually a teacher, is charged with establishing and maintaining a quality, individualized relationship with the students to engage in conversation and/or activities addressing important life questions, including academic, career and personal/social issues – an obvious link to the comprehensive school counseling program.

Overall goals of advisory programs can include:

- Providing one caring adult to whom the student can turn with questions and concerns
- Developing positive self images
- Linking students to the school and the educational agenda
- Providing the opportunity to develop relationships with peers and adults
- Facilitating the transition from one academic level or grade to the next
- Developing and refining study skills
- Identifying and exploring career interests
- Learning to set academic, career and personal goals

The support for well-functioning advisory programs comes from the research into resilience, persistence and community relative to schools. Studies have documented that these advisories, when well run, do indeed create meaningful learning communities that foster connection with teachers and peers, and address impediments to learning. When well structured and staffed with trained, committed adults, advisory programs can be a powerful venue for promoting the comprehensive school counseling agenda of academic, career and personal/social success for all students.

CHALLENGES TO ADVISORY PROGRAMS

While many advisory programs have been established by school counselors as a means of extending the comprehensive school counseling agenda to all students, research has found that not all teachers are equally prepared, equipped or motivated to be in personal mentoring/advising relationships with students. If counselors have not been involved in the development of the advisory program, it could be seen as usurping the counseling agenda. In addition, because of the many ways that advisory programs have been configured, there are many possible misconceptions about such programs.

The five most common reasons that advisory programs fail are the following:

- Insufficient planning
- Inadequate preparation of advisors
- Incomplete development of topics and activities
- Inappropriate time for meetings
- Lack of administrative and/or counselor support for the program

ADVANTAGES OF COUNSELING
INTERVENTIONS VIA ADVISORIES

When the advisory program, the comprehensive school counseling agenda and the national and/or state developmental competencies are aligned, advisory programs become powerful vehicles for providing comprehensive prevention and intervention to all students because of the following:

- All adults in the school are invested in the academic, career and personal/social development of all students, and fewer students will "slip through the cracks."
- The comprehensive school counseling agenda is seen as a full partner with the academic mission of the institution.
- Students have resources to support them in their educational journey.
- Students and teachers experience the school as a caring, supportive community; the entire school climate is conducive to learning.

DISADVANTAGES OF COUNSELING INTERVENTIONS VIA ADVISORIES

Disadvantages do exist, independent of whether counselors are involved in the development and ongoing maintenance of advisory programs. If counselors are not involved in the development and ongoing maintenance of advisory programs:

- The advisory program time could easily be usurped by the academic agenda, focusing on study skills and homework to the exclusion of career and personal/social issues.
- The advisory program could result in competition and turf issues with the counseling department, rendering the counseling department moot or doomed to focus on semi-clerical duties.

If counselors are involved in the development of advisory programs:

- Teachers will be functioning in quasi-counseling activities for which they have not been trained and may not be interested.
- Training, monitoring and evaluating so many professionals with advisory relationships with students is time- and labor-intensive.

TIPS FOR SUCCESS

- Be prepared to invest time in program design, advisor training and materials preparation
- Select advisors who are motivated and who naturally interact with students
- Address the academic agenda as well as career and personal/social issues, thereby helping teachers and administrators see the time as well spent and appropriate
- Meet regularly with advisors to monitor student progress and advisor feedback
- Explore the various models of advisory activities to create an advisory program that meets the unique needs of your school

REFERENCES AND RESOURCES

American Student Achievement Institute. (n.d.). *Guiding all kids: Implementing your local advisor-advisee program.* Bloomington, IN: Author. Available online at www.asai.indstate.edu/

Cole, C. (1992). *Nurturing a teacher advisory program.* Columbus, OH: National Middle School Association.

Compendium of Web sites about advisory programs for middle schools *www.middleweb.com/advisory.html*

Educators for Social Responsibility. (n.d.) *Partners in learning: Designing and implementing an effective advisory program.* Cambridge, MA: Author. Available online at *www.esrnational.org/hs/reform/ hsadvisory.htm*

Johnston, H. (n.d.). From advisory programs to restructured adult-student relationships: Restoring purpose to the guidance function of the middle level school. Tampa, FL: University of South Florida. Available online at *www.middleweb.com/johnston.html*

Summary of findings relative to high school advisories from the principal's perspective *www.principalspartnership.com/library.html*

How can school counselors and career guidance personnel assist more students of color and students from diverse cultures to participate in nontraditional career pathway programs?

José Villalba, Counselor Educator
University of North Carolina at Greensboro
Greensboro, N.C.
jose_villalba@UNCG.EDU

For female students and students of color, nontraditional career pathways are careers in medicine, law, engineering, pharmacy, higher education and architecture, to name a few. Some of the careers more common for these students are in the service industry, such as teaching, law enforcement, the military and nursing. Comparing the two lists, it is evident that there are disparities in salary and prestige between nontraditional and traditional career pathways.

If school counselors and career guidance specialists are to positively affect the career development of all students, then it stands to argue that these school professionals must become more involved in the career development, career self-efficacy, career information and career planning of diverse students in certain career tracks. Although the task is not an easy one, it is one school counselors and career guidance personnel can implement (and of which they already have the tools to do).

EXPAND NOTION OF CAREER OPTIONS

The career development of students starts at a very young age. Although most of us do not consider the importance of gender roles, parents' occupations and environmental factors, the facts are that children are exposed to jobs, occupations and careers very early on.

Therefore, elementary school counselors and career guidance specialists may assist all students by exposing them to a wide variety of career experiences, realizing that the more careers children learn about, the richer their career development. It is imperative that elementary school counselors and career specialists find video series, plan career field trips and organize career days with a specific emphasis on the level of gender and cultural diversity; they must make a concerted effort to infuse as much diversity as possible into these activities.

CHALLENGE LIMITED CAREER SELF-EFFICACY

Gender and racial/ethnic identity development is a major part of the middle school experience, which may have an impact on students' career self-efficacy. Career guidance personnel and school counselors would be wise to monitor students' identity development as it is related to career goals and aspirations, as well as belief in one's abilities. Through small group activities and large group guidance, school counselors and career specialists may challenge poor or limited career self-efficacy while fostering and encouraging a forum to freely discuss a multitude of career options.

INCREASE INTEREST IN
NONTRADITIONAL CAREER PATHWAYS

Finally, high school counselors and career specialists can help increase the interests of female students and students of color in nontraditional career pathways through diverse career information and career planning. School counselors are often seen as the multicultural experts within their schools due to their training. School counselors, therefore, must convert this knowledge into action by presenting gender, racial and ethically sensitive career materials and resources. Providing diverse career mentors and job shadowing in nontraditional settings for these students, locating scholarships for underrepresented students or simply challenging diverse students to look beyond their comfort zones are all effective ways of encouraging nontraditional careers for diverse students.

Also, career planning for many minority students entails discussions with parents and, perhaps, extended family members. For this reason, school counselors and career specialists may want to go outside the classroom and school to communicate with parents, thereby showing them respect while displaying a genuine interest in the careers of their children.

CONCLUSION

The most important ways school counselors and career guidance personnel can contribute to the diversity in all career pathways is to be aware and knowledgeable of gender and cultural differences. The simple act of increasing diversity awareness will lead to acquiring diverse career knowledge and augmenting career counseling and information delivery skills to benefit all students. School counselors and career guidance personnel must make the effort to apply all of their career development and diversity training to counseling and educating all students.

REFERENCES AND RESOURCES

Career Voyages
    www.careervoyages.gov

Diversity Working.com
    www.diversityworking.com

Leong, F. T. L., & Tan, V. L. M. (2003). Cross-cultural career counseling in schools. In P. B. Pedersen & J. C. Carey (Eds.), *Multicultural counseling in schools* (pp. 234–256). Boston: Allyn & Bacon.

Nile, S. G., & Harris-Bowlsbey, J. (2002). *Career development in the 21st century.* Upper Saddle River, NJ: Merrill Prentice Hall.

How can school counselors manage and protect their time so they have greater success in implementing a comprehensive program?

Linda Miller, Supervisor
Jefferson County Public Schools
Louisville, Kentucky
lmiller1@jefferson.k12.ky.us

I believe the most effective way to protect a counselor's time is to have a well-planned comprehensive program that is aligned and integrated with the mission of the school. The role of the counseling program can become integral and seamless if the plan is:

- Focused on student achievement
- Dedicated to removing learning gaps
- Based on school data
- Results oriented

The plan should not be developed in isolation but with the support and help of other stakeholders from the school community. These stakeholders become allies in helping to assure the counseling program is implemented fully and that the role of the counselor becomes a leadership role that is protected from "adminstrivia."

After the plan is developed, it becomes very important to get the word out. Make sure that teachers, students and parents are aware of the importance of having a comprehensive program and how vital it is to raising student achievement.

The final step is to evaluate the plan. Make sure that results are measured and reported to document the benefits of a having a program and a professional counselor to lead it.

As a former principal, I know that such a focused effort, showing positive student results and leading to the academic and personal/social success of students, would not go unnoticed. As the administrator, I would join others in becoming an avid and vocal protector of the counselor's time.

How do I deal with my principal who wants me to take care of discipline?

Jennifer Baggerly, Counselor Educator
University of South Florida
Tampa, Fla.
Baggerly@tempest.coedu.usf.edu

The proverbial three "R's" have been the guide in teaching students reading, writing and arithmetic. For school counselors, the three R's are also the guide in dealing with a principal who wants you to take care of discipline. What are the three R's for school counselors in this situation? Respect, role and responsibilities.

RESPECT

First and foremost, school counselors are to demonstrate respect for the position and person of their principal (ASCA, 2004). Respecting your principal's position entails understanding his or her role as the primary instructional leader that manages personnel assignment and evaluation, expenditure of funds, discipline, curriculum design, program evaluation, school safety and building related issues (National Association for Elementary School Principals, 2004). Respecting the person of a principal entails appreciating his or her unique characteristics such as age, experience, gender, ethnicity, personality, health and personal life events.

Consider the different needs of a 32-year-old, soft-spoken Hispanic male principal who only has two years of experience and is newly married versus a 58-year-old, outgoing African American female principal who has 25 years of experience and three grown children. Both deserve respect for their position and person, although the way you communicate that respect may be different.

For the former, respecting his need to appear competent and in control during a student crisis may be communicated through statements such as, "You are concerned with restoring order and getting this student under control. I'll help with that by assessing the crisis, consulting with teachers and parents, and counseling the student, and then I'll get back with you."

For the latter, respecting her experience and need for respect may be communicated through statements such as, "You've seen students do this before. They can be tiring and frustrating. I'll help by consulting with teachers and parents and counseling the student. Then I'll get back to you."

In both cases, respect is most effectively demonstrated by employing Carl Rogers' (1951) core conditions of unconditional positive regard, empathy and genuineness. Being genuine about your perspective and proposed actions requires you to be steadfast in your role.

ROLE

The school counselor's role is clearly defined in the ASCA National Model (2005). School counselors take "a leadership role in effecting systemic change in a school" (p. 2) by designing and implementing a comprehensive school counseling program to promote students' competencies in academic, career and personal/social development.

Within this role, appropriate counseling duties include, but are not limited to, counseling students, consulting with principals, teachers and parents, and coordinating resources. However, ASCA plainly states that inappropriate duties include "performing disciplinary actions" (2003, p. 3). Fortunately, more than 90 percent of principals surveyed by Perusse, Goodnough, Donegan, and Jones (2004) agree that performing disciplinary actions is not an appropriate duty for school counselors.

Giving your principal printed material regarding the ASCA National Model and research, such as Perusse's et al. (2004) study as well as Brigman and Campbell's (2003) study that indicates counselor-led interventions increase students' academic scores and behavior, may help you develop agreement on appropriate school counselor's roles and duties. Posting and disseminating your weekly calendar of scheduled counseling activities to students, parents, teachers and administrators will also help them respect your role. Providing teachers, administrators and school improvement teams with resources on discipline strategies will demonstrate your commitment to resolving school-wide discipline problems.

RESPONSIBILITIES

Finally, school counselors must be cognizant of their professional and ethical responsibilities. ASCA (2004) ethical standard A.1.a reminds school counselors that their primary responsibility is to the client, i.e., student, rather than the principal. Ethical guideline A.4.a. states that counselors are to avoid dual relationships with clients that could impair professional judgment. Being a student's counselor and a disciplinarian could be considered a dual relationship. Simply put, disciplining students compromises therapeutic relationships with students and hinders the school counselor's role of promoting the academic, career and personal/social development of students.

Given these guidelines of respect, roles and responsibilities, school counselors may respond to a principal's directive of "I need you to be in charge of discipline this year" with the following:

> *Thank you for your confidence in me. I know you have a lot to manage. I certainly will be a part of the team that addresses discipline strategies school wide. I'd like to share the ASCA National Model and some recent research with you to show you that the best use of my skills as a school counselor is to focus on appropriate duties such as classroom guidance, individual planning, counseling and consulting on issues such as discipline.*

According to my professional association, ASCA, directly disciplining students is considered inappropriate for school counselors because it compromises my professional and ethical responsibilities of maintaining a therapeutic relationship. However, what I can do is provide some helpful discipline resources to teachers and parents, counsel students on developing self-control, provide guidance lessons on respect of others and assess discipline referral data.

Perhaps we could discuss this further after you've had a chance to review the ASCA National Model and research. Could we set a time later in the week to discuss this?

REFERENCES AND RESOURCES

American School Counselor Association. (2005). *The ASCA national model: A framework for school counseling programs, second edition*. Alexandria, VA: Author.

American School Counselor Association. (2004). *Ethical standards for school counselors*. Alexandria, VA: Author. Available online at www.schoolcounselor.org

Brigman, G., & Campbell, C. (2003). Helping students improve academic achievement and school success behavior. *Professional School Counseling, 7*(2), 91–98.

Carnes, J. (Ed.). (1999). *Responding to hate at school: A guide for teachers, counselors, and administrators*. Montgomery, AL: Teaching Tolerance.

Cipani, E. (2002). *Positive behavioral support: Five plans for teachers*. Upper Saddle River, NJ: Merrill Prentice Hall.

Gysbers, N. C., & Henderson, P. (2000). *Developing and managing your school guidance program* (3rd ed.). Alexandria, VA: American Counseling Association.

Latham, G. (1994). *The power of positive parenting*. Milwaukee, WI: Northwest Publishing.

National Association for Elementary School Principals. (2004). NAESP platform. Alexandria, VA: Author. Available online at *www.naesp.org/client_files/platform04-05.pdf*

Perusse, R., Goodnough, G., Donegan, J., & Jones, C. (2004). Perceptions of school counselors and school principals about the national standards for school counseling programs and the transforming school counseling initiative. *Professional School Counseling, 7*(3), p. 152–161.

Rogers, C. (1951). *Client-centered therapy.* Boston: Houghton Mifflin.

Wittmer, J., & Adorno, G. (2000). *Managing your school counseling program: K-12 developmental strategies.* Minneapolis, MN: Educational Media.

How does a school counselor effectively help K-12 students to best understand his/her role at each level (elementary, middle and secondary)?

Bob Milstead, Supervisor
Orange County Public Schools
Orlando, Fla.
milster@ocps.k12.fl.us

The decision as to how best to help students understand the role of their counselor is one that is critical and often perplexing for school counselors. Over the years, most school counselors develop some materials/techniques to demonstrate the ways school counselors can help students. As with so many other areas involving schools and students, communication among all the parties involved is the primary ingredient.

ELEMENTARY SCHOOL

Determining what will work best at one's particular school setting is one of the first steps that need to be taken to help others understand the role of a school counselor. At the elementary school level, this often includes a book such at Katie Couric's "The Brand New Kid." After reading the book (designed for ages four to eight) to students, counselors can describe the kinds of activities and help they provide. Some counselors use a variety of hats or puppets to initiate a discussion of the roles they and other staff members play at the school. Frequently, counselors will hold a new student orientation every few weeks to meet with all the new students.

During this time together, counselors talk about ways they assist students in addition to covering the school rules, such as the dress code and specific policies for lunch time. Many counselors have begun using their school's Web site to answer the question, "What do counselors do?" The site often explains ways counselors assist not only children, but parents and teachers as well. This can also be a wonderful method to describe the school's comprehensive guidance program. Another technique that works well is to gather common objects to describe a counselor's role (for example, a rubber band to demonstrate flexibility and a paper clip to show how to hold things together).

MIDDLE SCHOOL

Middle school counselors have also begun to use the school's Web site to explain and clarify their comprehensive guidance program, explaining that a great deal of time might be spent on issues such as making decisions, solving problems and setting goals. Often counselors will go into classrooms to describe not only their role at school, but also that of the other student support services people available at the school, such as the police liaison officer and the school nurse.

Many schools have an in-house television system, and the counselors will use time during the morning announcements to clarify their role, describe upcoming events or to focus on a particular word of characteristic for the week. Many middle schools have also written a brochure (which is then distributed through both guidance and the main office) describing the role of the counselor and the ways assistance can be provided.

HIGH SCHOOL

High school counselors use many of the techniques listed above, especially the use of Web sites for the myriad of information sources to which high school students need access. Classroom presentations help clarify the kinds of services and assistance the school counselor(s) will provide. Frequently, school counselors will make a presentation to a variety of parent groups, such at the PTA or school advisory committee, to explain policies or procedures high school students need to be familiar with and to describe their comprehensive guidance program.

In schools that use a student planner, several pages can be inserted describing the guidance program and counseling policies and procedures. Many high schools offer summer orientation sessions for new students and their parents. These can be an excellent opportunity to discuss the comprehensive guidance program to be offered at the school. School newspapers and parent newsletters sometimes contain an article from the school counseling office about how counselors can help students.

Jennifer White, School Counselor
Burlington City Junior School
Burlington, N.J.
whiteje5@hotmail.com

As the sole, often busy school counselor for the urban junior high school I am fortunate enough to work for, the simple answer to that question is presence. Students best understand my role when they see me doing the critical tasks that define my role. Seventh and eighth grade students do not understand clinical terms like system support, consultation, collaboration or solution-focused therapy. Nor do they have readily definable task to characterize me with, such as college applications or recommendation letters. No, my middle school students know me by my presence, the ways I become involved in their lives. Quite simply, they know me by how my presence makes them feel – how reachable and attainable I am to them.

What kind of presence do I have in their lives, one might ask? During the school day, they know me as the person they can go to if they are in conflict. They know me as the smiling person who hurries them along to their next class, monitoring traffic through our narrow, busy hallway. They see me in their classes, talking about character development; they see me lead them through periodic awards assemblies where they receive recognition for everything from exemplary attendance to academic improvement to random acts of kindness I manage to "catch" them doing.

My role is larger than simply relating to students. I need to demonstrate my role and function to the other clients I serve – the faculty, the parents and the community at large. In some ways, this can teach students about my role in a more dramatic way than the services I deliver directly to them.

Often, the services I am involved with seek to compete with my presence to the children. As essential as these duties are, especially in an urban, impoverished district, it is important to distinguish between services and the ones that directly relate to the students. Students do not understand tasks like 504 committee meetings, school leadership council meetings or calls to community members trying to set up a career day for the students. What they see are closed doors and a person who can help behind those closed doors, unattainable and unreachable.

Therefore, as critical as my presence teaches them about my role and function, my lack of presence, my involvement in anything that is not student-centered, albeit essential, teaches my students about my role as well. When I first started counseling a few years ago, I began to see myself as the students were seeing me, with a phone attached to my ear, with paperwork exploding all over my desk, and with a smile for my students, but less and less time to free up for them. I realized, unfortunately, that I was teaching them who I wanted to be known as by what they saw me doing – phone calls, paperwork and meetings.

It became imperative to set boundaries, the kind that would let students in and release nonstudent-centered tasks out of my daily routine, at least as much as possible. Clearly, services for faculty and community maintain their demands on my time. I am still in the midst of creating a Web site for the counseling center at my school as a way to reach out to parents and community members. I just compiled a categorized list of community counseling practitioners available to parents on a sliding fee scale. Neither of these, however, needs to be done during school hours. That time belongs to my students.

Therefore, when the 504 committee, individual education plan and school leadership council meetings come up, and when the grade level team meetings surface (all important ways to demonstrate my role to teachers and administrators), I can feel a little less anxious that I am unavailable to students. I can feel confident that my presence is teaching them that no matter what else is going on, my time is, above all, reachable and attainable to them. They are the most important part of my presence.

REFERENCES AND RESOURCES

About your school counselor. (2000). South Deerfield, MA: Channing Bete. Ordering information online at *www.channing-bete.com*

American School Counselor Association
www.schoolcounselor.org

Couric, K. (2000). *The brand new kid.* New York: Doubleday.

The Education Trust
www2.edtrust.org/edtrust/

It's My Life/PBSKids Go
pbskids.org/itsmylife/index.html

Schmidt, J. (2004). A survival guide for the elementary/middle school counselor. San Francisco: Jossey-Bass.

Schwallie-Giddis, P., Cowan, D., & Schilling, D. (1994). *Counselor in the classroom: Activities and strategies for an effective classroom guidance program.* Torrance, CA: Innerchoice Publishing.

How does one find a balance among the many demands on the school counselor, such as individualized and group counseling, classroom work, consultation with parents and teachers, and crisis intervention?

Cynthia Francis, School Counselor
Chalmette Middle School
Chalmette, La.
cfrancis7@cox.net

Meeting the demands placed on the school counselor often resembles a balancing act. However, one of the most effective ways to get organized and eliminate some of the juggling is to make use of a basic calendar.

At the beginning of the school year, a master calendar can be set up for the counseling department. This calendar needs to correspond to the school calendar and list main topics that should be covered each month. Some of the items that might be included on this calendar include:

- Parent/teacher meetings
- Standardized tests dates
- Career or college nights
- Planned classroom guidance lessons
- Student groups

With the master calendar established, the counseling department can then identify priorities and make plans to address these items.

Setting up a monthly calendar and, subsequently, a weekly calendar further helps to organize the activities that are part of the counseling program. Time periods can be set aside for classroom guidance lessons and for individual and group counseling sessions. Establishing specific times for returning phone calls and meeting with parents and teachers is also essential.

When using calendars as a means of organizing the counseling program, it is important that these calendars be shared with students, parents and other school personnel. This is one way of publicizing the role of the school counselor, and it also allows others to know when the counselor is available for consultations.

Although calendars will help organize the demands placed on the school counselor, there will always be the unexpected and urgent needs that must be addressed. A school counselor, above all things, must be flexible and able to go with the flow. A good source for more information on the use of development of counseling program calendars is the ASCA National Model and its accompanying workbook.

Maryann Baldwin, Counselor
School District of Hillsboro County
Tampa, Fla.
maryann.baldwin@sdhc.k12.fl.us

The short answer to this question is, "I don't find a balance all the time." I work in a 90 percent free lunch, Title I urban middle school with 58 percent black students, 30 percent Hispanic students, 10 percent white students and two percent other. Some of my weeks are unbelievably busy, especially when I am the designated testing chairperson or have several cases of suspected child abuse. Some of my weeks are much more manageable, and I can catch up on seeing individual students and calling parents. Most of my weeks are a combination, depending upon what occurs at school, and what time of year it happens to be.

DIVIDE RESPONSIBILITIES

At my middle school of 900, we have three guidance counselors, one for each grade. We have tried to balance things by giving certain grade levels certain responsibilities, and then moving with our students through the three grade levels. In this way no one counselor gets "stuck" with the hardest job, and every counselor learns every job. A counselor starts with sixth graders and also has the responsibility for the child study team. In seventh grade, the counselor serves as testing chairperson. In eighth grade, the counselor does programming for high school, Limited English Proficiency and 504. All counselors register new students throughout the year, and each counselor chairs the a committee at his/her grade level for students who might be having academic or behavioral problems. All counselors participate in career education activities at his/her grade level, as well as notify students who are in danger of retention or who finally are retained.

Several positive results come from our format:

- Each counselor experiences all of the responsibilities of a middle school counselor, thus learning all aspects of middle school guidance.
- Students and parents get to really know their counselor, especially after two or three years. The cycle is only three years long, however, so counselors are never too far away from a particular grade level or guidance responsibility.
- Counselors work with all the teachers at a school over the course of three years. Since the administrators change grade levels each year, counselors work with all the administrators for all the grade levels over the course of three years.

KEEP A YEAR-LONG SCHEDULE

Each week brings surprises, no matter how well I may have planned. New registrations, teacher consultations, parents calling or dropping in, students having problems with other students or teachers, phone calls from other schools or state agencies, administrative requests and time of year all combine to make each week a unique experience. I have found having a year-long schedule, with certain events planned to occur throughout the year, keeps me on track and moving towards a successful completion to each school year.

In the beginning of the year, I go into all grade level classrooms to introduce myself and advertise groups. I have interested students sign up for groups and also have students suggest students who might benefit from groups. Group attendance requires a parent permission slip. My groups are ongoing throughout the year. At the semester change, I also go into all classrooms to discuss promotion and the after-school program to make up any failing courses. (This program meets for one hour twice a week after school. Attendance and completion results in a forgiveness grade of "D" to replace a grade of "F.") My third visit to classrooms occurs in early April when I introduce the career surveys and discuss the promotion policy from one grade to another.

COMMUNICATE

Communication is also very important. I meet with parents throughout the year, at conference nights (we have four) and on an individual basis. Weekly and sometimes daily I meet with individual students, parents and teachers. I attend all team meetings for my grade level and am a member of the steering committee. The principal meets with his staff, including guidance, twice a month, and I disseminate that information to my grade level teachers at team meetings.

How many hours per week should be spent engaged in each of the basic interventions (e.g., individual counseling, small group counseling, classroom guidance, peer helper programs, consulting and coordinating)?

Kenny Smith, School Counselor
Thatcher Schools
Thatcher, Ariz.
smith.kenny@thatcherud.k12.az.us

The ASCA National Model has been sweeping the country, and professional school counselors are embracing the concepts in districts, states and at individual schools. The reason for the excitement is the opportunity to answer the question, what do school counselors do? The ASCA National Model not only helps answer that question, but it provides the data to show why our schools run more efficiently and effectively because of professional school counselors.

Within the model is the delivery system, the portion of the model where professional school counselors can work with all students. The delivery system includes the following areas:

- Guidance and curriculum
- Individual student planning
- Responsive services
- Systems support

The difficult task within the delivery system is allocating time wisely for each of these areas. It is important to allocate specific time for each of the areas so that an adequate job can be done in each area.

The ASCA National Model recommends percentages of time to be spent in the four areas of the delivery system. Assuming an eight-hour day (480 minutes), minutes should be allocated as follows:

- 96 minutes spent on guidance an curriculum, such as classroom instruction, group activities, and parent workshops and instruction

- 144 minutes spent on individual student planning, such as individual or small-group appraisal and advisement
- 168 minutes spent on responsive services, such as individual and small group consultation, crisis counseling, referrals and peer facilitation
- 72 minutes spent on system support, such as professional development and partnering with staff, parents, community leaders, advisory council and district committees

The ASCA National Model can and will give professional school counselors confidence to do their jobs, direction to be most effective, and time frames and documentation to communicate with administrators about what they really do.

I am not good at statistics, so how can I do anything that supports the idea that my work is effective?

Madelyn Isaacs, Counselor Educator
Florida Gulf Coast University
Fort Myers, Fla.
misaacs@fgcu.edu

First of all, think about statistics as a language to communicate summaries of data. These summaries have to be prepared so that you fully understand what you are presenting and reading, and so that your audience (administrators, teachers, families and other stakeholders) can readily understand what you are presenting. In general, that means that you should be using simple statistics. The two phrases that come to mind are "simple is elegant" and "less is more."

USE SIMPLE STATISTICS

Since these are not research studies for generalizations to other populations, you do not need to be as concerned with sampling parameters and such. Simple statistics such as frequencies, percentages and means can be used to:

- Identify baseline data
- Drill down into all data and find smaller populations that require different services

- Compare groups or to compare performance between groups
- Provide simple evaluation (opinion) data

In addition, these simple statistics readily lend themselves to charts and graphs, which provide the easiest visual explanation of the data and can be easily transferred to other media such as newsletters, school Web pages and presentations via a spreadsheet program such as Microsoft Excel.

BEGIN WITH CAREFUL PLANNING

Any good data project needs to begin with careful planning. The first step is to identify the goal for your particular project or activity and the target population. Populations can be defined using data such as the entire school, grade, classroom or any subpopulation identified by factors such as gender, absolute or relative performance on classroom or standardized measures, absence/tardy rate, behavior infraction rates, students who are new to a school, or those who are referred by a colleague.

The characteristic that defines the population may serve as a baseline (for example, students who are selected because of absences). Target populations may be selected to receive a student development curriculum, intervention, services, consultation and the like for psycho-education or may receive these to remediate some performance factor. In either case, there is an initial expectation that by providing the intervention, service or curriculum, students will change in some way.

After you have identified your target population, decide on the most appropriate measurement:

- If you are comparing knowledge from one point to another, use pre and post testing.
- If you are comparing performance, you can either use frequencies (behavioral performance or number of grades) or you can group students and calculate the percentage of students in each category before and after.
- If you are measuring something to do with equity or access, you can compare relative percentages (e.g., proportion of girls in the school versus proportion of girls enrolled in advance placement (AP) math or science).

COMMUNICATE RESULTS

When reviewing, interpreting and reporting results in your school or to the public, make sure you are clear about:

- The groups you are measuring
- The change you were hoping for
- What you did (stated briefly)
- How the results affected students
- How the results will help form next year's student development program

To get started, consult resources such as any basic statistics text that helps you use descriptive statistics (those which describe rather than try to test inferences) and a good manual about using Excel spreadsheets.

REFERENCES AND RESOURCES

EZANALYZE: Data analysis software for educators
   www.ezanalyze.com

Microsoft: In and out of the classroom with Excel 97
   www.microsoft.com/Education/Excel97Tutorial.aspx

SchoolCounselor.com newsletter
   www.schoolcounselor.com/NEWSLETTER/

Support personnel accountability report card
   www.cde.ca.gov/ls/cg/re/sparc.asp

TechRepublic: 75 essential Excel tips
   techrepublic.com.com/i/tr/downloads/support/resource_doc/
   Excel_tips.pdf

I understand that the ASCA National Model emphasizes the importance of "systemic change." What does that mean and what is the school counselor's responsibility/role?

Mark Kuranz, School Counselor
Marquette University
Milwaukee, Wis.
kuranz@execpc.com

The ASCA National Model states that "...school counselors influence systemic change and advocate for students and their counseling programs..." (ASCA, 2005). Sounds nice, but what does it imply school counselors must do? What beliefs, knowledge and skills are required of school counselors to engage in this systemic practice?

First, school counselors must examine their belief systems. Beliefs drive behaviors, and therefore, require the school counselor to analyze the fundamental principles of the school counseling program. The beliefs, assumptions and philosophies of the program clearly articulate its essence to stakeholders. School counselors write a mission statement for the school counseling program to ensure it reflects the belief that all students are held to high academic standards. Remember, philosophically the school counseling program is for every student (ASCA, 2003), which means all students must receive instruction and support from highly qualified staff, be prepared to enroll in a rigorous curriculum and have access to the resources needed to be academically successful. A belief system is woven into the fabric of the school counseling program and drives the shift to a systemic perspective.

Second, a systemic perspective still expects school counselors to provide direct services to students in the form of individual counseling sessions, small-group sessions or classroom presentations, but also expects school counselors to be change agents (Perusse & Goodnough, 2004). Change agents are leaders who advocate for a school counseling program that focuses on what all students should know, understand and be able to do in the academic, career and personal/social domains. The program is sensitive to the developmental needs of the students, conducted in collaboration with school staff and connected to the mission of the school. It is no longer acceptable to work as a gatekeeper, providing information or knowledge to some students, assuming only some of them are motivated to learn. Critical in the systemic perspective and a program focus is the need to identify groups of students who are systematically not achieving.

For example, school counselors collect data that indicates the enrollment patterns in AP, international baccalaureate (IB) or honors courses are not reflective of the school demographics. The school counselor uses data, students' English and math scores at the proficient and/or advance level on the state test and minimum grade point averages of 2.75, to design strategies to increase enrollment in the AP, IB or honor courses to accurately reflect school demographics. Again, the school counselor's belief that every student should have access to a rigorous curriculum drives these strategies. This example is only a suggested starting point to begin to increase student enrollment in a rigorous curriculum.

After demonstrated success, the next step may be to open enrollment to all students with adequate resources in place to support student success. It is not the grade point average that is critical, but the monitoring of student progress and addressing the gaps in student performance. The systemic goal is for all students to be adequately prepared to be successful in a rigorous curriculum.

Third, a systemic perspective requires school counselors to be results-driven. This may be a paradigm shift for school counselors, but skilled school counselors use results in the form of data to demonstrate the program's effectiveness. It answers the question, "Do teachers, administrators, parents and community members view school counselors' work as contributing to academic success?" For example, school counselors can share how a student's grades improved, attendance improved, behavior referrals decreased, retention increased or school safety improved because of the student's participation in the school counseling program. It is based on simple percentages, such as, after a 10-week academic support group for seventh graders, their second quarter grades improved by 18 percent. A systemic perspective demonstrates improved results for all students.

In conclusion, school counselors believe they are critical members of the school team. A systemic perspective empowers them to advocate for every student to be academically prepared to choose from among a wide variety of post-secondary options and ultimately, to be contributing and productive members of society.

REFERENCES AND RESOURCES

American School Counselor Association. (2005). *The ASCA national model: A framework for school counseling programs, second edition.* Alexandria, VA: American School Counselor Association.

The Education Trust
www2.edtrust.org/edtrust

Perusse, R., & Goodnough, G. E. (2004). *Leadership, advocacy, and direct services strategies for professional school counselors.* Pacific Grove, CA: Brooks/Cole.

Tucson Unified School District
www.tusd.k12.az.us

I want to change my school counseling program to be more in line with ASCA's framework for comprehensive school counseling program. How do I begin to implement this in my middle school that serves more than 1,100 students and only employs two counselors?

Judy Bowers, Supervisor
Tucson Unified School District
Tucson, Ariz.
judybowers@cox.net

Because you serve more than 1,100 students, collaboration with teachers, administrators, community members, and even students is critical to your program's success. Always important in a comprehensive school counseling program, a team approach is essential in situations like yours where a small number of counselors serves a large student body.

As you begin to plan your transition to a program more aligned with the ASCA National Model, think about ways that you can get others involved. As discussed in the "ASCA National Model Workbook," people feel a sense of ownership when they are involved in the planning process. While some may resist change at first, their early involvement will enhance the delivery of your school counseling program and their commitment to change (ASCA, 2005).

Since you already have a school counseling program in place, the good news is that you don't have to start from scratch to develop a comprehensive program. Evolving your existing program will require you to assess where you are today and where you'd like to take the program in the future. A good place to start would be to determine what elements of the ASCA National Model already exist in your program. You can use the ASCA National Model Program Audit to complete this self-assessment. Review your program as evaluated by the audit and decide the vision for your school counseling program.

Another important component to aligning your program with the ASCA framework is to focus on the competencies that your program helps students develop. Competencies should be included from all three domains: educational, career, and personal/social. Spend some time studying the competencies that you feel are necessary for middle school students to achieve before they go on to high school. In addition, think about which competences should be taught at what grade level, and with what curriculum and teaching method(s).

In selecting the curriculum to use in teaching each competency, you can write lesson plans using your own materials, or you can look for lesson plans already written. Many resources are available on the Internet, including those listed on the ASCA Resource Web pages.

Who should teach these competencies? You have several methods available to you. If students are assigned by grade level, for example, you could teach the competencies to the grade you are responsible for supervising. Another method is for you and the other counselor to team up to teach all the competencies to all of the grade levels, dividing the students between you. A third method would be for the two of you to teach the lessons together. Perhaps the best solution in your situation would be to involve the teachers by team teaching and co-teaching. This collaborative approach would allow you to better leverage your resources and keep you from being spread too thin.

When planning for competencies, build in pre- and post-testing for students so that you can show the results of your lessons. Evaluation is a must to help your program grow and gain support. Refer to the ASCA National Model Handbook and Workbook for information on how to incorporate data-driven results into your overall approach.

It's important to take that first step to improving your school counseling program, and these are a few suggestions to help you get started along that path. Remember, your leadership and advocacy skills are important to the successful planning and implementation of your revised program. As a change agent, your role is pivotal to communicating and modeling to others the need for, and the effectiveness of, a comprehensive school counseling program.

In high schools where school counselors are not primarily responsible for scheduling, how is it done?

Marcia Price, School Counselor
Mobridge School District
Mobridge, S.D.
pricem@mobridge.k12.sd.us

School counselors in South Dakota register students for classes, including meeting with the students to check progress toward completion of requirements for a high school diploma and admission requirements to post-secondary educational institutions.

Most South Dakota school districts use a software program purchased by the state called "Infinite Campus" to handle scheduling, grades, transcripts, attendance and discipline reports. This program has replaced the traditional white boards used for creating master schedules. In smaller school districts, school counselors act as advisors in the creation of master schedules, but the primary responsibility is with administrative personnel.

Once a master schedule has been created and individual student schedules are generated, school counselors deal with the schedule conflicts. Our responsibility is to help students make informed decisions about course selections and explore all options for meeting the requirements for a high school diploma. School counselors will meet with transfer students to help them make course selections and determine their progression toward the completion of a high school diploma.

The overall opinion among South Dakota school counselors is that our responsibility is to our students, including helping them make good educational decisions. Our job is not to create a master schedule; that task belongs with administration.

My professor teaches that, as a future school counselor, I should be a contributor to the professional literature. Isn't this really the job of professors and researchers? If not, how do I learn more about how to write a scholarly paper? How would I even have time?

Martin Ritchie, Counselor Educator
University of Toledo
Toledo, Ohio
martin.ritchie@utoledo.edu

While scholarly research and writing is one responsibility of professors, you have real contributions to make as a practicing school counselor. There are three good reasons that you, as a professional school counselor, should contribute to the professional literature:

- No one is more aware of issues affecting school counselors than you. You are in the best position to evaluate programs and share what works and doesn't work with other counselors and counselor educators.
- Journal articles are the best way to share your ideas. Thousands of school counselors read journals. Published articles reach many more counselors than can be reached in conferences or workshops.
- Contributing to the literature necessitates that you keep abreast with the professional literature by reading what others are doing. This enables you to adopt best practices and improve your school counseling program.

Don't feel like you have to learn how to do this by yourself. Collaborate with a professor or peer who has already been published. For example, look at recent issues of Professional School Counseling. How many articles have a single author? Less than 10 percent. Team writing is more productive and more fun. Most professors are anxious to help because they depend on publications for promotion.

So how do you get started? First, familiarize yourself with the professional literature that's out there. Read recent issues. Talk to professors and peers. What are some counseling issues that need to be addressed? What are you doing that is working and may be worth sharing with others?

Before you even start writing, decide on the most appropriate journal for your manuscript, not just by title, but by content. Does your idea for an article look similar to the articles recently published in the journal? If you have questions about the appropriateness of your article or idea, call the editor. Editors cannot tell you whether they will publish your idea, but they can tell you if they think it is appropriate to submit.

Also, read the publication guidelines for the journal. They are available in the journal or on the journal's Web site. There may be different guidelines for different sections of the journal, and you must follow the guidelines exactly. If they specify APA format for references, make sure that you comply. Consult a professor if you have questions.

Before you submit your manuscript, proofread in addition to using spell check. Have others proofread your paper. Check every reference cited in the text and ensure that the same names and dates appear in the reference. Write a brief cover letter to accompany the manuscript and submit the correct number of manuscripts. Some journals use electronic submission. In your cover letter state if you are submitting for a specific section. If you have further questions, call or e-mail the editor.

After submitting your manuscript, it may take several months before you hear from the editor. Most journals use "blind review," meaning the author is not identified to the reviewers. Don't be disappointed if your manuscript is not accepted for publication. Rejection rates run between 60 to 90 percent in our field. Use the reviewers' comments to improve your work and your writing. If you are invited to rewrite and resubmit, do it. If you make the changes suggested by the editor, your manuscript will likely be published. It is gratifying to see your name in print, but most importantly, you are sharing your ideas with a wide audience.

REFERENCES AND RESOURCES

APA style guides are available from *www.apastyle.org/index.html*

Henson, K. T. (1999). *Writing for professional publication: Keys to academic and business success.* Needham Heights, MA: Allyn & Bacon.

Hiemstra, R., & Brier, E. M. (1994). *Professional writing: Processes, strategies, and tips for publishing in educational journals.* Malabar, FL: Krieger.

Hyff, A. S. (1999). *Writing for scholarly publication*. Thousand Oaks, CA: Sage.

Ritchie, M. (1996). *How to publish in our journal*. Counselor Education & Supervision, 36, 3–5.

Our director of student services does not have a background in school counseling. What are the professional, ethical and legal issues involved in receiving supervision? How can new and experienced counselors who work individually in schools obtain appropriate professional supervision?

Laurie Williamson, Counselor Educator
Appalachian State University
Boone, N.C.
wmsonll@appstate.edu

To answer this question, I first want to define the three types of supervision most appropriate in school settings: administrative, program and clinical.

- *Administrative supervision* refers to accountability, coordination and evaluation of the counselor's overall professional performance and effectiveness in the school. Administrative supervision is usually provided by the school principal.
- *Program supervision* ideally comes from the central office and coordinates the implementation of a comprehensive, developmental program across the district.
- *Clinical supervision* provides the counselor with a professional support system of trained professional counselors. Clinical supervision includes case management, clinical skill development and consultation regarding legal and ethical issues.

Clinical supervision is essential to the continued professional development of counselors, but, unfortunately, it is the type of supervision school counselors are least likely to receive.

Many experts in the field believe efficacy is best achieved through clinical supervision. The American Counseling Association recommends that counselors receive regular supervision to maintain and increase ethically their level of competence. Studies demonstrate that clinical supervision enhances effectiveness and accountability, improves counselor skills and increases levels of confidence and job satisfaction.

Many school counselors are unsure how to go about getting clinical supervision. First and most important is to educate yourself, your colleagues and your administrators. Get the word out about what supervision is and what it means to professional development, whether a counselor is new to the profession or has many years of experience. Options for direct on-site clinical and technical supervision include:

- Peer supervision by practicing counselors within the school system
- Supervision by counselors from other institutions, such as mental health counselors
- Supervision by central office coordinators who also provide program supervision
- Supervision by counselor educators from training programs in colleges and universities

A popular method of getting clinical supervision is group supervision. There are numerous benefits to group supervision. Group supervision is a specified requirement for practicum and intern students by the American Counseling Association, the American Psychiatrist Association, and the Council for Accreditation of Counseling and Related Educational Programs. It is considered to be an efficient and cost-effective use of supervisory time. Groups can provide a more comprehensive experience and help bridge the gap between the isolation of the school counselor and the activities of their colleagues. Many of these advantages are consistent with the current research on collaborative learning and cognitive skill development. Group supervision offers the participants the benefits of peer relationships, exposure to a greater number of cases, development of consultation skills and vicarious as well as direct learning.

When considering a supervisor, be aware that not all supervisors are created equal. If you are participating in individual or group supervision with a qualified supervisor, you may be able to count those hours to further your own professional credentials. School counselors can use supervision hours to document their pursuit of additional certification/licensure with the National Board for Professional Teaching Standards, Nationally Certified School Counselor and Licensed Professional Counselor.

School counselors are lagging behind other groups within the counseling profession in identifying supervision as an integral part of their professional routine. Poorly defined counselor roles and an unclear professional identity may contribute to the perception that school counselors do not have the same level of need for supervision as do clinical mental health counselors. And yet, school counselors routinely deal with acute counseling needs such as depression, suicidal ideation, substance abuse, pregnancy and school violence. School counselors need to take the initiative and actively pursue clinical supervision to ensure self-care and the provision of quality services to their clientele.

REFERENCES AND RESOURCES

Agnew, T., Vaught, C. C., Getz, H. G., & Fortune, J. (2000). Peer group clinical supervision program fosters confidence and professionalism. *Professional School Counseling, 4*, 6–12.

American Counseling Association. (2005). Code of ethics. Alexandria, VA: Author. Available online at *www.counseling.org*

Crutchfield, L. B., & Hipps, E. S. (1998). What a school administrator needs to know about school counseling professionalism: Ethics, clinical supervision, and professional associations. In C. Dykeman (Ed.), *Maximizing school guidance program effectiveness* (pp. 131-134). Greensboro, NC: University of North Carolina at Greensboro. (ERIC Document Reproduction Service No. ED421675)

Crutchfield, L. F., & Borders, L. D. (1997). Impact of two clinical peer supervision models on practicing school counselors. *Journal of Counseling and Development, 75*, 219–230.

Herlihy, B., Gray, N., & McCollum, V. (2003). *Legal and ethical issues in school counselor supervision.* In T. P. Remley, Jr., M. A. Hermann, & W. C. Huey (Eds.), Ethical & legal issues in school counseling (2nd ed., pp. 445-455). Alexandria, VA: American School Counselor Association.

Remley, T. P., Jr., & Herlihy, B. (2001). *Ethical, legal, and professional issues in counseling.* Upper Saddle River, NJ: Merrill Prentice Hall.

Peer helper programs are one possible delivery system for school counseling intervention. What are the advantages, disadvantages and tips for success?

Barbara Varenhorst, Consultant
Palo Alto School District
Palo Alto, Calif.
bvarenhorst@mindspring.com

More counselors are realizing that peer helping is meeting not only the need to supplement the scarcity of helping resources, at a minimal cost, but also the need to provide more services effectively. This is true if and when peer helping is solidly based on the National Peer Helpers Association's standards, which require the following:

- Defined purpose
- Quality, task-oriented training
- Appropriate service activities
- Continuous supervision
- Some type of evaluation

Peer helping includes many advantages, including the following:

- Provides services that counselors cannot provide
- Meets a need or resolves a problem so that counseling is not needed
- Alerts professionals to a problem before it becomes more severe

Prime examples of peer helping include suicide prevention, conflict mediation and academic achievement. For instance, a girl sitting alone during lunch is invited by a peer helper to eat with her group. Later the girl reveals that she had been planning to take her life that day, and now decides not to.

Schools who have trained peer helpers in conflict mediation find there is a significant reduction in conflicts in their schools. Peer programs have been called the "lodestone to prevention" based on research showing that such programs can play a major role in reducing the alienation and disconnectedness many youth feel, which often manifests in the social problems of alcohol/drug abuse, teen pregnancy and dropping out of school.

Research also documents the effects of peer helping in the area of academic achievement. The help that peers provide in tutoring and cross-age teaching serves as a powerful prevention strategy. For example, one 10th grade boy decided to study every night with the ninth grader he had been assigned to help. Both of the boys showed significant improvement in their grades as a result.

Peer helping is particularly powerful with at-risk youth. A boy returning to alternative school from prison took the training. Then he began befriending a seventh grader who was the school's scapegoat. Both boys turned their lives around. When youth are given the opportunity of assisting others through a problem, teaching the skills they have learned and seeing results of their work, they feel their life has worth and meaning. When these opportunities are given to at-risk youth, lives are salvaged.

Teaching the skills and attitudes of caring, respect for diversity and peace-making, school atmospheres are changed, bullying is reduced and cliques become less cruel. Counselors cannot do this alone, nor as effectively as with peer helpers. No matter how much a counselor may care about any student, he/she neither has the time, nor in many cases the credibility, of a peer to provide this kind of service.

Disadvantages of peer helping are not daunting. There is the fear of liability in terms of students taking on inappropriate tasks that might have tragic consequences. Although there have been no reported cases of this, preventing it from happening lies in appropriate training and excellent supervision. Establishing and implementing a program does take time and effort. It also requires knowledge and leadership training, which a counselor must secure. Programs fail when someone rushes into starting a program without being grounded in the basic requirements for a successful program.

Tips for success, in addition to preparation, include gaining the support of the administration and educating the faculty regarding the intent and purpose of the program. Establish a support system within the school and prepare others to take your place once you may leave.

REFERENCES AND RESOURCES

Benard, B. (1990). *The case for peers.* Portland, OR: Northwest Regional Educational Laboratory.

National Peer Helpers Association
    npha@peerhelping.org or (877) 314-7337
    www.peerhelping.org

Painter, C. (1989). *Leading a friends helping friends peer program.*
    Minneapolis, MN: Educational Media.

The Peer Resources Network
    support@peer.ca or (880) 567-3700
    www.peer.ca/PRN.html

Tindall, J. A. (1995). *Peer power, book 2: Strategies for the professional
    leader.* Bristol, PA: Accelerated Development.

Spirituality seems to be an important and missing piece in middle and high school. How do school counselors include spirituality in their comprehensive school counseling programs?

Linda Reynolds, School Counselor
The Sanibel School
Sanibel Island, Fla.
LindaR2@lee.k12.fl.us

The nurturing of the spiritual aspects of young people is as essential as the nurturing of their physical, emotional and mental well-being. If overlooked, young people often acknowledge that they are missing something. In my opinion, having had countless talks with students, "there is a God-shaped hole in all of us" (words of a song by Plumb off their Candy Coated Waterdrops album, 1999), a void in their lives, even if they cannot express this longing in words.

Students experience a certain sense of need, a desire to comprehend the purpose of life, to make sense of our reason for living and understand why bad things happen. That requires introspection and time to ask questions, particularly in times of trials, loss and changes. The school counselor can address these concerns to assist youth in bringing balance into their lives.

One's very core of being is associated with spirituality, and counselors are in a unique position to help students in this area. As trusted adults, they offer another perspective. Parents can frustrate their teenagers by not allowing them to make their own decisions about what to believe. For example, a 14-year-old requested to see me when his parents announced that they were getting a divorce. He wanted to know how this could happen. Was God punishing him? This led to an intimate conversation about his own personal beliefs. Perhaps more discussion at home with both parents would help him arrive at answers.

At times, a series of small group sessions offers another avenue to respond to students with similar issues. In the book "Seven Things Children Need" by John M. Drescher, the author noted that significance, security, acceptance, love, praise, discipline and God are all needed for a child to grow up healthy and well adjusted. These essentials can be topics of discussion in a small group setting.

Most recently, a 13-year-old female asked to meet with me as she was terribly frightened at the news that yet another hurricane might be on its way toward her home. That was shortly after Hurricane Charley destroyed her home, and they were living in temporary housing already. My job was to somehow calm her down enough to participate in class. Yet, her question to me was how could God send such an evil thing to destroy them. As written in "Talking To Your Kids in Tough Times" by Willow Bays, "There's nothing basically bad about an avalanche or earthquake (or a hurricane). They're just the way the earth breathes ... " Without getting scientific, I explained things in enough detail to give this child the comfort she needed.

Why didn't God protect my family when our house was robbed? How come some people are so much more blessed than others? Is my grandfather in heaven? Why did God make my sister handicapped? These are all questions that I have been asked at school. I feel the responsibility to discuss students' concerns and help them begin to resolve their problems of faith. It is part of growing up and coming to grips with the faith of your family.

Of course, I try to encourage young people to have similar discussions at home. This may or may not happen due to circumstances beyond my control. I simply have a responsibility to help them define who they are becoming by asking pointed questions and practicing reflective listening.

Youngsters often challenge us in our beliefs and bring us to a better place in our own lives. I have been blessed myself by counseling others. I pray that I make a positive difference in the lives of my students.

Kenyon Knapp, Counselor Educator
Troy University, Dothan Campus
Dothan, Ala.
kknapp@troyst.edu

There's the old adage that "people shouldn't discuss religion or politics in social settings" as these are thoroughly contentious topics. Add schools/education to that mix, and what arises is a minefield of "sacred cows," social agendas, frequently justified paranoia and angry parents. Also consider the fact that there are more than 33, 800 denominations in the U.S. and 4,200 recognized religions around the world, with each having their own view of spirituality (Adherents.com, n.d.). This makes religion and/or spirituality a very difficult issue for educators to address.

Spirituality is a vague, ambiguous and often carelessly used term (Koch, 2003; Whitney, 2001). The Association for Spiritual, Ethical, and Religious Values in Counseling (ASERVIC, n.d.) states that "the term spirituality is often vaguely defined or confused with the idea of religion or a particular sectarian belief system." When educators with multicultural zeal suggest discussing or teaching spirituality, the proverbial Tower of Babel experience occurs, where everyone speaks a different language (The Holy Bible, New International Version, Genesis 11:1-9), resulting in confusion, incoherence and disagreement.

Subsequently, what is often considered by some to be a happy compromise is to discuss "spirituality" in a very broad sense of the word. However, with the current and increasing variety of perspectives, especially in more urban areas, often no one is happy with discussions of spirituality. As spirituality is discussed and politically correct efforts are made to include numerous spiritual perspectives, the majority view of spirituality is often marginalized, and "the tyranny of the minority" occurs such that most are not satisfied with the discussion.

After reading numerous articles and books, and surveying school counselors, the following ideas may prove helpful when including spirituality in school counseling.

HAVE LOCAL SPIRITUAL/RELIGIOUS LEADERS ON-CALL FOR CRISIS SITUATIONS

This occurred at the school where my wife was the school counselor when a very loved and respected assistant principal died in an automobile accident. Local youth pastors, religious counselors and school counselors were available for students at the school. A number of schools allow local youth pastors to meet with parishioners in the cafeteria during lunch, thus providing spiritual support and positive role models for youth.

AVOID NEGLECTING OR IGNORING THE IMPORTANCE OF THE STUDENT'S SPIRITUAL/RELIGIOUS BELIEFS AND HOW THOSE BELIEFS AFFECT THE STUDENT'S THOUGHTS AND DECISIONS

The culture of secular imperialism has sought to marginalize or silence spiritual discussion. School counselors can change that moral climate by including discussion about spirituality and asking students how their belief system affects their academic, career and personal/social decisions (Aspy & Aspy, 1993). For example, when choosing career interest inventories, select ones that have a moral component, as many students' career decisions are influenced by their faith.

ATTEND STUDENT RELIGIOUS EVENTS

Attend events that address spiritual concerns of students, such as the annual "See you at the Pole" prayer meeting (See You at the Pole, n.d.). Also, attend meetings of spiritual/religious organizations such as the Fellowship of Christian Athletes (FCA, n.d.), Jewish studies and Bible clubs.

BECOME MORE AWARE OF YOUR OWN SPIRITUAL BELIEFS

This will help you be more respectful of others, not have unintentional biases and be more prepared to discuss how your spirituality/religion affects your life (ASERVIC, n.d.).

BE AWARE OF VARIOUS RELIGIOUS HOLIDAYS AND ACKNOWLEDGE THOSE HOLIDAYS TO STUDENTS WHO ARE OBSERVING THEM

As much as is possible within the parameters of school policy, provide some form of recognition of those holidays during the school day. For example, if you publish a counseling newsletter for parents or students, use this format to recognize the holiday.

HELP STUDENTS CONNECT THEIR ACTIONS TO THEIR MORAL COMPASS

When counseling students with dilemmas, ask them how they believe they should act such that they are morally at peace with their decision. This can help students live without regret, especially if their beliefs stem from a religious perspective.

The options for including spirituality in a comprehensive school counseling program are almost endless given the breadth of the topic. School counselors should also familiarize themselves with Section 9524 of the Elementary and Secondary Education Act (ESEA), which requires local educational agencies to certify in writing that it has no policy that prevents, or otherwise denies participation in, constitutionally protected prayer in public schools (U.S. Department of Education, 2003). Discussing spirituality, religion or prayer is constitutionally protected speech, and school counselors achieve a more comprehensive understanding of their students as they explore these issues together.

REFERENCES AND RESOURCES

Adherents.com, a collection of national and world religion statistics
www.adherents.com

Aspy, C., & Aspy D. (1993). Why religion should be an integral part of public school education. *Counseling and Values, 37*(3), p. 149.

Association for Spiritual, Ethical, and Religious Values in Counseling.
www.aservic.org/

Bay, W. (2003). *Talking to your kids in tough times.* New York: Warner Books.

Dobson, J. (1999). *Preparing for adolescence: How to survive the coming years of change.* Ventura, CA: Regal Books.

Doka, K. (2000). *Living with grief: Children, adolescents, and loss.* Washington, DC: Hospice Foundation of America.

Drescher, J. M. (1976). *Seven things children need.* Scottdale, PA: Herald Press.

Fellowship of Christian Athletes
www.fca.org/

Gordon, T. (1976). P.E.T. (Parent Effectiveness Training) in action. New York: G.P. Putnam.

Heller, D. (1988). *Talking to your child about God: A book for families of all faiths.* New York: Bantam Books.

Koch, G. (2003). Adolescent spirituality: An oxymoron?. In C. T. Dollarhide & K. A. Saginak (Eds.), *School Counseling in the Secondary School* (pp. 361–372). Boston: Allyn & Bacon.

Plumb. (1999). God shaped hole. On *Candy Coated Waterdrops* [CD]. Franklin, TN: Essential Records.

See You at the Pole
www.syatp.com/

U. S. Department of Education. (2003). Federal Register 68(40). Available online at *www.ed.gov/legislation/FedRegister/other/2003-1/022803b.pdf*

Whitney, D. S. (2001, November 15). *Defining the boundaries of evangelical spirituality.* Paper presented at the 2001 annual meeting of the Evangelical Theological Society, Colorado Springs, CO. Available online at *www.spiritualdisciplines.org/def.html*

World Almanac and Book of Facts. (1992). New York: World Almanac.

What are some recommendations for working with my district school board?

Gisela Harkin, Federal Official
U.S. Department of Education
Washington, D.C.
gisela.harkin@ed.gov

School counselors are in the best position to advocate for the academic success of every student. A recent noticeable trend in states is an effort to tie counseling programs to the learning process to promote student achievement – one of the tenets of No Child Left Behind (NCLB) Act. In a recent National Center for Education Statistics (NCES, 2003) report on high school guidance counseling, 77 percent of the counselors chose helping students with their academic achievement in high school as the first or second goal most emphasized by their guidance program (as compared to 58 percent in 1984).

Broadly speaking, school boards focus their efforts on issues related to student achievement. Therefore, it is essential for counselors to be informed about and active participants in the district/school reform efforts. As an active participant, counselors can contribute to building and sustaining effective collaborative relationships. These are not easy to establish or sustain, but counselors have the knowledge and skills to encourage collaboration, an essential element to get the job done.

First, counselors need to obtain school district commitment, as well as business/industry and parental support throughout the community, to the guidance program. Having this commitment beforehand facilitates collaboration in meeting the goals set out by the board. Strategies to obtain commitment to the guidance program include the following:

- Inviting board and community members to visit the guidance program
- Asking board members to adopt a policy supporting the guidance program
- Asking a representative to be part of the school guidance advisory committee

Once commitment and collaborative relationships are established, a proactive counselor determines how to best influence the school board agenda. Documenting change that is data-driven could align counseling programs with the school reform agenda. Therefore, one important element is for counselors to use quantitative and qualitative data to transmit information that would effect change and continuous improvement. Providing data and relevant materials assists the board in its advocacy role.

A second important element is assessing not only student needs and progress, but also what has been accomplished.

A third element is for counselors to be resource providers. Because of the work effective counselors do with parents, students, administrators and the community at large, they can become very useful in guiding the school board to internal/external resources that they may want to explore when dealing with issues and challenges.

Counselors need to play a strong leadership role when working with district school boards. They can be an asset to the board by staying current and keeping pace with changes, facilitating the work of the board, and providing information and resources useful to making decisions and improving programs.

REFERENCES AND RESOURCES

Gemberling, K. W., Smith, C. W., & Villani, J. S. *The key work of school boards*. Alexandria, VA: National School Boards Association.

National School Boards Association
www.nsba.org

Professional Development Resource Series: Public Relations and Advocacy published by ASCA
www.schoolcounselor.org

What are some specific strategies to lower the counselor/student ratio in my school?

Sally Woodruff, School Counselor
Hellgate School District
Missoula, Mont.
swoodruff@hellgate.k12.mt.us

My answer to this question addresses how to increase the number of people working with students, which would reduce the ratio. The district could hire more counselors. If your school is in a town that provides post-secondary training, interns and practicum students in any support service such as nursing, social work, school psychology, school counseling or private counseling could be used to cover parts of your counseling caseload. You could write grants to private or public institutions, including your state office of public instruction, to cover the wages of part-time assistance. Reducing ancillary duties, such as student discipline or clerical record keeping, also increases your time as a counselor.

Sharing components of your program with other staff in the school or in the community can reduce the counselor/student ratio. The teams you help create will essentially reduce the number of student contacts you must provide and reduce your counselor/student ratio. Identify the components of your program and then identify who in your school or community could be called upon to collaborate or share parts of your counseling program.

Community agencies, such as county mental health centers, juvenile justice offices, county health departments, county early intervention centers or local higher education programs, can be called upon to assist as team players in collaborating or sharing completion of program goals. Examples include:

- County mental health centers can set up school based mental health programs.
- The juvenile justice system in some communities can offer a staff person who can be a contact for students at your school who are at risk for becoming involved with the justice system.
- The health department can provide personnel who will do in-school group instruction on issues such as drug, alcohol or nicotine use.
- Early intervention centers can provide free training for parents, teachers, bus drivers and other school staff in the areas of behavior disorders or developmental challenges of students, through nationally known speakers or through their own staff.
- Universities and colleges have many support possibilities through either guest speakers for classes, such as a law school providing mediation support for students or a campus leadership group providing weekly classroom curriculum and instruction for leadership skills.

Other possibilities include the following:

- Classroom teachers can teach social skills curriculum, career curriculum, conflict resolution curriculum or grief/bereavement curriculum. There are several quality programs that are efficacy based through research. Social skills or conflict resolution, as well as personal/social development issues, can also be taught in physical education classes.
- Alternative learning centers can be utilized to provide a safe learning environment for behavior disordered students.
- Teachers can run classroom meetings or be mentors to any and all students to make them feel less isolated and more a part of a school team, which can reduce bullying behaviors.

Students and parents can also be involved in a developmental comprehensive program. Peer mediation teams made up of students can help to lower the rate of conflict on the playground or at other free-play times, and reduce the amount of crisis intervention you might spend on social issues. A career program in a classroom could be made up of parents who are recruited to each speak in the classroom to describe their employment setting and job duties. Community agencies, parents, students, school nurses, librarians, special education staff and virtually all school staff can be part of a team that addresses academic, career, and personal/social development of all students.

Jim Whitledge, Supervisor
Oakland Schools
Waterford, Mich.
Jim.Whitledge@oakland.k12.mi.us

Traditionally, counselor/student ratios receive attention when it comes to addressing change in school counseling programs for the purpose of improving student success. The supposition is that when school counselors have fewer students in their caseload, their programs will be successful. Many would like to see low caseloads mandated by state legislatures or local education bargaining agreements. This is not likely to happen because of the high financial commitments that are included in such agreements.

To provide quality school counseling programs for students, it is a better strategy to garner support for comprehensive guidance and counseling programs delivered by professional school counselors in which all students have equity and access, programs that measure how students are different as a result of participating in the program.

Historically, professional associations, consultants and lobbyists made recommendations for appropriate counselor/student ratios. ASCA recommends a ratio of 250-to-1 or better (ASCA, 2003; ASCA, 1997; ASCA, n.d.). The national average is cited by ASCA as 490-to-1. The National Association of College Admission Counseling (NACAC), describing best practices for pre-college guidance and counseling programs, recommends that the ratio be 100-to-1 as ideal, and 300-to-1 maximum (NACAC, 1990, Chapter 5).

ASCA indicates that ratios vary by level and state. States with high ratios in 2001-2002 include California at 971, Minnesota at 806 and Arizona at 759 (ASCA, 2002). These numbers and rankings are supported by NACAC (NACAC, 2004).

It is interesting that there does not seem to be research to show that counselor/student ratio makes a significance difference in relation to effective school counseling programs, even in California where the ratio is so high (Assembly Bill 722, 2003). Studies showed that while students' well being, ability to learn and academic achievement have a low correlation to ratios of pupils-to-pupil support personnel, they are not statistically significant.

In focusing on research regarding effectiveness of school counseling, ASCA reveals that ratios were not emphasized; rather, the emphasis is on results, leadership, counseling services and programs contributing to students' academic success (ASCA, 2004). These studies confirm that student behavior, attendance and achievement improve considerably, however, when adequate student support services are provided.

A strategy to lower the counselor/student ratio in the school is best addressed through student needs assessment, developing and maintaining a preventive, developmental, comprehensive guidance and counseling program that benefits all students and becomes an integral part of the entire school's education program. Results are measured to determine if students are different because of their participation in the counseling program.

The school's counseling program should align with the ASCA National Model (ASCA, 2003) so that counselor/student ratios might be lowered when school boards observe how students can improve their attendance, behavior and academic success through participating in the program. It is necessary for school counselors to collaborate with all stakeholders. Administrative support and understanding of the counseling program is essential for its success. Counselors provide leadership and advocate for their students as they help bring about change in the system to enhance students' academic success.

In addition, the four components of the ASCA National Model (ASCA, 2003) can fuel support for enabling school counselors to spend the majority of their time in direct student service, resulting in lower counselor student ratios. Many states have school counseling programs or models that align with the ASCA National Model, help contribute to student success and support lower ratios.

REFERENCES AND RESOURCES

Nonfiscal Public Elementary/Secondary Education Survey. (2002). State by state student-to-counselor ratio, 2001-2002. Retrieved April 29, 2004 from American School Counselor Association Web site: *www.schoolcounselor.org*. Also available at *http://nces.ed.gov/ccd/stNfis.asp*

American School Counselor Association. (1997). *The professional school counselor and comprehensive school counseling programs.* Alexandria, VA: Author. Available online at *www.schoolcounselor.org/*

American School Counselor Association. (2005). *The ASCA national model: A framework for school counseling programs, second edition.* Alexandria, VA: Author.

American School Counselor Association. (2004) *Effectiveness of school counseling.* Alexandria, VA: Author. Available online at www.schoolcounselor.org/

Assembly Bill 722. (2003). *Study of pupil personnel ratios, services, and programs.* Sacramento, CA: California Department of Education, Counseling and Student Support Office. Available online at www.cde.ca.gov/ls/cg/rh/

Education World Counseling Community *www.Educationworld.com/counseling/*

Fine, M. J., & Carlson, C. (Eds.). (1992). *The handbook of family-school intervention: A systems perspective.* Needham Heights, MA: Allyn & Bacon.

O'Callaghan, J. B. (1993). *School-based collaboration with families: Constructing family-school-agency partnerships that work.* San Francisco: Jossey-Bass.

National Association of College Admission Counseling. (1990). *Precollege guidance and counseling and the role of the school counselor.* Alexandria, VA: Author. Available online at www.nacac.com/downloads/policy_precoll_guidance.pdf

National Association of College Admission Counseling. (2004). *The state of college admission 2003-2004.* Alexandria, VA: Author. Available online at *www.nacac.com/research.html*

Wittmer, J. (1993). *Managing your school counseling program: K-12 developmental strategies.* Minneapolis, MN: Educational Media.

What are the best ways for school counselors to communicate to stakeholders how they contribute to student achievement?

Colin Ward, Counselor Educator
Winona State University
Winona, Minn.
cward@winona.edu

and

Tim Hatfield, Counselor Educator
Winona State University
Winona, Minn.
thatfield@winona.edu

Highlighting evaluative outcomes in relation to the effectiveness of school counseling services is crucial to developing an effective message to community and state stakeholders. The following is a brief overview of outcome evaluation for school counselors and the communication activities to highlight the effect school counseling services have on the overall academic success of students and the communities in which they live.

OUTCOME RESEARCH VS OUTCOME EVALUATION

Prior to developing communication strategies with school and community stakeholders, it is important for school counselors to understand the difference between outcome research and outcome evaluation. Outcome research provides general principles for selecting interventions and modes of practice. Grounded in the specific needs of a school or district, outcome research provides evidence needed to decide which services, interventions, programs and models will be selected for implementation.

Outcome evaluation, however, confirms the worth of these practices and the value of these services to local constituencies. It establishes the evidence needed to make judgments about whether the work of school counselors is having the desired effects at a specific site (e.g., improved academic achievement or reduced bullying). Evaluation results can be used to communicate the benefits associated with public expenditures for school counseling professional services.

USING OUTCOME EVALUATION RESULTS

In other words, outcome evaluation results establish counselor accountability. Adapted from the work of Stone & Dahir (2004), the following points can assist school counselors with demonstrating their accountability to the needs of all students and the schools in which they serve.

Understand the Mission
Connecting school counseling services to the mission of the district and the goals as outlined in the annual school improvement plan is essential for demonstrating the overall effect these services have on students. Establishing this link integrates school counseling services into the overall

curriculum of the school and guides the identification and analysis of the evaluative data elements.

Identify and Analyze Data Elements
A school's success, important to all stakeholders, is measured by those data elements critical to student achievement and school improvement. This can be accomplished by identifying the relevant student variables of demographics (such as gender, race, ethnicity, age/grade level and socioeconomic status) and known risk factors (such as depression, violence incidence and attendance/truancy patterns) to the specific counseling services in which they participated.

These data elements can then be correlated to the evaluative outcomes of student achievement (grades, test scores), knowledge units (bullying, wellness, social skills) and satisfaction ratings by students, faculty and parents.

Develop Long-Range Research Goals
Developing a timeline for evaluating school counseling services is central to maintaining an active research agenda in specifying how their activities contribute to the overall mission and purpose of the school. Besides providing good program organization for counselors themselves, it also communicates to stakeholders in a very concrete way a counselor's commitment to service and accountability. Creating research partnerships with counselor training programs and state/national school counselor organizations can assist with data analysis, research funding and support for sharing the results.

Identify Stakeholders
In a climate of diminishing resources, demonstrating to state decision makers the effect school counseling has on the learning and success of all students is vital. This is accomplished by identifying key stakeholders for school counseling services, including targeting individuals within the internal community (e.g, principals, teachers and school board members) and external community (e.g., parents, local and state public officials, businesses, and faith representatives). It is essential that school counselors use this "network of allies" to help distribute the effectiveness of school counseling on student success and advocate for maintaining those services within schools.

This is particularly important when the political climate within a school places inadvertent pressure on school counselors (and others) to remain silent on their effectiveness with students. This systemic oppression highlights the importance of maintaining an active external community. Additional external community stakeholders to consider are:

- State and regional counseling and school counseling organizations
- Parent groups
- Community mental health agencies that serve families and children
- City organizations and law enforcement agencies
- University leaders and counselor training programs
- Media (television, radio, newspapers)
- Churches

Communicate To Stakeholders
The following are essential elements when communicating to stakeholders about the effect school counseling services have on student success:

First, focus the message. Data speaks more loudly than words, and a clear message (as well as a few bar charts.) can demonstrate a concrete relationship between school counseling services and student learning outcomes. The H.A.N.D.S acronym can assist with framing the message to stakeholders:

- H–Highlight the problem being addressed, the impact it has on students and the consequences if not addressed promptly
- A–Address the problem by pointing out how the specific school counseling activity meets this gap in services and meets student needs
- N–Note the benefits this service has on students as demonstrated by the evaluative outcome data
- D–Data-based conclusions are framed in relation to program effectiveness
- S–State clearly requested action needed to prioritize the needs of students by supporting school counseling services

Second, distribute the results. Develop written materials that summarize the results of school counseling programming and the effect these services have on student success. Two important types of these summary materials are briefing papers and advocacy outlines:

- Briefing papers are designed for school board members, legislators and other decision makers related to school counselor funding. They present a brief outline of the program/service being evaluated, how it links to district/school goals and the results as related to student outcomes.

- Advocacy outlines are designed for supporters of school counseling and provide a summary of the school counseling program with supporting summary data as well as "talking points" that can assist with advocacy efforts when communicating with district decision-makers (district personnel, community allies, school board members and state legislators).

Developing a Web page and brochures that advertise the school counseling activities as well as the evaluative outcome results are also important marketing avenues.

CONCLUSION

Understanding how to identify, analyze and publicize evaluative outcomes that contribute to student success is paramount for school counseling professionals. The intentional effort to communicate with public school stakeholders provides a voice for the rights of all children. As guardians of the educational system and advocates for all students and families within the districts they serve, school counselors need to keep the focus on how they are demonstrably a part of student achievement and student success.

REFERENCES AND RESOURCES

Stone, C. B., & Dahir, C. A. (2004). *School counselor accountability: A MEASURE of student success*. Columbus, OH: Merrill Prentice Hall.

What are the most effective strategies/ interventions a school counselor can implement to help students with chronic absenteeism?

Alice Cryer-Sumler, Counselor
Louisiana Department of Education
Baton Rouge, Louisiana
asumler@stcharles.k12.la.us

A counselor can assist students in this area by first trying to involve the parents. However, if the parents cannot become involved, I have secured support from faculty and staff who could serve as mentors at school. These teachers were asked to check in with these students during the day. In fact, the student would report to them as soon as they arrived at school and during the day. These teachers were also encouraged to meet with the students for 10 minutes during their planning time to see if they needed special assistance with a problem.

Another strategy that I found helpful was to create a contract and check in with the students daily by simply chatting with them during transitions and at lunch.

Third, concrete rewards are always helpful. I gave the students a certificate of attendance. I began by rewarding them for coming one day in the beginning. Then I moved to giving certificates for coming three days at a time. I continued this process until we worked up to one week. In addition to the certificate, students worked toward having a pizza party with collective attendance. Finally, I called home to tell the students and parents thank you for coming to school.

Mary Pat McCartney, School Counselor
Bristow Run Elementary School
Bristow, Va.
mp.mccartney@verizon.net

When it comes to effective strategies/interventions for helping students with chronic absenteeism, the school counselor must first "consider the source." Is the student missing school because of a problem at home? Is it an academic, social or emotional issue at school? Talking with the student's teacher and parent will provide background information, but the most important means for discovering the source of the problem is to listen to the student. "What would make you want to come to school?"

Initially, the plan includes reviewing with the student (and the parent) a computer printout of the student's attendance record. In addition to making the student (and the parent) aware of the laws involving school attendance, explore the advantages of being on time every day. Seek student input and parent cooperation in the formulation of the behavior plan. Focus on strengthening the student's desire to belong in the class/school setting.

Each intervention plan should incorporate the student's individual needs, concerns, interests and talents. The following strategies have proven to be successful:

- Behavior contracts stating expectations and positive reinforcement (e.g., a student's interest in art used to devise a plan for earning extra one-on-one time with the art teacher)
- Positive incentives for the student and the parent (e.g., an early morning high-profile job, such as raising the flag or participating in the announcements, used to increase on-time attendance and foster parent pride
- Rewards such as daily stickers, prizes, a certificate, a special treat (e.g., special lunch times with the student and a few selected friends used as rewards, but also served to increase social standing)
- Mentors providing contact with another caring adult (e.g., a morning check-in routine with a mentor used to improve attendance and strengthen student's self-esteem)

Students must also perceive the classroom as a worthwhile place where they can meet with success. Here, the school counselor can consult with the teacher to determine if the work might be too easy or too difficult.

If the student completes the regular assignments quickly and accurately, arrangements can be made to allow the student access to the classroom computer or the opportunity to be a special "helper" for other students. An ongoing project of interest can also be made available to the student. If the work is too difficult, the counselor can encourage the teacher to take appropriate steps for making curriculum accommodations. Providing a parent volunteer tutor for the student is another option.

It is important to note that chronic student absenteeism can also be regarded as a school problem. A factor to consider is the school's policy. Are there significant consequences for missing class time? The school counselor is in a position to effect systemic change in this area. Working with the staff, the counselor can facilitate the development of a school-wide policy. Ideas to consider include a gradual set of consequences for unexcused absences, a grading system that incorporates points for participation and effort, and extra-credit work for missed instruction.

Efforts should be made to raise the level of awareness about the importance of daily attendance. Parents and students need to realize that attendance is important for achievement in school now and for job employability in the future. To this end, the school counselor might sponsor class or grade-level competitions for good attendance. A "media campaign" might be launched to include a report of the school's attendance rate in school announcements, the home/school newsletter and perhaps even the local paper, as chronic student absenteeism is a community problem as well.

REFERENCES AND RESOURCES

Capuzzi, D., & Cross, D. (1993). *Youth at risk.* Alexandria, VA: American Counseling Association.

Hallam, S., & Roaf, C. (1995). *Here today, here tomorrow: Helping schools to promote attendance.* London: Calouste Gulbenkian Foundation.

Jacobs, E. (1994). *Impact therapy.* Lutz, FL: Psychological Assessment Resources.

Murphy, J., & Duncan, B. (1997). *Brief intervention for school problems.* New York: Guilford Press.

Reid, K. (2002). *Truancy: Short and long-term solutions.* London: Routledge Falmer.

Sprick, R. S. (1985). *Discipline in the secondary classroom: A problem-by-problem survival guide.* The Center for Applied Research in Education, Inc.

Sprick, R. S. (2002). *Discipline in the secondary classroom: A problem-by-problem survival guide.* San Francisco: Jossey-Bass.

Wunderlich, K. C. (1988). *The teacher's guide to behavioral interventions.* Columbia, MO: Hawthorne Educational Services, Inc.

What can school counselors do to get parents more involved in the school and personal success of their children?

Beth McCann, School Counselor
Leon County Schools
Tallahassee, Fla.
mccannfsu@comcast.net

A school that embodies the spirit of a community of learners is on target for promoting student success. Education professionals know that it takes more than quality teaching to prepare students for the demands of the world. Although critical, a teacher cannot prepare a child for future success alone. The formula for success requires a team approach to the child's learning.

Many schools have teachers, counselors and support staff on their team, but fall short on a pivotal member: the parent. A community of learners is not complete without parental involvement. How can school counselors help to involve the parents? The answer lies in creating an environment that is welcoming and offering an array of options for involvement.

Research has shown that parent involvement is more important than income or educational level when it comes to student success (Starr, L., www.education-world.com, 2004).

The first step to encouraging parent involvement is for counselors to promote a positive environment that is nonthreatening and welcomes parents. This can be done in many ways, including hosting breakfasts on the first day of school for parents of kindergartners. The idea is to offer parents a warm and inviting place to go once they drop off their child. It can be a time to offer reassurance of the school's commitment to having an open door for parents to be involved with their student's education.

Creating a positive environment also comes in the form of communication. A parent will feel more comfortable and willing to volunteer if he/she is familiar with the faculty and staff. Familiarity can be achieved through simple avenues such as the faculty serving as friendly faces greeting parents and students in the morning and afternoon pickups.

It is also helpful to remember that the first communication with the parents needs to be a positive one. Calling a student's parent for the first time to tell them of problems could very well lead to walls being built between home and school. Tearing down those walls is much more laborious than building them. Bridging the home and school can also be done through school Web pages and regular e-mails. Some educators have found that parents are more likely to respond to e-mails than notes home or phone calls (Fischer, M., www-education-world.com, 2004). A counselor who is creating a nonthreatening parental environment must ask for participation and encourage parents to become involved. Parental involvement improves when they are invited to be a part of a nurturing environment.

There are many opportunities for parents to become involved in the schools. The National Parent Teacher Association has developed standards for parent and family involvement in school programs. The standards in their entirety can be viewed at www.pta.org. The six standards include:

- Communicating
- Fostering and promoting parenting skills
- Encouraging parent participation in learning
- Creating a positive environment
- Soliciting input in school decisions
- Collaborating with the community

Ideas that stem from these standards include open house spaghetti dinners, school carnivals, monthly counselor corners with parents, parenting classes, holiday clothing drives, mentoring programs and student recognition programs. All levels of involvement should be encouraged, from the parent who does something at home to the parent who comes in weekly to help at the school. No amount of volunteerism is too large or too small.

Conveying a message of welcome and appreciation is what parents will need to become interested in volunteering. Providing opportunity and encouragement will entice them to turn their interest into action. Counselors are skilled in creating both interest and action and are therefore the optimal people to promote successful volunteer programs.

REFERENCES AND RESOURCES

Clark, R., Hawkins, D., & Vachon, B. (1999). *The school-savvy parent.* Minneapolis, MN: Free Spirit Publishing.

Education World
www.education-world.com

National PTA
www.pta.org

ProjectAppleseed.org
www.projectappleseed.org

What is the optimal way to establish rapport with a client who does not want to work with you? (That is, the client is present because of a court order, principal's request, teacher or parent referral, etc.)

Gerald Sklare, Counselor Educator
University of Louisville
Louisville, Ky.
gbskla01@louisville.edu

Several approaches may be taken to help clients move from visitor status to that of becoming customers in the counseling process. First, I believe it's important to recognize that the client does not want to be meeting with you. Acknowledging this by telling clients something like, "My guess is that you really aren't interested in meeting with me today so it must be irritating for you to be here." Or, "I'm thinking that you're thinking how inconvenient this meeting is going to be and I would rather not be here at all." Comments like this show the referred clients that you can empathize with them. Being able to find a common ground with which to begin the session may help establish rapport and decrease clients' reluctance to discuss their difficulties with you.

After establishing rapport, it's essential that counselors find out clients' perceptions of why they think they have been referred to you. Comments like, "What is your understanding of why we are meeting today?" (Be prepared to share what you know about the referral.) Or, "What have you thought about trying next time you have this difficulty but haven't tried yet? How might that be helpful?" These types of questions may help set the stage for a more cooperative relationship between clients and counselors.

Another approach I have found that works effectively with referred and reluctant clients is solution-focused brief counseling (SFBC). With SFBC, clients determine their goals for counseling. When they decide what they want to work on rather than what counselors want them to accomplish, resistance decreases. When clients determine the agenda for counseling, clients become invested in the process. Counselors ask questions such as, "What do you want to accomplish as a result of meeting with me today?" or "What would your goal be meeting with me?" Other aspects of SFBC also encourage rapport in the counseling relationship with referred clients.

SFBC sessions focus on clients' experiences within their own frames of reference rather than the counselor's, and the sessions focus on discussion of solutions rather than problems.

In addition, SFBC uses the clients' terms and phrases rather than the counselor's, recognizes that clients are the best experts on themselves and focuses on strengths rather than weaknesses. This focus on client's successes rather than failures empowers clients to recognize that there may be a positive payoff in meeting with a counselor who practices SFBC. Sklare (2005) explains how to implement the SFBC approach and includes a chapter on working with mandated and reluctant clients.

REFERENCES AND RESOURCES

DeJong, P., & Berg, I. K. (1998). *Learner's workbook for interviewing for solutions.* Pacific Grove, CA: Brooks/Cole.

Sklare, G. B. (2004). *Brief counseling that works: A solution-focused approach for school counselors and administrators.* Thousand Oaks, CA: Corwin Press.

What tips do you have for starting and developing a successful peer mediation program?

Deborah Trust, School Counselor
Paul Laurence Dunbar Middle School
Fort Myers, Fla.
deboraht2@lee.k12.fl.us

Peer mediation is one of the most powerful tools students can use for preventing and solving conflict. It puts the responsibility of conflict resolution where it belongs: with students rather than adults. Peer mediation is a process of dispute resolution in which a neutral third party, two student mediators, assists two parties in order to help them achieve an agreement and find a positive, long-lasting solution to their problem.

At Paul Laurence Dunbar Middle School in Fort Myers, Fla., for example, peer mediation prevented conflicts that could have resulted in disciplinary action. Of the 306 situations mediated, 88 percent did not result in a subsequent disciplinary report.

Peer mediation is done as a preventative measure. Peer mediation can be requested by the students involved, by witnessing students or by adult referral. It is not punitive. It is not done after students have had a physical altercation unless the students want help in preventing future conflict. Students agree to work out their differences using mediation.

Pairs of combatants are mediated, not groups. It involves two trained student mediators who listen to each of the combatant's issues. One mediator focuses on one individual, asking questions and paraphrasing what the mediator has heard. This helps each individual to identify the problem. The other mediator focuses on the other student. The mediated students must identify their own solutions and sign an implementation contract. The mediators cannot provide the solution. This gives ownership of the conflict, and its solution, to the individuals involved.

Starting a peer mediation program involves training the mediators and having them practice their skills, including both listening and communication skills. Role plays and videotaping are helpful. The initial trainers can be professional mediators or teachers/counselors familiar with the process. It is empowering to allow the subsequent trainers to be the experienced students.

A peer mediation training retreat [called a lock-in] can be an excellent way to teach and practice the skills. The lock-in weekend is completely planned and run by students. They recruit chaperones, solicit restaurant and community sponsorship for meals and materials, plan team-building activities, schedule community agencies as speakers, and plan and run the training.

There are excellent materials available from "Peace Works" at the Peace Education International Foundation (1-800-749-8838) or from The Bureau For At-Risk Youth (1-800-99-YOUTH).

Students have to be given the autonomy to conduct the mediation sessions without adult intervention. An adult should be near, but not part of, the mediation. A "mediation table" and a quiet mediation space are needed because of issues of confidentiality. However, if the session becomes heated or loud, an adult may need to stop the mediation. Students can also be given the authority to stop a mediation that is not working. During mediation, mediators do not accept blaming or excuses. They put all responsibility back on the disputants.

When a counselor is dealing with an irate parent, what are the most effective techniques for calming him/her?

Carol Kaffenberger, Counselor Educator
George Mason University
Fairfax, Va.
ckaffenb@gmu.edu

An irate Mrs. Jones is at your office door. You have no idea why she is so upset. What does she want? What do you do? How do you calm her down? The most effective strategies involve hearing her out, using your counseling skills and working toward problem solving. It is helpful while working through these strategies to keep three goals in mind: diffuse the anger, build trust and address the issue.

Responding to an irate parent is often the responsibility of the professional school counselor. When meeting with an irate parent, it is important to separate the anger from the unstated fears and needs. Although it is not easy to be the recipient of a parent's anger, it is helpful to remember that expressions of anger typically stem from the parent's belief that the child's rights have been violated or that the child's needs have not been met in some way. Parents typically respond with anger when they believe that their children have been treated unfairly or will be harmed in some way by a school decision, policy or practice. The following strategies are offered for calming an irate parent and addressing the underlying issue(s).

HEAR THE PARENT OUT

If you address the issue or try to provide explanations before the parent has had his or her say, you may miss hearing the whole story. By allowing the parent the opportunity to tell his or her story, you also allow for catharsis that will result in lowering emotions and beginning the conversation about the issue. When a parent's voice is raised, it is also important for the school counselor to respond calmly and focus on listening for the underlying fears and needs instead of the way the message is being delivered. Valuable insights into the parent's perception of the problem will be gained. The information acquired from listening in this way can be used to understand the issue and begin problem solving.

USE YOUR COUNSELING SKILLS

Professional school counselors' training in active listening will provide the most effective strategy for defusing the anger and making the meeting productive. Active listening, involving respectful body language, minimal encouragers, and empathy (reflecting the content and the feelings expressed by the parent), will communicate that the counselor wants to understand the reason for the anger. Empathic responses like, "Mrs. Jones, you are furious with Mr. Samuels because you believe he humiliated your son in front of his classmates and other adults," will confirm your understanding of the parent's feelings and the issue.

Once the parent realizes that you are accurately reflecting the parent's perspective, the conversation will most likely take a different direction. The anger will be diffused and the issue discussed. Asking questions and summarizing what has been said are also effective counseling skills that will clarify the issue and may provide opportunities for the counselor to provide alternative perspectives about the issue.

WORK TOWARD PROBLEM SOLVING

The ultimate goal is to address the underlying issue, the problem that has caused the parent's anger. Throughout the listening phases of the meeting, separating the issue from the emotion will contribute to the problem-solving phase. If you have heard the parent out and used effective counseling skills to clarify the parent's perspective, then it is likely problem-solving strategies such as stating the primary issue, brainstorming for ways to address the issue, agreeing on steps to be taken and developing a work plan will be effective.

Although dealing with an irate parent can be challenging, the benefits can be enormous. Parents who remember the professional school counselor was willing to hear their story and help them address their concerns will become advocates of the school and the school counselor, and may be less likely to respond in anger in the future.

REFERENCES AND RESOURCES

Cicero, G., & Barton, P. (2003). Parental involvement, outreach, and the emerging role of the professional school counselor In B.T. Erford (Ed.). *Transforming the school counseling profession* (pp.191-207). Upper Saddle River, NJ: Merrill Prentice Hall.

Margolis. H. (1986). Resolving differences with angry people. *The Urban Review, 18*(2), 125–136.

Margolis, H. (1991). Listening: The key to problem solving with angry parents. *School Psychology International, 12*(4), 329–347.

McEwan, E. (1998). *How to deal with parents who are angry, troubled, afraid or just plain crazy.* Thousand Oaks, CA: Sage.

Whitaker, T., & Fiore, D. (2001). *Dealing with difficult parents.* New York: Eyeon Education.

School Counseling Research

The responsibility of school counselors to both conduct and be consumers of research has been an ethical obligations for quite some time. Section F.1.c of ASCA's Ethical Standards (ASCA, 2004) states that the professional school counselor conducts appropriate research and report findings in a manner consistent with acceptable educational and psychological research practices. The counselor advocates for the protection of the individual student's identity when using data for research or program planning.

This makes a great deal of sense. Research provides critical information we need to make important decisions that affects all aspects of practice, including what we believe (our foundation) and in what ways we manage, deliver and are accountable for our work. Research can produce important discoveries for best practices in producing systemic change, providing effective leadership, collaborating and advocating.

This chapter encompasses frequently asked questions and answers related to accessing existing data, collecting data, conducting action research and providing an empirical basis for school counseling.

REFERENCES AND RESOURCES

American School Counselor Association. (2004). *Ethical standards for school counselors*. Alexandria, VA: Author. Available online at www.schoolcounselor.org

How do I access existing data so that I can most efficiently make decisions about my program?

Linda Webb, Counselor Educator
Florida Atlantic University
Boca Raton, Fla.
lwebb@fau.edu

Data, data, data. As school counselors are being asked to become more accountable, the use of data becomes increasingly important. From national standards to federal, state and local initiatives, school counselors are being advised to use data to inform decisions related to their program and student outcomes. The good news is that data exists just about everywhere and is easily accessible.

Two types of data that can help schools counselors make decisions about their programs are:

- Best practice data
- Local data

Both are important when developing programs that reflect the needs and mission of schools, and both maintain their effectiveness over time.

BEST PRACTICE DATA

Best practice data provides evidence about the programs and approaches that have been most successful in helping students become academically and socially more successful. One of the best ways school counselors can keep a pulse on best practice data is through professional affiliation.

For example, ASCA provides its members publications that include data about what works, such as Professional School Counseling, a journal that emphasizes data-driven programs and strategies, including articles on how to use data to develop and maintain effective programs. In addition, ASCA's Web site provides listserv directories to support best practice networking among members with similar interests.

LOCAL DATA

Local sources provide a second type of data useful for making decisions. Local data is embedded in obtainable documents such as school reports and records, school improvement plans and accreditation studies that are used for local and state accountability.

Survey Feedback

Local data includes feedback surveys from students, parents and teachers. Feedback generally covers a wide range of topics including school safety, quality of instruction, school climate and communication. Counselors familiar with the surveys being used in their schools can target items to guide counselor intervention.

One example might include using school climate data from students and teachers as a basis for planning a teacher workshop on building encouraging, supportive classrooms. This data could also be used as an outcome measure the following year.

Trend Reports

Other sources of local data are generated from reports reflecting trends in student test scores, grades, attendance, discipline data, graduation and retention rates. Frequently found in electronic databases, these reports tend to drive much of the school-wide decisions and should be considered an important part of guidance program planning.

In addition, trends can be identified and linked to guidance program goals. For example, in one school, counselors and administrative staff used existing test score, attendance and discipline data to identify ninth grade students who would benefit from increased academic and social support as they transitioned to high school.

Increasingly, schools and districts are adding technology and staff to help counselors download, arrange and analyze data trends that help keep the focus on identified need and student outcomes while supporting the school's overall mission.

Also, Internet searches on "school improvement" provide links to regional sites and programs such as Toolbelt (National Central Regional Educational Laboratory, 2004) and SPSnapshot (Etraffic Solutions, 2003), both targeting improved access and management of existing data.

Building an effective guidance and counseling program is a process. School counselors can use many sources of data to inform their program decisions and support the improved academic and social success of all students.

REFERENCES AND RESOURCES

Etraffic Solutions, SPSnapShot (student performance snapshot): An online tool for analysis of standardized test scores for Florida educators *www.etrafficsolutions.com/products/spsnapshot/index.html*

Isaacs, M. L. (2003). Data-driven decision making: The engine of accountability. *Professional School Counseling, 6*(4), 288–295.

Levesque, K., Bradby, D., Rossi, K., & Teitelbaum, P. (1998). *At your fingertips: using everyday data to improve schools.* Berkeley, CA: MPR Associates.

North Central Regional Educational Laboratory, Data use: School improvement through data-driven decision making *www.ncrel.org/datause/*

I want to collect data from students, parents and teachers, although I don't have the resources to type it all in after I collect it. Is there a better way?

Russell Sabella, Counselor Educator
Florida Gulf Coast University
Fort Myers, Fla.
sabella@schoolcounselor.com

There are several great alternatives for collecting data, such as using online survey tools, handheld computers and optical recognition software for scanning data into spreadsheets. Local colleges and universities can be also a significant survey resource. In addition, software packages and online services are available to help with the survey design process.

ONLINE SURVEYS

Online surveys in particular are a viable and relatively easy method for collecting data, and they are already in the realm of capability of virtually all schools.

Advantages
Conducting surveys online comes with many advantages:

- Data is stored and collated immediately after the respondent clicks the Submit button. With one or two clicks of the mouse, the counselor can analyze the data or create graphs of the data at any time during collection, getting a snapshot of the results as they come in.

- The time for the entire survey process is significantly diminished, especially if the same survey is periodically conducted over time.
- An online survey can be conducted with a few people in one locale or many people around the globe, reducing or even eliminating traditional barriers of space, place and time.
- Online surveys can include an array of multimedia elements including sound, animation and photos, making them more interesting to respondents and perhaps increasing response rates.
- Copies of online survey results can be sent to more than one person or place, facilitating collaboration between the counselor and researchers helping with the analysis.

Disadvantages
Possible disadvantages for conducting online surveys include:

- If some of the desired respondents do not have Internet access, they cannot participate, rendering the sample of participants not truly representative of the population under study. Providing access in a mental health agency or school would minimize this problem.
- Limited controls over who responds to an online survey could threaten the validity of survey results. For instance, without proper controls, participants could respond more than once or perhaps may more easily misrepresent their identity. Password protecting an online survey could help, though not necessarily solve, this problem. Online services may help by identifying and tracking who responds to a given survey.
- Respondents may encounter technical problems (computer, survey access or survey itself), possibly hindering appropriate data collection procedures.

In general, however, most people would agree that conducting surveys online provides powerful advantages that make this option quite attractive.

OPTICAL RECOGNITION SOFTWARE

In recent years, new optical mark recognition (OMR) software has been developed that allows counselors to design their own surveys, including questions and room for responses, and then scan the completed surveys using a simple and relatively inexpensive document scanner.

For example, the Remark OMR allows users to:

- Design survey forms using any word processor
- Print survey forms
- Scan completed survey forms and recognize data with an off-the-shelf image scanner
- Analyze or export the data to the applications such as spreadsheets

Distinct advantages of these software products are that they are cost efficient, make creating customizable surveys very easy and reduce human error.

LOCAL COLLEGES OR UNIVERSITIES

Counselor educators have needs that lend themselves well to collaborating with school counselors for conducting all types of research.

First, conducting research is an important part of many counselor educators' jobs. For many, it is a scholarly endeavor of particular interest. For others, it may be a less desirable condition of employment for which they are duly evaluated.

Second, counselor educators are interested in providing their pre-service students with valuable and realistic learning experiences. Helping counselors with the accountability and decision-making process can often become part of a supervised class assignment in which students and instructor collaborate with school counselors, providing guidance and much-needed help.

DESIGN SERVICES

Some school counselors create online surveys using Web authoring programs such as Microsoft FrontPage™ or Macromedia DreamWeaver™. These programs make creating surveys as easy as word processing.

Other school counselors find that online Web survey services, some free and some for a nominal fee, require minimal technical skills and provide excellent results. While the free versions are usually limited in power and scope as compared to the purchased versions, they have proven sufficient for counselors who want to survey a limited number of clients. Many of these services also provide the ability to conduct analyses online and download the data for importing into software such as a spreadsheet.

REFERENCES AND RESOURCES

Free Online Surveys.com
  www.freeonlinesurveys.com

Handheld Survey Software
  www.handheld-systems.net/

National Center for Education Statistics, Create a Graph site
  nces.ed.gov/nceskids/graphing/

OmniPage Pro 14 Office
  www.scansoft.com/omnipage/

Pocket PC Survey and Handheld Survey System
  www.pocket-surveys.com/

Quia
  www.quia.com

SurveyMonkey.com
  www.surveymonkey.com

Tyler, J. M., & Sabella, R. A. (2004). *Using technology to improve counseling practice: A primer for the 21st century.* Alexandria, VA: American Counseling Association.

Ultimate Survey Software Enterprise
  www.prezzatech.com/UltimateSurvey-surveysoftware.asp

Zoomerang
  www.zoomerang.com

I've heard of "action research." What is this and why should I do it?

Deryl Bailey, Counselor Educator
University of Georgia
Athens, Ga.
dbailey@coe.uga.edu

As I see it, action research is research that stems from "real issues" schools, where schools identify the issues or problems and research grows from there.

Why should you do it? The answer is simple. Our public educational system has failed to address adequately the needs of all students, especially those from underrepresented groups, such as students of color and poor students. Action research is needed to determine best approaches to educating all students.

Action research requires a stronger collaboration among public schools, families and higher education than exists today. Rather than traditional research, where higher education researchers determined the type of research to be conducted, action research evokes a collaborative effort to determine the type of research necessary. Schools present the problems and/or challenges they're facing, and the researchers are there to help address those issues.

Working together, researchers, teachers, counselors, administrators, parents and even students form research teams to design studies based on intervention strategies. When the studies are completed, the results are taken back to the schools to bring about change and solutions.

What types of empirical evidence exist that support the idea that participation in a school counseling program results in higher academic, personal/social and career success?

Greg Brigman, Counselor Educator
Florida Atlantic University
Boca Raton, Fla.
gbrigman@fau.edu

Three of the most important categories of research that address the empirical basis for school counseling are:

- Large reviews of research on various school counseling interventions and their effect on students
- Large studies of comprehensive school counseling programs and their effect on students
- Randomized comparison group validation studies of counselor-led interventions and their effect on student performance

LARGE REVIEWS

Large reviews are important because they synthesize many studies over a period of time. Three of the most extensive and respected reviews are Borders & Drury (1992), Whiston & Sexton (1998) and Hughes & Karp (2004):

Borders & Drury (1992) published a landmark review of 30 years of research pertaining to school counseling. After examining the results of hundreds of studies, they concluded that individual and small group counseling as well as classroom guidance and consultation:

- Contributed directly to students' academic success
- Improved behavior and attitudes toward school

Whiston & Sexton (1998) found tentative empirical support for:

- Career planning
- Group counseling
- Social skills training
- Peer counseling
- Consultation

Hughes & Carp (2004) reviewed 50 studies that focused on the effect of career guidance programs on academic and vocational achievement. Several of the studies reviewed included other large reviews of research. Major findings include:

- Guidance activities related to junior high students had the largest effects.
- Students benefit both vocationally and academically from participating in career courses.
- Academic counseling or advising had positive results.

LARGE STUDIES

Large studies that look at the effect of comprehensive school counseling programs is another important category to consider when examining the empirical basis for school counseling.

Lapan, Gysbers & Sun (1997) examined the effect of comprehensive school counseling programs. They investigated 236 Missouri high schools

(22,964 students) and found that students in schools with more fully implemented guidance programs reported:

- Earning higher grades
- Being better prepared for their futures
- Having more college and career information
- Believing their school had a more positive climate

A follow-up study conducted by Lapan, Gysbers & Petroski (2001) looked at seventh grade students and teachers in 184 Missouri middle schools. Students in schools with more fully implemented guidance programs reported:

- Feeling safer in school
- Having better relationships with their teachers
- Believing their education was more relevant
- Being more satisfied with the quality of their education
- Having fewer problems related to their school environment
- Earning higher grades

Nelson, Gardner, & Fox (1998) examined school counseling programs in 14 Utah high schools. Students in schools with more fully implemented guidance programs reported:

- Higher ratings for their school counseling services
- More advanced math and science courses
- Higher ACT scores in all areas
- Higher ratings for their overall educational preparation

Sink & Stroh (2003) examined 150 elementary schools (20,131 students) in the state of Washington. One important difference in this review of research is that student performance in reading and math on standardized achievement tests was used to compare students in schools with comprehensive school counseling programs versus noncomprehensive programs.

The conclusion was that elementary students enrolled for several years in schools with comprehensive programs scored significantly better than students in schools with noncomprehensive programs.

RANDOMIZED COMPARISON GROUP VALIDATION STUDIES

The third important category of research that addresses the empirical basis for school counseling involves randomized comparison group validation studies.

One of the key questions frequently asked by various educational decision makers is, "How can you tell that it was the school counselor intervention or program that made the difference?" To answer this question, special care must first be taken when designing the research. Recently, the U.S. Department of Education's National Center for Education Evaluation established what it considers strong evidence of programs that work – randomized, comparison group designs with multiple sites.

In response to the need for this type of research, Brigman & Campbell (2003), Campbell & Brigman (2004), Webb, Brigman & Campbell (2004), and Brigman, Webb and Campbell (2004) conducted four studies involving a total of 50 school counselors and more than 800 students in fifth, sixth, seventh and ninth grade in 36 schools located in two counties. This series of randomized comparison group studies looked at the effect of school counselor-led small group and classroom guidance interventions on student performance in math and reading on standardized tests. The interventions focused on helping students develop key cognitive, social and self-management skills associated with school success.

The researchers found that, related to comparison students, students receiving the school counselor-led interventions achieved significantly higher math scores in all four studies and significantly higher reading scores in two of the four studies:

- In math, 86 percent of students improved in math by an average of 30 scale score points.
- In reading, 75 percent of students improved an average of 25 scale score points.

According to Whisten & Sexton (1998) and Sink (2003), randomized comparison group research is in short supply, and more such research is needed.

In conclusion, school counselors have a solid empirical base that supports the idea that school counseling programs have a positive effect on student academic, personal/social and career success.

REFERENCES AND RESOURCES

American School Counselor Association. (2004). *Effectiveness of school counseling*. Alexandria, VA: Author. Available online at www.schoolcounselor.org/

Brigman, G., & Campbell, C. (2003). Helping students improve academic achievement and school success behavior. *Professional School Counseling, 7*(2), 91–98.

Center for School Counseling Outcome Research at the University of Massachusetts, Amherst *www.umass.edu/schoolcounseling*

Lapan, R. T., Gysbers, N. C., & Petroski, G. F. (2001). Helping seventh graders be safe and successful: A statewide study of the impact of comprehensive guidance and counseling programs. *Journal of Counseling & Development, 79*(3), 320–330.

Nelson, D., Gardner, J., & Fox, M. (1998). *An evaluation of the comprehensive program in Utah public schools.* Salt Lake City, UT: Utah State Office of Education.

Sink, C., & Stroh, H. (2003). Raising achievement test scores of early elementary school students through comprehensive school counseling programs. *Professional School Counseling, 6*, 352–364.

Whiston, S. C., & Sexton, T. L. (1998). A review of school counseling outcome research: Implications for practice. *Journal of Counseling and Development, 76*(4), 412-426.

School Counselor Roles and Responsibilities

Admittedly, the school counseling profession suffered throughout its early development from a lack of consistent identity, lack of basic philosophy and, consequently, a lack of legitimization. In recent years, however, there has been an acute focus among school counseling leaders throughout the country on standardizing the practices of school counseling. As a result, ASCA has published (and continually updates) the following documents:

- The ASCA National Model®
- Ethical Standards
- Role Statements
- Position Statements
- The National Research Agenda and Work Plan

In this chapter, experts share their perspectives about topics such as the responsibility of accountability, how the school counselor role is evolving, appropriateness of school counselor duties, differences of duties among grade levels, similarities and differences with related professionals, ratios, specific roles in different areas of practice (e.g., special education and diagnostics), and factors contributing to the growth and development of the profession.

Accountability seems like an ominous task; how do I even get started?

Jay Carey, Counselor Educator
University of Massachusetts at Amherst
Amherst, Mass.
careyandassoc@attbi.com

and

Carey Dimmitt, Counselor Educator

University of Massachusetts at Amherst
Amherst, Mass.
cdimmitt@educ.umass.edu

Accountability has been a theme in school counseling professional literature for the past 30 years. Over this time, an impressive series of articles has both cautioned counselors about the potential consequences of failing to become accountable and provided concrete suggestions for practitioners to increase their accountability. Most recently, ASCA has incorporated an accountability system into the ASCA National Model in order to help align school counseling programs with standards-based educational reform initiatives.

FAILURE OF ACCOUNTABILITY TO EMERGE AS A STANDARD PRACTICE

In spite of 30 years of discussion about the importance of accountability, however, widespread changes in accountability practices have failed to emerge in either the practice of school counseling or in the preparation of school counselors. What explains our profession's inability to reorganize our work to produce more local accountability data in spite of widespread recognition of the necessity of doing so? Why is "accountability" such an ominous goal?

In the real world of public schools, school counselors constantly juggle their time because there are more good things that need to be done than there is time to do them. Accountability activities drop off the to-do list because they do not directly relate to the work of helping students, and they require an expensive initial investment of precious time. Busy practitioners fail to initiate the data collection activities that are needed to demonstrate accountability, even through they believe that having such information is essential to ensuring their continued professional existence and vitality.

At the National Center for School Counseling Outcome Research, we help the profession establish the research base that is needed for responsible and effective practice. We also help school counseling programs develop the data skills that are needed for standards-based school counseling practice. Through our work in school counseling reform, we have come to believe that the most salient reason that school counseling programs fail to become accountable is that "accountability" is the wrong goal. School counselors do not see how becoming accountable will help them serve students. The reasons for becoming accountable revolve around the terrible thing that will happen if we do not become accountable. The motivation to become accountable is "all stick and no carrot."

DATA-BASED MANAGEMENT SYSTEMS

We recommend changing the accountability goal. Rather than trying to demonstrate accountability, we focus our work on helping school counseling programs develop data-based management systems. These systems enable counselors to:

- Use institutional data to identify needs
- Focus interventions
- Select evidence-based interventions
- Monitor the effects of interventions
- Evaluate outcomes
- Document impact
- Report accountability results

School counselors find that most of the activities of a data-based management system actually enhance their ability to be efficient and effective in helping students. Implementing a data-based management system requires an initial investment of time and effort. However, once it is implemented and integrated into school routines, it is relatively easy to maintain and continues to generate needed accountability data as an important byproduct of the program management process.

If you recognize the need to produce accountability information, we recommend that you commit to implementing a data-based management system. If you implement the ASCA National Model management system, the accountability system will follow naturally. The following steps are very helpful:

- Learn about data-based management systems by consulting recent sources such as Dahir and Stone (2003), Isaacs (2003), Johnson (2002), and Love (2002)
- Identify the system tools and skills you will need in order to develop and implement a data-based management system, including consulting the Web sites of the National Center for School Counseling Outcome Research, the American Student Achievement Institute and the Center for Students Support Systems Studies and Services

- Seek needed professional development at state and national conferences and contact local partners who can provide the needed hands-on professional development support and technical consultation
- Contract with administrators to have the development of a data-based management system identified as a major district priority and to reallocate the system support time that will be needed to develop and implement a data-based management system. In one district we work with, for example, the school counselors initiated their implementation by exchanging the development of action research projects for lunch room duty. This exchange was possible because the district formally recognized the importance on moving to a data-based school counseling program.

In spite of the initial costs, the implementation of a data-based management system will solve more problem than it creates, enhance school counselors' abilities to serve all students well and generate the accountability data that we all need to thrive in a standards-based school environment.

REFERENCES AND RESOURCES

American Student Achievement Institute
  asai.indstate.edu/

Center for Student Support Systems
  www.sandiego.edu/soe/instcenter/studentsupp

Dahir, C. A., & Stone, C. D. (2003). Accountability: A MEASURE of the impact school counselors have on student achievement. Professional School Counseling, 6, 414–221.

Isaacs, M. (2003). Data-driven decision-making: The engine of accountability. Professional School Counseling, 6, 228–295.

Johnson, R. (2002). Using data to close the achievement gap. Thousand Oaks, CA: Corwin Press.

Love, B. (2002). Using data/getting results: A practical guide for school improvement in mathematics and science. Norwood, MA: Charles-Gordon.

National Center for School Counseling Outcome Research
  www.umass.edu/schoolcounseling/

How has the role of the school counselor changed over time and in what ways will it continue to change?

Chris Sink, Counselor Educator
Seattle Pacific University
Seattle, Wash.
csink@spu.edu

Probably no topic within the school counseling profession has generated so much debate as the role of the counselor. By performing an online search of publications from 1980 to present, I received nearly 1,750 hits on this issue. With so many writings on the topic, it is obviously not possible to catalog here all the responsibilities school counselors have had over the years. Even so, I attempt to respond briefly.

First, I tackle how the school counselor's roles have evolved through the years. Even though there are numerous historical reviews in the school counseling literature documenting the various counselor functions, they essentially reflect the duties associated with specific eras in the life of profession (Sink, 2005, pp. 1-42).

FORMATIVE ERA

Early on, during the profession's formative era (early 1900s to 1930s or 1940s), guidance personnel (e.g., classroom and vocational teachers) assisted students with their vocational and career-related needs. Around the 1930s and 1940s, this focus was extended to provide educational support as well. Guidance "counselors" became more involved, for instance, with student assessment, conducting individual counseling on nonvocationally related issues and coordinating pupil-personnel services (e.g., administrative duties, referral, counseling, consultation) more holistically.

TRANSITIONAL ERA

Subsequently, during the profession's transitional era (1940s to 1970s), guidance counselors continued to provide pupil-personnel services, but with emergence of developmental psychology during this time, school counselors' roles again began to shift. By no later than the 1960s, school counseling programming and services were directed to a broader range of student developmental needs and concerns.

CONTEMPORARY ERA

Nowadays, the contemporary era is really a fuller expression of the developmental guidance and counseling movement. Not only are school counselors paying attention to students' developmental needs, they are adopting a more systemic and prevention-oriented approach to their work through the implementation of comprehensive school counseling programs, such as the ASCA National Model (ASCA, 2003).

More specifically, the key functions of today's school counselors are to:

- Conduct their comprehensive guidance and counseling programs and related services with professionalism (e.g., act ethically and advocate for the welfare of students and their caregivers)
- Use individual and group counseling to support the healthy development of all students
- Facilitate large group guidance lessons to help students reach their educational, personal/social and career goals
- Consult with other professionals inside and outside the school to advance the interests of students and their caregivers
- Coordinate their school's comprehensive program in such a way that program and student outcomes are attainable and verifiable

If these roles are closely attended to, school counselors are fostering a positive and safe learning environment, helping to create a collaborative community of learners, and safeguarding and advocating for the human rights of all members of the school community (ASCA, 2003).

LOOKING AHEAD

I now consider the second part of our initial question. From my perspective, for at least the near future, school counselors will need to be well attuned to the patterns of societal change (Sink, 2005, pp. 390-405). For example, with the dynamic nature of the family constellation, the support services provided must be flexible and wider in spectrum.

In addition, how school counselors effectively assist their diverse student bodies (e.g., cultural, ethnic and sexual orientation) will continue to occupy the center stage as well. Undoubtedly, school counselors must be involved with the accountability movement in education. This requires them to be active "players" in school reform, evaluating their programs and services, and making a concerted effort to help close the achievement gap among groups of students.

Finally, school counselors should:

- Implement fully the ASCA National Model
- Consider how school/community/home service/integration models might be successfully used in educational settings of the future
- Use technological advancements to assist in their work

REFERENCES AND RESOURCES

American School Counselor Association. (2005). *The ASCA national model: A framework for school counseling programs, second edition.* Alexandria, VA: Author.

Baker, S. B., & Gerler, E. R., Jr. (2004). *School counseling for the twenty-first century* (4th ed.). Upper Saddle River, NJ: Merrill Prentice Hall.

Erford, B. T. (2003). Transforming the school counseling profession. Upper Saddle River, NJ: Merrill Prentice Hall.

Sink, C. A. (2005). *The contemporary school counselor: Theory, research, and practice.* Boston: Houghton Mifflin.

Thompson, R. A. (2002). *School counseling: Best practices for working in the schools* (2nd ed.). New York: Brunner-Routledge.

Is there a recently published, comprehensive list of appropriate and inappropriate duties for school counselors?

Trish Hatch, Counselor Educator
San Diego State University
San Diego, Calif.
thatch@mail.sdsu.edu

The most current list of "school counseling program activities and non-school counseling program activities" is contained on page 56 of the ASCA National Model (ASCA, 2003). This list reflects one clarification and the addition of three new items to an earlier list. The clarification addresses testing, a hot topic for school counselors these days. The prior list states that "administrating cognitive, aptitude, and achievement tests" is an inappropriate task for school counselors.

The new list adds that the "coordination" of these tests is also inappropriate. Three newly added appropriate roles for school counselors are the following:

- Serve students in small and large group counseling, rather than working with only one student at a time in a therapeutic, clinical mode
- Be a student advocate at student meetings (such as special education and student study teams), rather than simply the preparer of the paperwork for the meeting
- Analyze and interpret student data, rather than be the one who performs the clerical function of data entry

These new additions are helpful to school counselors who are seeking opportunities to educate themselves, their administration and staff as to the appropriate role of the school counselor. Without a clearly defined role and function, school counselors often find themselves in the position of "utility players." Anyone who has coached sports knows the role of utility players who "play wherever the coach tells them - for the good of the team." They are not assigned a specific position. School counselors who embody this belief system often agree to perform clerical and administrative functions, contributing to role confusion, which is not a new problem for school counselors.

For decades, school counselors have been frustrated and disillusioned by the gap between the theory and practice within the school counseling profession. Stewart writes, "They listen to speeches and read articles by guidance leaders and are inspired by the high-level nature of the work counselors should be doing. Then they face the cold reality of the tasks their administrator assigns them, and the comparison is quite traumatic" (1965). At a meeting held for secondary counselors in 1965, the following comments were shared:

"I have never had such a frustrating job in my life. I have no time to do real counseling."

"I am primarily a clerical worker. Yesterday I was too busy programming to be able to take time to talk with a junior who is in real trouble."

"My principal seems to feel that it is more important to discipline a student than to counsel him." (Stewart, 1965, p. 17).

Unfortunately, many school counselors still feel this way. The ASCA National Model (ASCA, 2003) was written to serve as "One Vision, One Voice" for the profession of school counseling. The inclusion of the lists was intended to educate and assist school counselors as they clarify for themselves and their constituents their proper role in schools. Rather than perform disciplinary actions, counselors provide prevention education and counsel students who have disciplinary problems; rather than signing tardy slips, they counsel students who are tardy; rather than substituting when teachers are absent, they collaborate with teachers to provide classroom guidance lessons.

Each of the "non-school counseling program activities" listed in the ASCA National Model is accompanied by an appropriate "school counseling programs activity" option. It is hoped that school counselors will use the list intelligently. Rather than flagging the page for the principal saying, "See, I don't do discipline," the preferred method might be to share the school counselor's appropriate role in the discipline process.

APPROPRIATE SCHOOL COUNSELING PROGRAM ACTIVITIES

According to the ASCA National Model, appropriate school counseling program activities are the following:

- Individual student academic program planning
- Interpreting cognitive, aptitude and achievement tests
- Counseling students who are tardy or absent
- Counseling students who have disciplinary problems
- Counseling students as to appropriate school dress
- Collaborating with teachers to present guidance curriculum lessons
- Analyzing grade point averages in relationship to achievement
- Interpreting student records
- Providing teachers with suggestions for better management of study halls
- Ensuring that student records are maintained as per state and federal regulations
- Assisting the school principal with identifying and resolving student issues, needs and problems
- Working with students to provide small- and large-group counseling services
- Advocating for students at individual education plan meetings, student study teams and school attendance review boards
- Disaggregated data analysis

INAPPROPRIATE SCHOOL COUNSELING PROGRAM ACTIVITIES

According to the ASCA National Model, appropriate school counseling program activities are the following:

- Registering and scheduling all new students
- Coordinating or administering cognitive, aptitude and achievement tests
- Signing excuses for students who are tardy or absent
- Performing disciplinary actions
- Sending students home who are not appropriately dressed
- Teaching classes when teachers are absent
- Computing grade point averages
- Maintaining student records
- Supervising study halls
- Performing clerical record-keeping duties
- Assisting with duties in the principal's office
- Working with one student at a time in a therapeutic, clinical mode
- Preparing individual education plans, student study teams and school attendance review boards
- Performing data entry

What are the major differences between school counselors at each of the levels: elementary, middle and secondary?

Debra Ponec, Counselor Educator
Creighton University
Omaha, Neb.
dlponec@creighton.edu

Debate has raged far and wide and for many years regarding the role and function of school counselors. At one time, secondary school counselors were consulted only for career education information; middle school counselors aided with scheduling and helping those adolescent blues; and elementary school counselors were a figment of one's imagination. Since the introduction of a developmental guidance and counseling model, a lot has changed ... and continues to change. It has now been realized that guidance and counseling programs must focus on the dynamic status of educational reform and human development. These programs, which are systematic, sequential, clearly defined, data-driven and results-based, must provide direct proactive and preventive services to students, families and faculty.

The counselor must not only be a change agent within the school, but an advocate for students and their academic success. As part of the larger, collaborative team within the school and community, school counselors seek to support student learning and success with a focus on assisting students to reach their highest potential and productivity within society. Although the overarching goal of a comprehensive, developmental guidance and counseling program may be similar from PreK through grade 12 levels, its implementation is different at each level.

ELEMEMENTARY SCHOOL COUNSELOR

The elementary school counselor offers a program that is aligned with the school's mission statement and is an integral part of the total education program. The counselor provides proactive leadership in forming a team of educational professionals within the school to create a caring climate and atmosphere conducive to student learning and school achievement.

Typically a school counselor's role includes activities in counseling, teaching, consultation and coordination. At the elementary school level, the focal point of the program (as determined by time allotment) and the counselor's role are to nurture, teach, and promote personal/social, academic/educational, and career/occupational skills within the classroom.

In addition, the awareness of the impact of developmental issues in combination with academic scope and sequence competencies provides the impetus for teaching, developing and practicing coping skills through individual or small group counseling activities.

MIDDLE SCHOOL COUNSELOR

The middle school counselor is faced with students who are in the midst of rapid growth and development that may impede academic success due to fatigue, exploring interests and identity, and developing an understanding of how learning connects to "real" life and the world of work. In addition, these students – out of a sense of belonging and identity – have assigned their peers the major influence over their decisions and life choices.

The middle school counselor begins to make the shift from the "nonjudgmental teacher" who teaches proactive and preventive coping skills to a mentor and crisis confidant who guides students in achieving academic success, places a greater focus on career exploration, models the importance of networking within the community, and facilitates connections with needed information and community resources.

SECONDARY SCHOOL COUNSELOR

The secondary school counselor aids students in developing a vision of the future through formalizing career and education goals, identifying key components in relationship formation and defining personal identity. Secondary students are beginning the normal separation from their parents and beginning to define their independence. Peers continue as a major influence in the lives of high school students who are at an increased risk for societal ills.

The secondary school counselor becomes a guide when these high school students begin to transition into adulthood and the world of work. This guidance is essential for high school students to reach their potential and become contributing members of a global society.

REFERENCES AND RESOURCES

American School Counselor Association. (2004a). *Why elementary school counselors?* Alexandria, VA: Author. Available online at www.schoolcounselor.org

American School Counselor Associaton. (2004b). *Why middle school counselors?* Alexandria, VA: Author. Available online at www.schoolcounselor.org

American School Counselor Association. (2004c). *Why secondary school counselors?* Alexandria, VA: Author. Available online at www.schoolcounselor.org

Ponec, D. L., & Brock, B. L. (2000). Relationships among elementary school counselors and principals: A unique bond. *Professional School Counseling, 3*(3), 208–217.

Ponec, D. L., Poggi, J. A., & Dickel, C. T. (1998). Unity: Developing relationships between school counselors and community counselors. *Professional School Counseling, 2*(2), 98–102.

Zalaquett, C. P. (2004, June). *Principals' perceptions of school counselors' role and function.* Paper presented at the meeting of the American School Counselor Association, Reno, NV.

What are the similarities and differences among school counselors, school social workers and school psychologists?

Stanley Baker, Counselor Educator
North Carolina State University at Raleigh
Raleigh, North Carolina
stanley_baker@ncsu.edu

Based on my experience, the roles and functions of school counselors are more general and broadly defined in practice, while school social workers and school psychologists have more specific and clearly defined roles and functions. School counselors are usually assigned to a specific school or set of schools while school social workers and psychologists are itinerant professionals housed in a central location who work with clients on an assignment or appointment basis. Because they are assigned to schools, the roles and functions of school counselors are more likely to be influenced by the views and needs of their principals and faculty members, and they are expected to serve all students at their schools in a variety of ways.

Therefore, individual school counselors may have different roles and functions, depending upon the culture and characteristics of their schools. On the other hand, because of their central location, the roles and functions of school social workers and psychologists are usually more narrowly and specifically defined. They probably have one supervisor who clearly understands why they were hired and how they were trained. The supervisor, having a limited number of social workers and psychologists to share, desires to be certain that the social workers are doing what they were hired to do.

SIMILARITIES AMONG THE THREE PROFESSIONS

Similarities these groups of professionals share are that they:

- Usually have graduate degrees, most often at the master's level
- Are represented by national professional associations that provide codes of ethics, role statements and advocacy for the professions
- Are trained to work in school settings in order to help students be successful in school and in life through interventions and advocacy
- Have national accreditation standards that govern their professional training

- Have the opportunity to acquire professional licenses above and beyond the certificates and licenses required to work in school settings

Their respective professional associations are the following:

- School counselors: ASCA
- School social workers: School Social Work Association of America
- School psychologists: National Association of School Psychologists

Their respective accrediting associations are the following:

- School counselors: Council for the Accreditation of Counseling and Related Educational Programs
- School social workers: Council on Social Work Education
- School psychologists: American Psychological Association

Their respective professional licenses are the following:

- School counselors: Licensed professional counselor
- School social workers: Licensed clinical social worker
- School psychologists: Licensed psychologist

In addition, some of the skills taught and acquired across the training programs for these three professions are similar. All three professionals are trained in basic interpersonal communication skills for individual counseling and group counseling. Other areas common to the respective training programs are advocacy, assessment, cultural sensitivity, crisis intervention, referrals, prevention programming (e.g., social skills training), consultation, behavioral management and evaluation/accountability.

DIFFERENCES AMONG THE THREE PROFESSIONS

Differences exist as well. While school psychologists draw primarily from psychology for their foundation, school social workers draw primarily from sociology and social work. Although school counseling probably primarily drew from psychology initially, other behavioral sciences such as sociology, social work, anthropology and political science have become influential as well. Often school counselors were teachers before being trained as counselors. On the other hand, many school counselors have undergraduate backgrounds and work experience outside of education, especially in psychology, sociology and social work.

Therefore, school counselors probably come from more varied undergraduate degree and work experience backgrounds than do school social workers and psychologists. Some school psychologists and social workers may have had undergraduate degrees in education; however, the majority of these professionals move from undergraduate degrees in their primary discipline (i.e., psychology, sociology or social work) to acquire graduate degrees therein as well.

Looking at the training and roles and functions closely, it appears as if one area that differentiates school counseling from the others is career counseling and guidance. This emphasis on understanding career development and choice, and translating that knowledge into helping students prepare for work and careers is not found in the other two professions.

The area that seems to differentiate school social workers from the others is working within communities and with parents in order to achieve home, school and community collaboration. School psychologists seem to be differentiated from the others by an emphasis on individual assessment of academic skills, learning aptitudes, personality and emotional development, and social skills in order to make recommendations for individual education plans (IEPs); educational placements; and primary, secondary, and tertiary prevention programming.

Understanding the roles and functions of these three groups of professionals is important for schools and for students. Educational systems are challenged and encouraged to allow them to apply their knowledge as they were trained to do.

REFERENCES AND RESOURCES

American School Counselor Association
  www.schoolcounselor.org/index.cfm

Baker, S. B., & Gerler, E. R., Jr. (2004). *School counseling for the twenty-first century* (4th ed.). Upper Saddle River, NJ; Pearson Education.

Freeman, R. D. (2004). *What is a school psychologist?* Cartersville, GA: Bartow County School System Office of Psychological Services. Available online at www.bartow.k12.ga.us/psych/whatis.htm

National Association of School Psychologists
  www.nasponline.org/index2.html

North Carolina State University, Department of Social Work. (n.d.). *School social worker job description.* Raleigh, NC: Author. Available online at www.ncsu.edu/chass/SocialWork/SchoolSocialWorker.html

School Social Work Association of America
www.sswaa.org/

What does the elementary school counselor's day typically involve?

Marie Geyer, Counselor Educator
Cider Mill School
Wilton, Conn.
mariegeyer@sbcglobal.net

One of the reasons I love this job is that no day is truly "typical." On a job description I can list things such as:

- Individual counseling
- Small-group counseling
- Classroom guidance lessons
- Conferring with teachers, administration and staff about students
- Collaborating with teachers, service providers and parents
- Networking with the district and colleagues about programs and services to benefit our students
- Researching information on diagnosis, behaviors, treatments, learning styles and resources to meet our students' needs

All these things happen frequently, but not every day, not in a set percentage of time and not (often to my frustration) on a schedule. I think of an elementary school counselor as an advocate for children, helping them to cope with and navigate in our 21st century world. I weave "getting along with each other" into my counseling sessions and classroom guidance lessons. This includes coaching in civility, dealing with bullies (as a target, a bully or a bystander), resolving conflicts with others, and coping with frustration and anger.

I chose the elementary level as my area of interest because we can be proactive here; children are able to learn and enhance skills, parents still are able to manage their children (or more readily regain control), and life is still fun and exciting.

At the start of this year, in our prep week before school opened, I met and started to establish relationships with new teachers; reconnected with teachers I've worked with before; read IEPs and 504s; reviewed incoming students' files; discussed potential issues with administrators, teachers, and parents (separately and in combinations); attended in-service programs; met with colleagues to discuss needs and plans for this school year; and readied my office an files for a new start.

Then when students arrived, I kept an I eye on children new to the school – making sure they knew how to get to the gym, media center, bus and so on and were not wandering lost in hallways. I wound up spending a week in lunch lines in the cafeteria helping work out snarls in the computerized payment system (One of those "looked good on paper" ways to simply buying lunch). I observed classes, looking for those students (and teachers) who were in need of immediate attention. I spoke with our local service providers about status of children receiving services, and those who should if we could work out the details. I saw some of my students for individual sessions to catch up on events of the summer and hear their concerns and excitement about this new school year.

Three weeks later, I'm still spending time helping with the lunch line. I am scheduling and holding groups. I put together a brochure explaining what counselors do for our new parents PTA meeting. I attend PPTs and 504 meetings and confer with teachers and specialists about services for our students. I try to find out how I can pay for materials. I talk with parents about all kinds of things, including concerns about student performance, attention issues, family issues impacting education, referrals to outside support, and catching up on news with them. Soon I'll start contacting teachers about fitting guidance lessons into their schedules.

Schedules seem to be created just so they can be changed – field trips, snow days, special activities on the class side, and emergencies, IEP and 504 meetings, training sessions and any number of other things on my side. Next week, it will be more of the same, and new and exciting things, too.

REFERENCES AND RESOURCES

Coloroso, B. (2003). *The bully, the bullied, and the bystander: From preschool to high school – How parents and teachers can help break the cycle of violence.* New York: HarperCollins.

Doleski, T., & McNichols, W. H. (1983). *The hurt.* Mahwah, NJ: Paulist Press.

Munsch, R., & Martchenko, M. (1980). *The paper bag princess.* Buffalo, NY: Annick Press.

Sunburst Visual Media
www.sunburstvm.com/

Uno card game by Mattel
www.mattelgamefinder.com/

What does the middle school counselor's day typically involve?

Cindi Carlisle, School Counselor
Chief Joseph Middle School
Richland, Wash.
cindi_carlisle@rsd.edu

Not long ago I looked carefully at all the miniature graffiti on the courtyard wall of our middle school. A student had reported that she had seen some offensive words written on the wall, so I checked it out. It was not difficult to find the swear words. However, amidst all the junk and trivia that had been etched on the wall I discovered this gem, which I think is typical of middle school thinking: "Life is short, love is long. Let's do both."

How children choose to experience middle school can be nothing short of an adventure for any adult who is willing to work with them. Although I have worked at this level for more than 15 years, I am still amazed at the energy, joy and depth of feeling that adolescents can generate. Counselors who embrace these children and their challenges are not just in for an adventure, but are in for a satisfying journey. Such a journey starts with a typical day in the life of both the student and the counselor.

A DAY'S JOURNEY

In framing this journey, I could not help but think of it in terms of the ASCA National Model. The ASCA National Model addresses the structure of the school counselor's day, the amount of time spent delivering service, and an accountability component to evaluate the effectiveness of each program or service. The model recommends that 80 percent of our time be devoted to student contacts (individual, classroom, small groups, etc.) and the remaining 20 percent to address system support (communications, collaborations and other contacts).

The start of my day is split between systems support and individual student planning activities. If I do not begin my morning by checking e-mail and reviewing my calendar, I often overlook important communications that affect my day. If I do not begin with communications, I am in parent/student/teacher conferences that meet before school starts.

ACADEMICS, PERSONAL/ SOCIAL, CAREER COMPETENCIES

The mornings are usually spent in individual planning or guidance curriculum. I visit as many as four classrooms per week to address guidance curriculum needs. My counseling partner and I have presented this year on: long-term career assessment and school goals, social skills necessary to achieve career goals, understanding high school registration, accessing appropriate Internet sites to conduct individual career interest inventories, finding occupational information and browsing prospective schools for post-secondary planning.

Academic counseling receives major emphasis all four grade periods of the year. Counselors are in a continual feedback loop between the school, the parents and the child. At our school, we have almost 800 students. One of our goals has been simply to touch base with every child and do a brief conference on his/her academic goals.

We have a huge investment in our students' ability to learn personal and social strategies for middle school survival. Unfortunately, we spend approximately one hour each day doing lunch duty. Our administration is not convinced that children are better served in the counseling offices during lunch. The main advantage of student supervision is that we can observe children in less structured environments. I have learned important things about a child simply from lunch duty observations.

OTHER PROGRAMS AND DUTIES

The two longest and most complex activities in our counseling department are coordinating state assessments and scheduling grade-level registrations. Each fall, we do computer assessments of children's reading and math skills. Each spring is spent conducting the Washington Assessment of Student Learning (WASL). We are expected to respond to any directives or requests from administration, even if the requests are not connected to counseling duties. We perform such tasks as substitute teaching, extra yard duty when asked and elementary school visitations to enroll fifth and sixth graders in the spring.

THE MODEL WILL BRING ORDER TO CHAOS

Now that I am well versed in the systems of the ASCA National Model, I find it easier to present alternatives to our administrators. It has been a slow journey from the old system into the rubrics of the new system; however, the rewards are indisputable. I look back on the past 16 years of counseling at middle school and am grateful that I can use the language and paradigms of the ASCA National Model to justify increases in direct services.

As we work with more students and their families, the level of gratification increases. Children see our energy levels rise and are more enticed to take the journey with us.

Although our district has not embraced the Model, our parents, teachers, office staff and even our students have welcomed the shift in counseling emphases. Just talking with students on a daily basis is enough to keep our momentum and re-affirm why we became counselors in the first place.

Vicki Crawford, School Counselor
Vinton Middle School
Vinton, La.
vicki.crawford@cpsb.org

As a counselor in a small middle school, my typical day would probably vary from many other counselors. My role is more "jack of all trades" with curriculum support, administrative tasks, committees and counseling. I begin with my arrival at school at about 7:20 a.m. answering phones, fielding questions and writing student admits for previous absences. Once the secretaries arrive, my attention then shifts to helping substitute teachers find their lessons and talking with students coming into the building. I make arrangements to meet with any students who request a visit.

Then the day progresses with multi-tasking, including:

- Meeting with students
- Talking to parents about grades
- Discussing student progress with the teachers
- Setting up and attending parent/teacher conferences

- Completing various reports on tutoring, school improvement and testing/accountability
- Requesting and sending student records
- Monitoring/talking to students in the hallway between classes

I try to visit with the students who have first lunch during their lunch period, either in session or casually while they are eating. My lunch is eaten, when possible, in the next 15 minutes. Then when second lunch period begins, I am on duty in the cafeteria. I have been able to use this time to touch base with the students informally. Often this is a time when students request a formal visit, and I can set it up for later in the day.

The multi-tasking continues in the afternoon. In addition to maintaining student records, I am responsible for everything pertaining to the students on the computer network: grades, accountability and reports. After classes have ended, I typically help out in the office with the phones and meeting with students and teachers until about 3:45 p.m. The next 15 to 30 minutes are spent trying to tie up some of the tasks that were started earlier in the day and not finished. I rarely leave before 4:00 p.m. or with my desk cleared.

What does the secondary school counselor's day typically involve?

Barbara Blackburn, School Counselor
Greenbrier East High School
Lewisburg, W.Va.
bbblackburn@earthlink.net

INDIVIDUAL COUNSELING

First of all, there is no such thing as a typical day. Our roles change from day to day and week to week. I see students through scheduled appointments for counseling sessions such as individual planning and personal social issues. I also see students for impromptu crisis counseling such as boyfriend/girlfriend problems, social issues with peers, conflicts with teachers and family crisis.

CLASSROOM GUIDANCE

Providing classroom guidance allows me to address a variety of student counseling needs. I find the more classroom guidance I do, the fewer fires

I put out. A major topic of classroom guidance is in the areas of academic advisement, curriculum planning and career guidance, which is usually done in a computer lab where students do individual career, post-secondary, financial aid and scholarship searches. I precede these guidance sessions by giving PowerPoint presentations about the current career market, educational requirements and so forth. These guidance sessions also include information on interpreting tests, completing financial aid forms, developing portfolios and preparing for senior interviews.

I also provide classroom guidance lessons on personal/social topics such as goal setting, dating, domestic violence, suicide prevention and communication/mediation skills.

GROUP COUNSELING

I also set up and conduct group counseling sessions. These are usually topic-specific, such as anger management, dealing with grief, substance abuse and divorce. I also bring in experts from the community to do groups and train teachers to work with me and eventually take over the groups.

PROGRAM MANAGEMENT

In addition to counseling activities, I am also responsible for managing various school activities, including: organizing school-wide programs such as college day, registering students for their classes, scheduling the arena and testing my grade level (setting up the dynamics and doing make-up testing). I also help coordinate senior interviews, developing the educational part and bringing professionals in to work with students on their resumes and interviewing skills. In addition, I handle the logistics for college field trips, peer mediation training and natural helper training.

SYSTEMS SUPPORT

I also do a lot of systems support, where I work as part of the team to meet student needs. This includes developing staff members' awareness of counseling-related initiatives and the various issues our students face. For example, I train them on new programs our students use for career, financial aid and scholarship searching. I also in-service teachers about school-wide programs such as college day and addressing substance abuse issues. I keep teachers informed about who I'm bringing in to work with students. I also develop lessons related to academic planning, career development and personal/social development for our advisor/advisee program. I also sit in on all IEP and 504 meetings for my students.

And the list goes on and on. Each day is different. Some days I am in my office all day seeing students and managing my program. Other days I am in the classroom all day. Other days I am on a field trip with students. Other days I am training peer mediators. Other days I am working with feeder schools to train students and teachers about our curriculum.

What are the differences among counseling, guidance and therapy?

Michael Karcher, Counselor Educator
University of Texas at San Antonio
San Antonio, Texas
mkarcher@utsa.edu

How guidance differs from counseling and therapy is an easier question to answer than how counseling differs from therapy. To make these distinctions, it may be best, perhaps, to consider some of the similarities and differences among these three approaches. Counseling and guidance, unlike therapy, emphasize normal developmental processes and how to facilitate them. Therapy typically focuses on the remediation of a problematic behavior or enduring emotional state, whereas counseling may be initiated by a concern about such a state. However, the counselor has traditionally been trained to focus on ways to help the client or student re-engage in normative developmental growth processes, the achievement of which typically negates, eliminates or lessens the presence of the negative state.

However, it is true that both counseling and therapy are problem-focused, in general. Unlike guidance, in which prevention is the target and which occurs through the provision of skills training, knowledge, or experiences that can change attitudes, both therapy and counseling necessitate that both the healer and sufferer agree that there is a problem to be dealt with.

Consider Jerome Frank's universal definition of therapy, first described in "Persuasion and Healing" in 1961, includes four elements: a healer, a healing context (e.g., therapist's office), a rationale for the problem (also called a "shared myth" about the problem), and rituals based on that rationale that the "sufferer" believes will facilitate their own healing.

One of the greatest problems faced by school counselors is that a therapy approach, and to a lesser degree a counseling approach to problem remediation, requires (at least based on Frank's definition) requires that the student share and counselor hold a similar belief about the presence of a problem. The therapy or counseling approach also requires that the student view the counselor's techniques or intervention method (i.e., counseling rituals) as having the potential to lessen their problem. But when students do not believe that "hanging out with that crowd," engaging in particular risk-taking behavior or persisting in underachievement is problematic, then it is unlikely that they will view the therapist (or counselor) as a healer with valuable techniques.

Bruce Wampold conducted a meta-analysis of available research on adult psychotherapy and reported in the great psychotherapy debate that, in general, up to 25 percent of the effectiveness of psychotherapy results from:

- Therapist's allegiance to an approach
- Client's hope and belief that the therapist, in that place and with those techniques, can help them
- Alliance that develops between client and therapist when these elements are present

In work with youth, it can sometimes be hard to develop this therapeutic alliance when youth do not agree with the counselor's assessment of the youth's problem, the method of change or the counselor's ability to help them. Therefore, many who work with youth have emphasized the importance of first working with them to identify what the counselor and student can both agree is an important problem in the youth's life.

Guidance, on the other hand, does not depend on the youth's acceptance of having a problem. Instead, its effectiveness is determined in large part by its ability to engage youth in changes in attitudes or facilitate the development of skills or knowledge that change attitudes (and subsequently change behavior).

Prevention programs often serve as the backbone of guidance programs used by school counselors. Robert Selman, after watching the emergence of school-based prevention programs over the last quarter of the 21st century, observed that such programs evolved through the following periods:

- In the 1960s and 1970s, there was a heavy push to instill in youth knowledge about the dangers or risky behavior (e.g., showing youth the rotting lungs of adult smokers).

- In the 1980s and early 1990s, there was an emphasis on skill development, such as refusal skills (e.g., the "Just Say No" campaign of the Reagan era).

After observing the limited effectiveness of these programs, Selman commented that only those programs that targeted the personal meaning youth make of behaviors in their lives seemed to have lasting effects.

Schorr's summary of effective prevention programs (Schorr, 1989) also emphasized that such programs almost always were:

- Enduring over time
- Involved a close relationship between youth and some caring adult or older person

That is, personal meaning was most often shaped through long, lasting relationship-based interventions.

Guidance, then, like therapy and counseling, also may depend on the quality of the school counselor's relationship with youth and how they together make meaning of that relationship and what is learned through the course of its development.

REFERENCES AND RESOURCES

Durlak, J. A. (1997). *Successful prevention programs for children and adolescents*. New York: Plenum.

Frank, J. D., & Frank, J. B. (1991). *Persuasion and healing*. Baltimore, MD: Johns Hopkins Press.

Schorr, L. B. (1989). *Within our reach: Breaking the cycle of disadvantage*. New York: Doubleday.

Wampold, B. E. (2000). *The great psychotherapy debate*. Mahwah, NJ: Erlbaum.

Yeates, K. O., & Selman, R. L. (1989). Social competence in the schools: Toward an integrative developmental model for intervention. *Developmental Review, 9,* 64–100.

What is the role of the counselor in the 504 program?

Deb Hardy, School Counselor
Irvington School District
Irvington, N.Y.
nyssca1@aol.com

The school counselor has many tasks as a student advocate. School counselors must be aware of how students learn and when obstacles occur that prevent adequate access to learning. The importance of understanding the regulations for a 504 Plan is essential for students to be served appropriately under the law.

A 504 Plan is developed as an educational plan when the student is showing an impairment substantially limiting learning or another major life activity. These students are eligible for referral, evaluation and educational services under 504.

A child who may have a disability, but is not classified as learning disabled, may be able to qualify under the 504 Plan. To be eligible for a 504 Plan, the student must show a physical or mental impairment that limits at least one life activity, such as walking, breathing, seeing, hearing, speaking, writing and performing math calculations.

When students are being reviewed for a 504 Plan, school counselors should:

- Know who referred the student and the reasons for referral
- Understand the barrier to learning for that student
- Understand how the accommodations will assist the student in overcoming the barrier
- Identify learning support devices that may be needed for the student to learn, such as a computer, scribe or calculator
- Be able to read and interpret test results as needed
- Obtain teacher reports that will assist in identifying the concerns towards learning
- Participate in the initial and annual review of the plan

Once the student has obtained a 504 Plan, school counselors should:

- Communicate with the student's teachers regarding the accommodations
- Maintain contact with parents on the student's progress
- Be knowledgeable on how the accommodation affects testing, state and standardized
- Develop an appropriate career plan
- Assist the student in a career search that matches the student's interests
- Work on resume writing
- Work on a transition plan for college
- Develop a list of colleges that match the student's interests
- Investigate colleges and their support services according to the student's needs

If a student transfers into a new district, the school counselor should be made aware of any former plans from the previous school that are still in effect. The new school must adhere to the previously established plans until the student has had an updated review meeting.

Janna Scarborough, Counselor Educator
Syracuse University
Syracuse, N.Y.
scarboro@syr.edu

Professional school counselors advocate for, and contribute to, the academic, career and personal/social development of all students. Consequently, providing services to students with disabilities is an essential role of school counselors.

Section 504 of the Rehabilitation Act of 1973 is civil rights legislation that protects individuals from discrimination, based on disability, in programs and activities receiving federal financial assistance. Within schools, the intent of Section 504 is to provide students with disabilities equal access to educational programs, services and activities. Students may not be denied participation in school programs and activities solely on the basis of disability, and students with disabilities must be afforded the opportunity to obtain the same results, to gain the same benefit, or to reach the same level of achievement as students without disabilities.

Section 504 has complementary, albeit different objectives than the Individuals with Disabilities Act (IDEA) that addresses special education. IDEA is a federally funded statute that ensures that a free, appropriate public education in the least restrictive environment is provided to students who qualify under the 13 categories of disability defined by the IDEA.

Students who meet the definition of a person with a disability under Section 504 are those who:

- Have a physical or mental impairment that substantially limits one or more major life activities, such as walking, seeing, hearing, speaking, breathing or learning);
- Have a record (history) of such an impairment; or
- Are regarded as having such an impairment.

Therefore, Section 504 is broader in its scope, and many students who qualify for protection under 504 do not qualify for Special Education.

Unlike regulations applied to special education, it is the responsibility of the general education program to ensure both compliance and funding of Section 504 requirements. It is important that a response program, including policies and procedures for 504 referral, evaluation and decision-making, be developed. As part of the educational team ensuring Section 504 response program implementation, school counselors may refer students for evaluation, assist with evaluation procedures, aid in the development of accommodation plans and provide direct services to students.

Generally, school counselors should not have the authority to be solely responsible for making placement or retention decisions, nor for coordinating the multidisciplinary team or supervising the implementation of accommodation plans.

Because the focus of school counseling programs is the development, implementation and evaluation of planned interventions and strategies that meet the diverse needs of all students, school counselors utilize the primary interventions of consultation, coordination and counseling to assist with the Section 504 response program.

As consultants and collaborators, school counselors serve as a member of the school's multidisciplinary team to:

- Identify students with special needs
- Assist in developing accommodation plans

- Work with staff and parents to understand the special needs of these students
- Collaborate with others in the delivery of services

As coordinators, school counselors:

- Make referrals to other appropriate specialists within the school system and community
- Address academic, career and personal/social competencies by providing individual and small group counseling and classroom lessons to students
- Ensure that all students have equal access to their services
- Provide specific direct services to students with disabilities as part of accommodation plans

School counselors provide a variety of services, in cooperation with regular and special education personnel, to address the needs of regular education students with disabilities.

Perhaps the most important role of school counselors within the school is to adhere to the spirit of developmental school counseling programs by working as leaders, advocates and collaborators to promote academic achievement for all students.

REFERENCES AND RESOURCES

American School Counselor Association. (1999). *The professional school counselor and students with special needs.* Alexandria, VA: Author. Available online at www.schoolcounselor.org

Baumberger, J. P., & Harper, R. E. (1999). *Assisting students with disabilities: What school counselors can and must do.* Thousand Oaks, CA: Corwin Press.

Council of Educators for Students with Disabilities, Inc. (2000a). §504 placement. Austin, TX: Richards Lindsay & Martin, L.L.P. Available online at *www.504idea.org/504_placement.html*

Council of Educators for Students with Disabilities, Inc. (2000b). §504 resources. Austin, TX: Richards Lindsay & Martin, L.L.P. Available online at *www.504idea.org/504resources.html*

Glenn, E. E. (Ed). (1998). Counseling children and adolescents with disabilities [Special issue]. *Professional School Counseling, 2*(1).

Learning Disabilities Online
    www.ldonline.org/ld_indepth/teaching_techniques/504_plans.html

Richards, D. (1994). *A step-by-step process for developing a §504 program from scratch.* Austin, TX: Richards Lindsay & Martin, L.L.P. Available online at www.504idea.org/StepbyStep.pdf

U.S. Department of Education, Office for Civil Rights
    www.ed.gov/about/offices/list/ocr/index.html?src=oc

U.S. Department of Education, Office for Civil Rights. (1991). *The guidance counselor's role in ensuring equal educational opportunity.* Washington, DC: Author. Available online at
    www.ed.gov/about/offices/list/ocr/docs/hq43ef.html

U.S. Department of Education, Office of Special Education and Rehabilitative Services
    www.ed.gov/about/offices/list/osers/osep/index.html

U.S Department of Education. The Office for Civil Rights. Implementation of Section 504 of the Rehabilitation Act of 1973. *www.ed.gov*

Wright, P. W. D., & Wright, P. D. (2005). Discussion of section 504, the ADA and the IDEA. Richmond, VA: Wrightslaw. Available online at *www.wrightslaw.com/info/sec504.summ.rights.htm*

What is the role of the school counselor in special education?

Emily Snyder, Consultant
Know Your Options
Fairfax County, Va.
emasnyder@aol.com

ASCA's position statement on special needs students is clear. Professional school counselors are responsible for providing guidance and counseling services to all students in their caseload, regardless of need.

Federal mandates such as Public Law 94-142, IDEA and 504 Plan legislation require that all students receive equitable educational opportunities. The passage of this legislation, intended to address learning style differences and concerns particular to special needs students, along with the resulting inclusion movement, has created new and challenging opportunities for professional school counselors.

School counselors now have an ethical and legal responsibility to utilize their unique skills within a team process to ensure that special needs students receive educational services appropriate for their individual learning styles. They must work with others to provide prevention and intervention strategies that will help students progress and achieve to the best of their abilities (Baker, 2000).

As part of their schools' established multi-disciplinary teams, professional school counselors can focus on all facets of student IEPs and provide support services that enhance parent involvement in the special education process (The Council for Exceptional Children, 1994).

Specifically, professional school counselors should participate with their students' teachers and special education staff and administrators in their school's pre-referral process. They should attend all IEP meetings; doing so provides them with the opportunity to work collaboratively with others to offer individual support services (such as social skills training, behavior management, individual counseling and group counseling) that support the classroom teachers' role of making accommodations and modifications that help students achieve successfully in school.

Professional school counselors can use their communications training to enhance parent involvement in the special education process. To do so effectively, they must:

- Know and understand federal, state, and local policies and regulations involving parental rights and the special education process (Tarver-Behring, Spagna, and Sullivan, 1998)
- Be knowledgeable enough to communicate with parents intelligently and provide them with information for support services

School counselors can also:

- Provide families with resources within the school district and community, such as contacts for advocacy and support groups, school contact information, and local and state testing requirements
- Advocate establishing a special parent association for those interested in taking an active role in their schools

- Offer (in conjunction with teachers) workshops on meeting academic targets through organizational and study skills sessions, as well as provide information and resources on post-graduation opportunities

Any discussion about the role of school counselors in the special education process must include an emphasis on the need for school districts to provide appropriate and continuous staff development training (Baker, 2000). All graduate education programs should mandate course work and practical experience in special education law, special education identification measures and procedures for diagnosis.

Additionally, school districts and lawmakers must focus on ways to reduce caseloads so that professional school counselors have the time to fully participate as advocates for all students and their families, regardless of their individual needs.

REFERENCES AND RESOURCES

Anderson, W., Hayes, D., & Chitwood, S. (1997). *Negotiating the special education maze: A guide for parents and teachers* (3rd ed.). Bethesda, MD: Woodbine House.

Baker, S. B. (2000). *School counseling for the twenty-first century* (3rd ed.). Upper Saddle River, NJ: Prentice Hall.

The Council for Exceptional Children. (1994). *Creating schools for all students – What 12 schools have to say: A product of the working forum on inclusive schools.* Reston, VA: Author.

Friend, M. P., & Bursuck, W. (2001). *Including students with special needs: A practical guide for classroom teachers* (3rd ed.). Boston: Pearson Allyn & Bacon.

Levine, M. D. (1998). *Educational care: A system for understanding and helping children with learning disabilities at home and in school.* Cambridge, MA: Educators Publishing Service.

Siegel, L. M. (2001). *The complete IEP guide: How to advocate for your special education child.* (2nd ed.). Berkeley, CA: Nolo Press.

Tarver-Behring, S., Spagna, M. E., & Sullivan, J. (1998). School counselors and full inclusion for children with special needs. *Professional School Counseling, 1*(3), 51–56.

What is the school counselor's responsibility and role in diagnostics?

Angie Stansell, School Counselor
Hatton High School
Town Creek, Ala.
akounsel@yahoo.com

In understanding the school counselor's responsibility and role in diagnostics, the school counselor should be come very familiar with Section A.9. of "ASCA Ethical Standards for School Counselors." It provides a guide for all aspects of diagnostics. School counselors are to adhere "to all professional standards regarding selecting, administering and interpreting assessment measures and only utilize those within the scope of practice." (A.9.a)

Many assessments are to be utilized only after one has received the needed training in administering and interpreting the assessment. Usually this training involves much time in practicing with students and adults the details and techniques of the administration. Likewise, it is highly important to be trained in the scoring and interpreting of the assessment.

The same skills are equally needed in the commonly used achievement tests in the school setting, since the school counselor may be called upon to interpret or provide professional input in meetings involving parents, teachers and students, and then use that information to make decisions regarding academics, special education and other areas. The counselor can provide meaningful, understandable results. So, administering the assessment and interpreting the results are equally important in the area of diagnostics.

Confidentiality issues should always be a priority when utilizing information and collaborating with staff. (A.9.c) Both used and unused assessments should be stored in a locked area.

Many school systems have a preference of assessments to be used for various needs. Many also contract with psychometrists to administer and score them. It appears that the school counselor would follow the school system's practice for assessments and make referrals as needed. Many school counselors are involved in their school's assessment program as test coordinator for the yearly state required tests in achievement.

However, when called upon to select and administer a test to an individual student for a particular problem (such as reading or math skills, behavior or attention), the school counselor should take caution that the instrument is standardized and measures those areas for which it is being administered. (A.9.f) A school counselor's diagnostic skills can help students in various needs that affect students' academic, career and personal/social development (A.9.g).

What is the school counselor's role during a school crisis?

Brenda Melton, School Counselor
Navarro Academy
San Antonio, Texas
meltonbrenda@msn.com

The school counselor's role in a crisis is to ensure the well-being and safety of the students through leadership, collaboration and advocacy. A crisis, defined as a sudden death or traumatic event that impacts an entire school or community, is a powerful occurrence. Examples include a human crisis (such as a suicide, murder, bomb threat or accident) or a natural catastrophe with widespread effects (such as a hurricane, tornado or fire). With this continuum of crises, school districts rely on the professional expertise of the school counselor as well as administrative and police interventions.

Students, school staff and parents should be aware of what is involved in a sudden death or similar crisis and how it affects the school and community. If there is not a crisis management plan that involves the school counselor's role, then one needs to be developed. In developing an effective plan, prevention, intervention and postvention strategies are imperative. It is also critical to recognize individuals with self-destructive behavior and provide support and appropriate interventions. After a plan has been developed with all stakeholders, professional development should be implemented on a regular basis to review the plan and provide resources and information.

PREVENTION STRATEGIES

The school counselor needs be preventive by including crisis management in the comprehensive school counseling plan. Students and staff will need to practice and know how to respond in different situations where evacuation or containment are necessary. School counselors need to provide resources to staff such as information on:

- Reflective listening
- The need for clear information regarding the crisis
- Responses to grief
- Student needs in grief
- What to look for in identifying students who are at risk
- Process for referring at-risk students

During prevention, the counselor's role is to:

- Provide workshops for the staff on crisis management, depression and suicide prevention /intervention
- Provide information for parents on crisis management, suicide prevention and ways to help their child

INTERVENTION STRATEGIES

The school counselor will need to know what responses to anticipate (denial, anger, blame, crying, depression) and be prepared with age-appropriate interventions. Have a resource file available for students, teachers and parents, using resources such as The Dougy Center. The school counselor should be available to help students process their feelings. Cheri Lovre of The Crisis Management Institute suggests that counselors may be need to stay in their usual offices so students and staff know where they are. The school counselor will need to assist with peer counseling activities. Lovre recommends that peer counselors be used for a limited time during the day to roam the halls and hang-outs, encouraging peers to be in rooms with adult supervision.

During intervention, the counselor's role is to:

- Provide crisis counseling for students
- Identify students who need more intense counseling and post-traumatic intervention for grief/loss
- Provide information to the media on the incident (without revealing personal information about the child) and the role of school counselors in providing support to the students (as needed)
- Support parents, teachers and staff in providing for the students
- Stabilize the school environment and assist students in returning to normalcy

- Provide expertise in long-range intervention and crisis response for the district
- Join in the community efforts to improve the school environment

POSTVENTION STRATEGIES

The period following a crisis is a critical time for analyzing what worked, and didn't work, about implementing crisis management plan. The plan should be revised and updated based on lessons learned. It's also a time to ensure appropriate follow-up support is provided all those affected by the crisis.

During postvention, the counselor's role is to:

- Evaluate and assess the information received about the emergency
- Call a consultant to come to the school if necessary
- Provide follow-up support at intervals (three months, six months and on anniversary dates)

Linda Eby, School Counselor

Gordon Russell Middle School
Gresham, Ore.
LindaCE@aol.com

Every day in America, school counselors report to their school buildings expecting to carry out another day of their counseling program – a classroom presentation, a parent meeting, a group or a meeting to help a student find new ways to be successful with their academics. But, every day there is at least one counselor who arrives to school to find that an emergency, tragedy or crisis will supercede all other activities for that day. Whether a student or staff death, violence on the campus, or a natural disaster, school counselors are uniquely trained to offer services in managing the crisis.

The ASCA National Model outlines leadership, advocacy, collaboration and systemic change as key counselor skills. These skills are equally critical in developing a district crisis plan, implementing the plan and recovering in the aftermath of a crisis.

LEADERSHIP

School counselors provide leadership in developing and maintaining a comprehensive district crisis plan that includes an appropriate developmental response to the emotional needs of students, while also considering the support needed by staff, families and the community.

Many districts have mobilized their school counselors into flight teams that enter a school in crisis, establishing safe rooms for students and/or staff, coordinating communication with parents and providing valuable information regarding community resources. School counselors monitor the recovery process after a crisis by meeting with students who were most affected by the event, and educating students, parents and staff about typical reactions following a crisis.

ADVOCACY

School counselors advocate for student success through a crisis, just as at any other time. Emotional first aid to victims of a tragedy has proven to be a key factor in facilitating the recovery process. School counselors' skills in diffusing and processing highly charged emotional situations make them expert advocates. Teachers and other staff have special needs also, depending upon the crisis. The school counselor's sensitivity to need of the staff to have time away from their classroom for grieving and processing, time with their own personal support systems and help with students in the classroom is crucial. Advocating for staff is advocating for students, as students will be impacted tremendously by the reaction of their teachers and other adults in the school.

It's important for school counselors to remember staff that may not be initially considered, such as bus drivers, custodial and cafeteria staff, and parent volunteers who work in the building. Secretarial staff members also need support during a crisis with the increased volume and emotional level of phone calls coming in from parents, media and others in the community. Advocacy must also extend to administrators, as they feel much of the responsibility to get their school community through the crisis. School counselors can help by offering their expertise and resources to administrators. They can also help by participating on the safety and crisis management teams, both in planning for and responding to a crisis.

COLLABORATION

Collaboration is vital to an effective crisis response, and a particular strength of school counselors. As school counselors participate in crisis planning meetings, their skills in collaboration can facilitate the content of crisis planning as well as the process of the meeting itself. School counselors excel in communicating with grieving parents, and can provide a valuable service in the collaboration between the school and the family in the case of a student death.

SYSTEMIC CHANGE

As mentioned earlier, school counselors need to be members of their district's crisis planning teams, developing and maintaining a viable, comprehensive response plan. As leaders in systemic change, school counselors are the catalysts in changing procedures and policies to best meet student needs, even in looking at effective responses to a crisis.

Specialized training equips school counselors to maximize their response as flight team members and district crisis planning team participants, as well as when tragedy strikes within their own school communities. Excellent resources exist to assist school counselors in fulfilling their roles as leaders, advocates, collaborators and systemic change agents.

REFERENCES AND RESOURCES

American School Counselor Association. (2003). Crisis response. *ASCA School Counselor*, November/December

Crisis Management Institute
www.cmionline.org

David Baldwin's Trauma Information Pages
www.trauma-pages.com

The Dougy Center
www.dougy.org

Gordon, N. S., Farberow, N. L., & Maida, C. A. (1999). *Children and disasters*. New York: Routledge.

Oates, M. (1993). *Death in the school community: A handbook for counselors, teachers and administrators*. Alexandria, VA: American Counseling Association.

SAFE: Teen Suicide Prevention
www.safe-teen.com/

Trauma Intervention Program
www.tipnational.org

Yellow Ribbon Prevention Program
www.yellowribbon.org

What is the school counselor's role in testing?

John Galassi, Counselor Educator
University of North Carolina
Chapel Hill, N.C.
jgalassi@e-mail.unc.edu

TESTING PURPOSES

Tests are used for a variety of purposes in schools, and the school counselor has an important role in almost all of them. Within the school counseling program, tests are used to:

- Help students gather information about interests, abilities, skills and achievement in order to make immediate and long-term decisions and to set goals for educational, personal and career development
- Diagnose students with special learning needs (often conducted by school psychologists or educational diagnosticians trained in the administration of individual intelligence and other specialized tests)

Standardized tests frequently form the basis of institutional decision-making such as:

- Evaluating curriculum
- Classifying students into instructional tracks
- Comparing the achievement levels of students in different schools
- Assessing teacher effectiveness

In what is referred to as high-stakes testing, tests increasingly are being used as benchmarks for student progress, instructional accountability and the evaluation of individual school performance.

SCHOOL COUNSELOR'S ROLE IN TESTING

Some of the assessment purposes for which tests are used, as well as the counselor's role in those areas, are controversial. For example, Baker and Gerler (2004) asserted that the only legitimate assessment functions for counselors are those that are used to achieve counseling goals. They believe testing to classify and track students and to determine levels of student academic achievement is not a legitimate activity for school counselors because those functions are designed to achieve instructional and administrative goals.

The school counselor's role in testing will vary from school to school. According to the North Carolina Department of Public Instruction, for example, that role includes interpreting test results and other student data and assisting teachers with the educational placement of students by using appropriate educational assessment strategies.

A variety of other professional testing roles have also been identified for the school counselor, including:

- Interpreting test results to students, faculty and parents
- Helping teachers prepare their students for academic assessment through classroom guidance activities such as teaching effective test-taking strategies and conducting small groups for underachieving or high anxious students
- Selecting appropriate tests
- Ensuring the proper administration of tests in accordance with standardized instructions
- Assisting administrators in understanding and using school-wide testing results

In order to accomplish these functions, the school counselor must possess a variety of assessment competencies including knowledge of principles of measurement, of standardized and nonstandardized assessment procedures, of selecting, administering, and scoring assessment instruments, and of interpreting and communicating test results (ASCA, 1998b). Moreover, the school counselor subscribes to ethical standards with regard to the selection, administration, and interpretation of testing materials (ASCA, 1998a).

With the advent of outcomes-based school reform and the passage of legislation such as the No Child Left Behind (NCLB) Act, a high-stakes testing environment has emerged. Even though ASCA (ASCA, 2002) opposes the use of a single test to make decisions about student and/or school success, school counselors frequently must function as testing coordinators for the standardized achievement tests on which these decisions are based. This role involves a number of clerical and other time-consuming, non-professional responsibilities such as counting test booklets, organizing makeup tests and monitoring test takers.

Research has indicated that these responsibilities interfere with the school counselor being able to deliver a comprehensive counseling program and may adversely affect the counselor's relationships with teachers, students and other school personnel (Brown, Galassi, & Akos, in press). Moreover, many of these duties can be carried out by clerical workers, trained volunteers or other support staff (ASCA, 2001), thus freeing the school counselor to attend to testing and other program responsibilities that require professional expertise.

LaBarbara Sampson, Counselor Educator
Greenville County Schools
Greenville, S.C.
lsampson@greenville.k12.sc.us

In the area of student appraisal and assessment, the school counselor assists by using strategies such as helping students plan their educational program, interpreting test data with teachers to make appropriate decisions about academic placement and sharing occupational information with students. The school counselor's role as it relates to assessment is to:

- Conduct an annual needs assessment involving students, parents and staff
- Plan program initiatives using the Comprehensive Developmental Guidance and Counseling Program Model
- Plan for the delivery and evaluation of comprehensive developmental guidance and counseling program initiatives
- Prepare and submit required program accountability reports
- Respond appropriately to requests for counseling services
- Identify and use appropriate evaluation tools
- Utilize evaluation results to reassess program goals and objectives
- Interpret standardized tests to teachers, parents and students

NO CHILD LEFT BEHIND LEGISLATION REGARDING TESTING

Focused on promoting success for all students, NCLB includes legislation regarding testing. In grades three through eight, for example, the NCLB legislation references required testing. The school counselor is integral to making sure that the school is a supportive learning environment for that required testing. In addition to continuing activities that ensure that students are ready to learn, the guidance and counseling program can institute activities school-wide that promote a supportive learning environment during the pre-testing months and weeks, and even year-round. Some of the programs and activities the school counselor would implement include:

- Reducing stress, including math phobia and test phobia reduction
- Improving study and testing skills
- Boosting self-confidence

In grades nine through 12, the NCLB legislation stresses accountability for the results of learning activities and a system that supports all students graduating from high school. In states with high-stakes testing for grade promotion and/or graduation requirements, students with performance anxiety may need strong support to keep them confident and in school. Some of the programs and activities the school counselor would implement include:

- Coming to school ready to learn
- Developing a graduation plan
- Beginning the path toward success outside of high school
- Preventing and recovering high school dropout students

OUTCOME RESEARCH

The school counselor should base all of these activities on NCLB accountability requirements and current research. Counseling outcome research is a potentially useful source of this information because it is designed to provide guidance on which techniques and activities produce positive changes for students. It is critical that school counselors be informed about outcome research and know which activities are supported and which are not supported by research. Outcome research can assist school counselors in selecting counseling interventions and guidance activities that have been shown to be effective.

REFERENCES AND RESOURCES

American School Counselor Association. (1998). *Competencies in assessment and evaluation for school counselors.* Alexandria, VA: Author. Available online at www.schoolcounselor.org

American School Counselor Association. (2001). *The professional counselor and use of support staff in counseling.* Alexandria, VA: Author. Available online at www.schoolcounselor.org

American School Counselor Association. (2002). *The professional school counselor and high-stakes testing.* Alexandria, VA: Author. Available online at www.schoolcounselor.org

American School Counselor Association. (2004). *Ethical standards for school counselors*. Alexandria, VA: Author. Available online at www.schoolcounselor.org

Baker, S. B., & Gerler, E. R., Jr. (2004). *School counseling for the twenty-first century* (4th ed.). Upper Saddle River, NJ: Pearson Education.

Brown, D., Galassi, J. P., & Akos, P. (in press). *School counselors' perceptions of the impact of high-stakes testing*. Professional School Counseling.

What would you say are the top five significant events contributing to the growth and development of the school counseling profession?

Tamara Davis, Counselor Educator
Marymount University
Arlington, Va.
tamara.davis@marymount.edu

The significant events that have contributed to the growth and development of school counseling combine the historical impact of federal legislation, the current emphasis on the ASCA National Standards and ASCA National Model and the influence of current events.

HISTORIC LEGISLATION

Based on a historical review of significant events, it is undeniable that the passage of the National Defense Education Act (NDEA) of 1958 greatly affected the school counseling profession. School counselors were, for the first time, valued as integral to the academic progress of students. In general, the NDEA increased the number of full-time counselors in schools, increased the number of consultants at the state level who focused on school counseling, funded training opportunities for school counselors and increased the amount of funding for school counseling services (Schmidt, 2003).

Perhaps the most significant growth and development has occurred in the last two decades as a result of comprehensive school counseling program development, management and implementation. The comprehensive program model provided by Gysbers and Henderson in 1988 (Baker, 2000) and their work in the early 1990s (Gysbers & Henderson, 2000) provided a framework for school counseling services in terms of planning, implementation and evaluation. School counselors finally had a blueprint that they could follow and model in their programs.

DEVELOPMENT OF NATIONAL STANDARDS

In 1998, ASCA released national standards for school counseling programs (Campbell & Dahir, 1997). The standards addressed the three domains that promote the overall development of students: academic, personal/social and career development.

Providing specific objectives and guidelines for school counselors helped define the role of the school counselor and guided practice in a professional manner. The standards were touted throughout the country as the manual for school counseling practices and provided specific objectives that should be achieved in order to promote success for students.

Most recently, the growth and development of school counseling has occurred as a result of the ASCA National Model (ASCA, 2003). The model has accomplished the paramount task of integrating all of the components that constitute an effective counseling program. Each component of the ASCA model is a part of the comprehensive program, with the four major areas (foundation, accountability, delivery system and management system) feeding into and influencing each other.

CURRENT EVENTS

While these events have been monumental in school counseling, societal events have also affected the growth and development of school counseling programs. In April 1999, the horrific violence at Columbine High School in Littleton, Colo., forever changed how school personnel (school counselors, in particular) must be more involved in the emotional and social well-being of students. School counselors were recognized as key personnel to help assess the mental health of students and support for school counseling appeared to increase.

Another act of violence that forever changed how students feel about safety was the 9/11 attacks on the World Trade Center and the Pentagon. Accepting the vulnerability of our nation to such attacks requires that school counselors address the fears and insecurities that surround the daily lives of students, faculty, parents and communities. The school counselor's role is not limited to the traditional roles of counselor, consultant and coordinator; it has transformed to include leadership, advocacy and accountability (The Education Trust, 2003).

While the ASCA National Model gives us a foundation for a prosperous future in school counseling, we should be ever mindful that much of the growth and development of the profession depends on the people who choose the path. The profession will only continue to grow and develop if we assume responsibility for its promotion and demonstrate the efficacy of its practices.

REFERENCES AND RESOURCES

American School Counselor Association. (2005). *The ASCA national model: A framework for school counseling programs, second edition.* Alexandria, VA: Author.

Baker, S. (2000). *School counseling for the twenty-first century* (3rd ed.). Upper Saddle River, NJ: Merrill/Prentice Hall.

Campbell, C. A., & Dahir, C. A. (1997). *Sharing the vision: The national standards for school counseling programs.* Alexandria, VA: American School Counselor Association.

The Education Trust. (2003). Transforming school counseling initiative. Available online at *www2.edtrust.org/EdTrust/Transforming+School+Counseling*

Gysbers, N. C., & Henderson, P. (2000). *Developing and managing your school guidance program* (3rd ed.). Alexandria, VA: American Counseling Association.

Schmidt, J. J. (2003). *Counseling in schools: Essential services and comprehensive programs* (4th ed.). Needham Heights, MA: Allyn & Bacon.

Technology

Technology underpins our fastest growing industries and high-wage jobs, provides the tools needed to compete in every business today and drives growth in every major industrialized nation. Recognizing this trend, Former President Bill Clinton stated, "All students should feel as comfortable with a keyboard as a chalkboard; as comfortable with a laptop as a textbook. The rest of society would fall behind if it did not get a grounding in the rudiments of computers at a early age." To effectively work with students and other educational stakeholders, school counselors too must maintain adequate levels of technological literacy.

Progressively powerful computers, sophisticated software and expanding networks are rapidly changing traditional school counseling approaches and standards of performance. Although no one is truly certain if or when the exponential growth of technology will taper, it is well recognized that we are immersed in a new age of information, communication and collaboration (Sabella & Tyler, 2001). For better or worse, computers are changing the ways in which we conduct our work, interact and especially make decisions.

Counseling professionals must adapt to new ways of interfacing with machines and the people that use them in a way that promotes the goals and objectives of their work. No aspect of society or economy can function effectively and compete without such tools. School counselors that decide to "opt out" of information technology will be working with students who perceive them to live in a world that no longer exists. Information and networking technologies are now essential tools for manipulating ideas and images and for communicating effectively with others – an important component of the counselor's job (Sabella, 2003).

Examples of technology issues covered in this chapter include developing and learning about school counseling related Web sites, listservs, relevant technological competencies for school counselors and software.

REFERENCES AND RESOURCES

Sabella, R. A. (2003). *SchoolCounselor.com: A friendly and practical guide to the World Wide Web* (2nd ed.). Minneapolis, MN: Educational Media.

Sabella, R. A., & Tyler, J. M. (2001). School counselor technology competencies for the new millennium. In D. S. Sandhu (Ed.), *Elementary school counseling in the new millennium.* Alexandria, VA: American Counseling Association.

How do I find helpful and resourceful Web sites among the millions available on the Web?

Russell Sabella, Counselor Educator
Florida Gulf Coast University
Fort Meyers, Fla.
sabella@schoolcounselor.com

The easiest way to find helpful and resourceful Web sites is to let others do the work for you. Various organizations and individuals have dedicated time and work compiling short descriptions of Web pages with accompanying Web site addresses for a specific topic. Users can e-mail the organization or visit the organization's Web site to receive these compilations (known as subscribing to a listserv). Here are several resources which are of interest to school counselors.

ASCA

ASCA provides a free monthly e-newsletter to all members that includes many resources and tools available on the Internet.

BLUE WEB'N

Blue Web'n (*www.kn.pacbell.com/wired/bluewebn/*) is an online library of more than 1,700 outstanding Internet sites categorized by subject, grade level and format (lessons, activities, projects, resources, references and tools). Search parameters are by grade level, broad subject area and subject area. New sites, along with their descriptions, are added weekly.

EDUHOUND

EduHound (*www.eduhound.com*), a division of *T.H.E. Journal*, is a highly specialized educational directory with built-in resource links offered free to educators, students and parents. EduHound.com seeks to harness the vast information resources of the Web, while enabling educators to use the Internet as a classroom tool. Since its launch in January 2000, the site boasts thousands of visitors per week and an ever-growing list of subscribers to their weekly newsletter.

LOCKERGNOME

Lockergnome (*www.lockergnome.com*) provides a variety of free newsletters that point to Web sites of interest related to technology solutions.

RESEARCHBUZZ

ResearchBuzz (*www.researchbuzz.com*) covers the world of Internet research. This site provides almost daily updates on search engines, new data-managing software, browser technology, large compendiums of information, Web directories and more.

SCHOOLCOUNSELOR.COM

SchoolCounselor.com (*schoolcounselor.com/newsletter*) provides a free newsletter to advance technology literacy and application among school counselors.

SCOUT REPORT

Scout Report (*scout.cs.wisc.edu/scout/report/*) is a weekly publication of the InterNIC Net Scout project at the University of Wisconsin – Madison. It provides a fast, convenient way to stay informed about valuable resources on the Internet. It combines in one place new and newly discovered Internet resources and network tools, especially those of interest to researchers and educators.

While using Web site compilations is the easiest way to find helpful information on the Web, it does have potential drawbacks:

- Waiting for others to present URLs may not be very timely.
- This method leaves to others' judgment the value and usefulness of the information.

Therefore, counselors need to supplement this information with more immediate and personalized Web sources. I recommend that counselors learn how to become proficient in finding and processing online information, resources and tools.

I consider conducting effective searches similar to playing golf – mostly skill and some luck. The integrity of search results will depend in part on the search engine used and the skill with which the search is performed. To become more proficient at Internet searches, I recommend spending some time practicing searches as espoused by tutorials such as those listed below.

REFERENCES AND RESOURCES

Beginners' Central, a users' guide to the Internet
northernwebs.com/bc/

Evaluating Web Resources, teaching modules for effectively evaluating Web resources
www2.widener.edu/Wolfgram-Memorial-Library/webevaluation/webeval.htm

Finding information on the Internet – A tutorial
www.lib.berkeley.edu/TeachingLib/Guides/Internet/FindInfo.html

Google Tutorial
www.google.com/help/index.html

Internet Literacy
www.udel.edu/interlit/

Sabella, R. A. (2003). *Schoolcounselor.com: A friendly and practical guide to the World Wide Web* (2nd ed). Minneapolis, MN: Educational Media.

SchoolCounselor.com
www.schoolcounselor.com

How do I find out about useful school counseling online communities or listservs?

Theresa Hawkins, Counselor Educator
University of Iowa
Iowa City, Iowa
tshawkins@hawkportal.com

and

Pat Partin, Counselor Educator
Gardner-Webb University
Boiling Springs, N.C.
ppartin@shelby.net

Several approaches are useful when searching for school counseling online communities and listservs:

- Join listservs that are directly associated with local, regional, state and national professional organizations
- Search the professional organizations' Web sites for information regarding their listservs
- Use search engines such as Google to find links to school counseling communities that may have resources for current issues
- Ask other professional counselors what they find useful on the Internet

A number of sites list multiple listservs for counselors. Among them are:

- ASCA
- American Counseling Association
- SchoolCounselor.com
- Some state departments of education

Another way to find school counseling listservs is to check your state's school counselor Web site. An increasing number of state organizations are providing listservs as a service to members and a way for counselors in the state to communicate and share with each other. Selected school counselor listservs are listed below.

ASCA LISTSERVS

ASCA members can join targeted listservs that can be a goldmine of support and ideas. Information about ASCA's listservs states, "Regardless of whether you work at the elementary or post-secondary level, or anywhere in between, there are often times when you need to discuss issues with and garner ideas from other practicing school counselors working at the same level. ASCA's targeted listservs allow you to do just that." ASCA has 12 targeted listservs, including by job setting, ASCA region, international and student.

INTERNATIONAL COUNSELOR NETWORK

This is one of the first listservs, moderated by Ellen Rust and housed at the University of Tennessee, to include a large network of school counselors and mental health counselors.

REFERENCES AND RESOURCES

American Counseling Association
www.counseling.org

American School Counselor Association Listserv
www.schoolcounselor.org

Indiana Department of Education Listserv
www.doe.state.in.us/sservices/list.htm

International Counselor Network Listserv
listserv.utk.edu/archives/icn.html

SchoolCounselor.com
www.schoolcounselor.com

Student Iowa School Counselor Association Listserv
www.uiowa.edu/~sisca/Distribution_List.htm

Virginia Department of Education Listserv
www.people.virginia.edu/~mgd2u/listserv.html

How do I set up my own Web site?

Tarrell Portman, Counselor Educator
University of Iowa
Iowa City, Iowa
tarrell-portman@uiowa.edu

and

Kathleen Kellum, Counselor Educator
University of Iowa
Iowa City, Iowa
kathleen-kellum@uiowa.edu

Setting up your own Web site can be a daunting task for many professional school counselors. However, some school counselors may have received advanced technical training during their counselor education programs. Whether you identify more with one group or the other, be assured that an active, updated Web site is an invaluable tool when marketing school counseling programs. These Web sites:

- Provide a method of disseminating information to students, parents, faculty, staff, administration and community leaders
- Encourage home/school/community collaborations
- Increase public relations
- Unite stakeholders in support of school counseling programs

How do you set up your own Web site? There are four stages to the process: planning, design, implementation and evaluation.

PLANNING

In the planning stage, lay the groundwork for your Web site by conducting the following activities:

- Explore other school counseling program Web sites to help you identify and select specific components you would want on your Web site
- Assess the technical resources available for creating a Web site (e.g., What technical support do you have available in your building or district? Your school may have a specific technical person with the responsibility, and often the only authority, of placing information on the school's Web site.)
- Determine the scope of your Web site (e.g., What Web space is available? How much of your time can you spend creating and maintaining a Web site?)
- Explore Web publishing software available at your school

DESIGN

Don't be afraid to be creative in the design stage. In this stage, you conduct the following activities:

- Conceptualize what you want to accomplish with your Web site
- Explore prepackaged Web sites available on the Internet that can be reworked for your site
- Experiment with color schemes, logos and interactive components
- Gather content and decide what information is to be included on your school counseling site and what information can be received via links to the school and district Web sites
- Develop a template that shows the site's overall "look and feel"
- Have internal and external stakeholders give direct, honest feedback about your site; be sure to include a special education teacher or someone knowledgeable in assistive technology so you will be serving all ability levels through your program

IMPLEMENTATION

The third stage, implementation, becomes a reality after the stakeholders have provided feedback for your Web site template. During the implementation stage you:

- Gather support from stakeholders
- Get the word out that a new school counseling Web site is coming
- Place the Web site on a server. This can be as simple as handing the content information to a school technology employee or uploading an attachment

EVALUATION

The final stage, evaluation, is an ongoing process. During this stage, you can:

- Request feedback on the site and link responses directly to your e-mail account
- Keep an ongoing record of comments you receive about the Web site from people who use the school counseling program – positive or negative
- Use feedback to update your site as appropriate

Many resources are available on the Internet and in your library to help you get started. Creating a Web site does not have to be a lonely process. Consult with a technology specialist and your peers to gain the information you need to set up a Web site in your area. School counseling program Web sites are beneficial to program delivery. You just need to take the plunge.

REFERENCES AND RESOURCES

How to Create Your Own Web site
www.freewebhostingtips.com

Lynch, P. J., & Horton, S. (2002). *Web style guide: Basic design principles for creating Web sites* (2nd ed.). New Haven, CT: Yale University Press.

W3Schools' full Web building tutorials, all free
www.w3schools.com

Web Design Group ... Making the Web accessible to all
www.htmlhelp.com

Williams, R., & Tollett, J. (2000). *The non-designer's Web book* (2nd ed.). Berkeley, CA: Peachpit Press.

In addition to e-mail, how do school counselors use technology to collaborate or connect with each other and with stakeholders?

Edward Coyle, Retired School Counselor
Neenah, Wis.
edcoyle@ameritech.net

Technology provides effective collaboration tools to connect school counselors and stakeholders. Two good examples are listservs and Web sites.

LISTSERVS

One way to increase communication with other counselors is to use a listserv. A listserv is simply a way to send information or questions to other members of the list. An e-mail is sent to an address and then transmitted to all list members, who can then reply. This has been a wonderful resource for being able to access advice and resources for unexpected problems encountered at school.

Most listservs are set up for specific populations. For example:

- ASCA has listservs for different levels in schools (elementary, middle and high).
- State counseling associations have listservs for counselors in their state or region.

- Individuals can set up their free listservs using companies such as Yahoo or MSN.

WEB SITES

Another use of technology for collaboration is publishing a Web site for the counseling department in your school, or even publishing your own site. Web sites provide an efficient way to distribute information, freeing your time and resources for other needs. They also open communication to parents or students who might be afraid to ask questions.

School counseling Web sites can provide readily available information such as:

- Scholarships
- Summer opportunities
- Counselor's schedule
- Counseling newsletters
- Information about specific issues such as divorce, nightmares and eating disorders
- Emergency information such as how to respond to a crisis

The school district will have a technology coordinator to help you create and maintain a Web site. Many programs are easy to use and older students are more than willing to help. Web page design programs, such as Microsoft FrontPage, are readily available and often cost less than $100.00. A company that offers Web space to schools and educators for a fee is www.myschoolonline.com. It also offers templates and clipart.

Here are some tips when putting together your Web site:

- Make your site informative, easy to use and frequently changing so that students and parents will use it
- Be very careful about getting too fancy when designing your site. Some backgrounds and fonts make reading difficult, and high-resolution pictures, music and animation may take too long to download
- Advertise your site so that parents and students will know about it and use it. Advertising ideas include placing an article in your school's newsletter and mailing letters to parents
- Provide a way for students without Internet access at home to receive important information

REFERENCES AND RESOURCES

American School Counselor Association
  www.schoolcounselor.org

Journal of Technology in Counseling
  jtc.colstate.edu/

MySchoolOnline
  www.myschoolonline.com

Sampson, J. P., Jr., Carr, D. L., Panke, J., Arkin, S., Minvielle, M., & Vernick, S. H. (2003). *Design strategies for need-based Internet Web sites in counseling and career services* (Tech. Rep. No. 28). Tallahassee, FL: The Florida State University, Center for the Study of Technology in Counseling and Career Development. Available online at www.career.fsu.edu/documents/technical reports/Technical Report 28/TR-28.html

Wisconsin School Counselor Association
  www.wscaweb.com

Sometimes I e-mail sensitive student information to teachers and other counselors, and I am worried about the ethical implications of this. Should I be worried, and what measures can I take to continue using this convenient form of communication?

Paul Meyers, Principal
Ferndale Elementary School
Ferndale, Calif.
meyers@humboldt.k12.ca.us

and

Bob Tyra, School Counseling Consultant
Los Angeles County Office of Education
Downey, Calif.
tyra_bob@lacoe.edu

School counselors should use caution whenever they are handling confidential student information. Many attorneys consider e-mail to be an educational record and subject to the Family Educational Rights and Privacy Act (FERPA). Therefore, school counselors should handle electronic files with the same care they would hard copies of student records.

First, using e-mail to transmit confidential information can be safe and ethical if the following precautionary steps are taken:

- Pretend that anything you write in an e-mail will be on the front page of your local newspaper
- Only make statements in writing that are professionally necessary and required as a part of employment and responsibility to students
- Strip all e-mail messages of all information that identifies the student by name or student identification number

Second, confidential information should not transmitted via e-mail without a guarantee of privacy. Your e-mail and files should be password protected and secure enough to prevent someone from unauthorized access. It is also recommended that your school use confidential taglines on e-mails to reduce the possibility of someone inadvertently seeing confidential information. For example:

> CONFIDENTIALITY NOTICE: This communication and any documents, files, or previous e-mail messages attached to it, constitute an electronic communication within the scope of the Electronic Communications Privacy Act, 18 USCA 2510. This communication may contain non-public, confidential, or legally privileged information intended for the sole use of the designated recipient(s). The unlawful interception, use, or disclosure of such information is strictly prohibited under USCA 2511 and any applicable laws.

By following these guidelines, you will eliminate potential confidentiality problems.

What are the relevant technological competencies for school counselors?

Carlos Zalaquett, Counselor Educator
University of South Florida
Tampa, Fla.
zalaquet@tempest.coedu.usf.edu

During the mid 1990s, I created one of the first counseling center Web pages in the country and believed we were reaching a "new frontier." I soon realized that this frontier provided the basis for a lifelong learning affair. To prevail as viable professionals in today's schools, counselors should become literate in information technology (Sabella, 2000).

To provide effective services and become leaders in their schools, counselors need to have the following technological competencies.

BASIC COMPUTER LITERACY

Counselors need to be "au fait" in the current and emerging uses of technology in education and counseling, as well as its effect on students, teachers and families (especially low-income and minority). The Journal of Technology in Counseling provides a good starting point.

Counselors need to be proficient in either a Windows or a Macintosh platform, including familiarity with:

- Educational computing and technology terminology
- Keyboarding and operation of computer peripherals (printers, CD-ROM/DVDs, scanners)
- Application software (word processing, spreadsheets, and presentation software)
- Telecommunication (e-mail, videoconferencing, listservs)
- Operational skills such as accessing files, installing software, using online help menus and creating spreadsheets/databases
- Web publishing and graphics software

COUNSELING SERVICES

Today's global society depends on information technology to conduct everyday activities. This paradigm shift demands that counselors develop competencies to enhance their counseling services, including the following:

- Recognize how technology is changing various aspects of current duties, including interactions with students, parents and colleagues
- Learn about best practices in using technologies, including when and when not to use technology with clients
- Help clients properly interpret and apply information gained through technological applications
- Construct group and virtual guidance activities
- Implement synchronous and asynchronous online activities to help students exercise judgment, develop values, and analyze and evaluate information and opinions
- Use educational technologies for data collection, information management, problem solving and decision-making

- Use multimedia and hypermedia software to support individual and/or group interventions
- Use computerized statistical packages
- Use computerized testing, diagnostic and career decision-making programs with students
- Help clients search for various types of counseling-related information, including careers, employment and educational opportunities, financial assistance/scholarships, mental health, and social and personal information

INTERNET

The Internet is the major communication tool available to schools and families. For this reason, school counselors must know how to utilize all major Internet components in counseling and guidance activities, including how to:

- Use mailing lists and file transfer protocol (FTP)
- Evaluate the quality of information on the Internet
- Access professional and academic information
- Communicate with other school counselors worldwide
- Participate in Internet forums and distance-learning activities
- Design and maintain Web pages
- Design Web-based activities for families, with a focus on how parents can assist their child's academic and personal development
- Use proper Internet etiquette (known as "netiquette")
- Comply with federal guidelines to ensure access to all students (such as Bobby™ at www.watchfire.com/products/desktop/bobby/default.aspx and Section 508 of the U.S. Rehabilitation Act)

ACCOUNTABILITY

The use of data in assessing, planning, treating and evaluating the outcome of counseling services is critical. The following competencies will facilitate collecting and analyzing students' data:

- Use relational databases to monitor and articulate student progress
- Be knowledgeable and proficient in software that collects the aggregated and disaggregated data needed to review, monitor and improve performance in areas such as student achievement, attendance, standardized test results and college scholarships

- Use data from state and national sources, such as the U.S. Department of Education (www.ed.gov)

PARADOX OF CHANGE

Technology is constantly changing. Paradoxically, this cycle of renewal creates stress and anxiety. Paradox of change competencies include the following:

- Learn techniques for relaxing and managing stress and anxiety
- Be an educated consumer; learn how to objectively analyze the features, functions and benefits of new technologies before using them
- Learn and use software that reduces the time spent on administrative tasks, allowing more time for working with students and families

ETHICAL APPLICATION OF TECHNOLOGY

Technological advances are constantly testing the boundaries of ethics and standards of practice. For this reason, school counselors should:

- Know the legal and ethical guidelines for providing technology-based counseling services
- Know professional standards (such as ASCA, the Association for Counselor Education and Supervision, and the National Council for Accreditation of Teacher Education) for using technology
- Know the pedagogical, social and cultural inequity issues raised by the access and use of computers
- Consult with colleagues and legal experts to ascertain what new guidelines are needed when working with emerging technologies
- Use the Internet for finding and using continuing education opportunities in counseling

TO INFINITY AND BEYOND...

School counselors can assume a leadership role in their school if they are technologically savvy, using their technical know-how to help schools revise technology plans and present clear rationales behind equipment/training requests. Examples include:

- Understand the language and the various components of a technology plan
- Know how to collect the data needed to review, monitor and improve performance in school

- Contribute to the development of school and district technology plans
- Know how to develop an effective technology component for your guidance department
- Learn to evaluate school-based technology plans.
- Identify national, state and private funding for technology

Now is the time to proactively engage in learning these technological competencies. Although this is a long list, the good news is that there are many resources available to learn these competencies. School counselors are uniquely positioned to move beyond the basics and lead the way for an ethical, humane and effective use of technology in counseling. I strongly believe that school counselors modeling the efficient and educationally sound use of technology will possess leadership positions in their schools.

REFERENCES AND RESOURCES

About Education/Adult Continuing Education, Computer literacy articles and resources
www.adulted.about.com/cs/computerliteracy/

Association for Counselor Education and Supervision Technology Interest Network (1999). Technical competencies for counselor education students: Recommended guidelines for program development. *www.acesonline.net/index.asp*

American School Counselor Association. (2004) Ethical standards for school counselors. Alexandria, VA: Author. Available online at *www.schoolcounselor.org/*

Berry, T., Srebalus, D. J. , Crome, P. W., & Takacs, J. (2004). Counselor trainee technology use skills, learning styles, and preferred modes of instruction. *Journal of Technology in Counseling, 3*, 1.

Chandras, K. V. (2000). Technology-enhanced counselor training: Essential technical competencies. *Journal of Instructional Psychology, 27*, 224–227.

Digital Divide Network
digitaldividenetwork.org/content/sections/index.cfm

Henderson, M. V., & Scheffler, A. J. (2003). New literacies, standards, and teacher education. *Education World, 124*, 390–395.

Journal of Technology in Counseling
jtc.colstate.edu/

National Center for Technology Planning
www.nctp.com/

Netiquette
www.albion.com/netiquette/index.html

Sabella, R. (2000). School counseling and technology. in Wittmer, J. (Ed.). *Managing your school counseling program: K-12 developmental strategies* (2nd ed.). Minneapolis, MN: Educational Media.

Springfield Township High School Virtual Library, Online activities promoting computer literacy
mciu.org/~spjvweb/infolitles.html

Webopedia, Online dictionary and search engine for computer and Internet technology definitions
webopedia.com/

Zalaquett, C. P. (1994). *Counseling center help screens.* Tampa, FL: Sam Houston State University, Counseling Center. Available online at www.shsu.edu/~counsel/hs/

Some technology and education organizations and general resources of regular information:
- Association for the Advancement of Computing in Education at *www.aace.org*
- Campus Technology at *www.syllabus.com/*
- International Technology Education Association at *www.iteawww.org/*
- Milken Family Foundation Education Technology at *www.mff.org/edtech/*
- T.H.E. Journal at *www.iste.org/*

School Counselor Training

Whether you are considering becoming a school counselor, have already decided and are looking for an appropriate graduate program or are a professional school counselor engaging in continuing education, you are interested in high-quality, relevant school counseling training.

This chapter offers expert advice for frequent questions about a variety of school counselor training issues such as: finding online or distance learning school counseling programs, dealing with noncounseling-related duties, understanding popular professional development areas of interest, preparing for your school counseling job interview, understanding accreditation standards and choosing a quality program.

REFERENCES AND RESOURCES

Council for Accreditation of Counseling and Related Educational
    Programs
    www.cacrep.org

Are there any online or distance learning school counseling programs available yet?

Jill Cook, Director of Programs
ASCA
Alexandria, Va.
jcook@schoolcounselor.org

Online coursework and degree programs have been around since 1994 (Levy 2003), and according to All Online Schools (www.allonlineschools.com), there are three million people enrolled in distance education programs worldwide. Programs offered range from certificates in workplace Spanish and gunsmithing to PhDs in accounting and chemistry.

Because of the nature of the subject, however, not many online degree programs are available in school counseling. The following list overviews online schools counseling programs that are available. Please note that Arkansas, California, Illinois, Missouri and Oregon do not recognize or accept degrees earned through distance learning for counselor licensure.

Capella University
225 South 6th St., Ninth Floor
Minneapolis, MN 55402
(888) CAPELLA
www.capella.edu

Master of Science with in Human Services – Mental Health Counseling Specialization

This program focuses on counseling theory and the development of psychological testing skills. It requires three one-week master's degree colloquia. Degree requirements do not prepare graduates for licensure as counseling psychologists.

Doctor of Psychology – Counseling Psychology Specialization

This program requires a two-week extended seminar followed by nine weekends in residence. It concludes with a second two-week extended seminar.

Liberty University
1971 University Blvd.
Lynchburg, VA 24502
Keith Miraldi (krmiraldi@liberty.edu)
(800) 424-9596
www.liberty.edu

Master of Arts in Professional Counseling

This program is available via video-based lectures and online courses. Students are required to be on campus for three weeks.

Doctor of Philosophy in Professional Counseling

This program centers on one-week residential intensive formats with an on-campus schedule that requires students to be on campus a few times a year.

Seton Worldwide
400 South Orange Ave.
South Orange, NJ 07079
John E. Smith (smithjoh@shu.edu)
(888) SETONWW
www.shu.edu

Master of Arts in Counseling

This program requires two four-day residencies during the 48-hour program. Residencies are designed to provide direct skills practice and training under supervision.

UMassOnline
University of Massachusetts Boston
100 Morrissey Blvd.
Boston, MA 02125-3393
Rick Houser (rick.houser@umb.edu)
(617) 287-7668
www.umb.edu

Master of Education in Counseling – School Guidance

The program operates on a cohort model where all participants complete the same program of study over a two-year period. Clinical courses are taught during the first summer, and all participants must be present on campus for the months of July and August. The remaining courses are delivered in a Web-based, online format following a semester calendar. Participants must follow the program of study exactly.

University of Missouri – Columbia
302 Hill Hall
Columbia, Missouri 65211
(573) 882-4972
mudirect@missouri.edu
schoolmentalhealth.missouri.edu/index.htm

Master of Education - Mental Health Practices in Schools

All courses are offered online. This program does not provide certification in school counseling.

Educational Specialist - Mental Health Practices in Schools

All courses are offered online. This program does not provide certification in school counseling.

Walden University
1001 Fleet St., Fourth Floor
Baltimore, MD 21202
(866) 4WALDEN
www.waldenu.edu/

PhD in Education – General Program

This program is intended for students whose professional practice and career goals cover a range of educational topics or are interdisciplinary, combining specific education subjects with complementary subjects from the humanities or social, natural and behavioral sciences.

PhD in Psychology – Counseling Psychology

This program prepares students to practice as a licensed psychologist who works with clients to promote functional relationships, healthy lifestyles, and positive career choices and roles. Counseling psychologists work with clients of all ages in various therapeutic settings to facilitate growth and development by building on client strengths.

REFERENCES AND RESOURCES

Bear, J., Bear, M., & Head, T. (2003). *Bears' guide to earning degrees by distance learning* (15th ed.). Berkeley, CA: Ten Speed Press.

Criscito, P. (2002). *Barron's guide to distance learning* (2nd ed.). Hauppauge, NY: Barron's.

Distance Education and Training Council
www.detc.org/

Edu Directory
www.edu-directory.org/online.php

eLearners.com
www.elearners.com/

Levy, S. (2003, Spring). Six factors to consider when planning online distance learning programs in higher education. *Online Journal of Distance Learning Administration, 6*(1). Available online at *www.westga.edu/%7Edistance/ojdla/spring61/spring61.htm*

Mills, D. Q. (2001). *The Internet university: Your guide to online college courses* (4th ed.). Los Angeles: BNi Building.

Peterson's guide to distance learning programs (7th ed.). (2002). Lawrenceville, NJ: Thomson Peterson's. See also *www.petersons.com/distancelearning/*

Philips, V., & Yager, C. (2003) (1998?) *The best distance learning graduate schools.* New York: Princeton Review Publishing.

WorldWideLearn
www.worldwidelearn.com/

How do we teach pre-service school counselors to deal with being assigned duties not related to counseling?

John Littrell, Counselor Educator
Colorado State University
Fort Collins, Colo.
john.littrell@colostate.edu

Implementing a comprehensive school counseling program is a full-time responsibility. When school counselors are assigned noncounseling activities, their professional contributions are diminished, and their students suffer. ASCA (2003) has clearly stated that "although school counselors are team players who understand fair-share responsibilities within a school system, they cannot be fully effective when they are taken away from essential counseling tasks to perform noncounseling activities…" (p. 167).

Duties inappropriate for counselors include:

- Assuming master schedule duties
- Acting as testing coordinators

- Providing detention room and classroom coverage
- Administering discipline
- Carrying out clerical responsibilities

To deal with being assigned these inappropriate duties, three approaches need to be taught to pre-service school counselors:

- Employ prevention
- Master the art of saying "no"
- Creatively accept an inappropriate assignment

EMPLOY PREVENTION

Prevention is the starting point. Being proactive and prevention-oriented in establishing appropriate parameters for practicum and internship students helps to avert related problems. First, counselor educators are responsible for ensuring that pre-service school counselors are placed in sites that acknowledge the legitimate role of counselors (ASCA, 2004).

In addition, written guidelines that delineate the legitimate roles of professional school counselors should be included in the contract between the preparation program and the school district. These written guidelines should be discussed when the pre-service counselor is placed in a school setting.

Finally, pre-service counselors have a responsibility to know the legitimate roles of school counselors and to be able to provide a rationale for those roles.

MASTER THE ART OF SAYING "NO"

Despite their best prevention efforts, however, pre-service counselors may still be pressured by school personnel to accept noncounseling duties in the interest of being a team player. How can pre-service counselors respond to these gentle or heavy-handed requests to deviate from professional standards? It is useful for counselors-in-training to learn to say "no."

For most pre-service counselors, saying no to performing noncounseling duties during their field experiences generates fear–fear of being seen as uncooperative, fear of not being accepted and fear of failing the course.

A powerful antidote to fear is courage. Saying no requires courage. Brendan Francis once said, "Many of our fears are tissue-paper-thin, and a single courageous step would carry us through them." What, then, are some possible courageous steps pre-service counselors can take?

Listen to Your Inner Voice
One courageous step is listening to the professional inner voice that asks, "What is best for students, and what is appropriate, given my professional training?" That inner voice knows that the answer is straightforward: Act as a professional school counselor. The inner voice should also be prepared to state that utilizing school counselors in nonprofessional activities is economically wasteful of taxpayers' dollars (Portman, 2004).

Discover the Unsaid
A second courageous step is taking time to discover the unsaid. What is the person in authority really asking? A useful response can be, "Help me understand how this activity promotes my growth as a professional school counselor."

Explore Alternatives
A third courageous step is exploring alternatives with the person making the request. One question might be, "Looking at what's already on my plate, what can I put on hold?"

Offer Solutions
A final courageous step is offering to help the person think of alternative solutions. For example, "Let's work together to come up with a solution to this problem that respects my professional role and yet gets the job done."

CREATIVELY ACCEPT AN INAPPROPRIATE ASSIGNMENT

A third approach that needs to be taught to pre-service counselors is how to creatively accept an inappropriate assignment. If the pre-service counselor slips and says "yes" to an noncounseling assignment, then the assignment can become an opportunity to do productive counseling work. Supervising study hall? Turn this inappropriate assignment around by organizing the study hall into tutoring groups, helping students help other students.

Employing prevention, learning to say no and creatively accepting the inevitable are three skills that help pre-service counselors avoid being assigned noncounseling duties.

REFERENCES AND RESOURCES

American School Counselor Association. (2005). *The ASCA national model: A framework for school counseling programs, second edition.* Executive summary. *Professional School Counseling, 6*(3), 165–168.

American School Counselor Association. (2004*). The role of the professional school counselor.* Alexandria, VA: Author. Available online at *www.schoolcounselor.org/*

Jensen, B. (2003). *The simplicity survival handbook: 32 ways to do less and accomplish more.* New York: Basic Books.

Portman, T. (2004, April). *Accountability data: Utilization of district school counseling personnel.* Paper presented at the meeting of the American Educational Research Association, San Diego, CA.

What are the top five professional development areas of interest for school counselors?

Bob Tyra, Consultant
Los Angeles County Office of Education
Los Angeles, Calif.
Tyra_Bob@lacoe.edu

The California Counselor Leadership Academy, a program sponsored by the Los Angeles County Office of Education, recently completed a comprehensive survey of nearly 160 school counselors throughout California. The entire survey is published on the Web at www.lacoe.edu/ccla.

When asked whether their school district included professional development for school counselors, 39 percent of our respondents said "no." A number of anecdotal comments associated with this question indicated that school counselor professional development is often not a priority for school districts. Counselors said that they often use designated district staff professional development days to catch up on paperwork or attend inservices primarily designed for teachers.

PERSONAL/SOCIAL

When asked in what domain (personal/social, career, or academic) they would like to receive more professional development, counselors responded as follows:

- Personal/Social (39 percent)
- Career (33 percent)
- Academic (28 percent)

Counselors indicated that within the personal/social area, they want more information on confidentiality, suicide prevention, life after loss issues and child abuse reporting.

STUDENT RESULTS

In an era of increasing statewide demand for academic success and high test scores, a recent Internet survey of school counselors showed that more than 70 percent of respondents chose Student Results as a first, second or third priority for professional development needs. It stands to reason, then, that professional development efforts need to take into account how the information shared in these development efforts can be translated into student results.

LEGAL ISSUES

In 2003, we ran a series of county-wide regional forums on legal and ethical issues in school counseling using the 20 question survey in "Legal and Ethical Considerations in School Counseling" by Remley, Hermann and Huey as a starting point of discussion. This topic was very well received and the question-and-answer format made for a lively forum with considerable debate and numerous requests for more professional development in this area.

PERSONAL ACCOUNTABILITY

Given the lack of state funding for school counseling and support services in general, our academy has focused professional development efforts on assisting more than 150 school counseling programs throughout the state develop and produce a school support personnel accountability report card (SPARC).

The SPARC has been used as an advocacy tool and an accreditation evidentiary document to support the mission of school counseling and its relationship to school safety and academic success. More than 60 current SPARCs may be reviewed at www.lacoe.edu/sparc.

Robert Bardwell, Supervisor
Monson Public Schools
Monson, Massachusetts
bardwellr@monsonschools.com

Listing the top five areas of interest for professional development for all school counselors is no easy task, for a number of reasons:

- School counselors are at different stages of their careers and, therefore, their professional development needs vary widely.
- School counselors with areas of expertise or interests such as technology will not need as much professional development in that topic as others would.
- Professional development needs depend on work level (e.g., play therapy for elementary and college admissions for secondary).

Therefore, this "top five" list of professional development areas merely scratches the surface:

- Legal and ethical issues
- School violence/bullying
- Technology
- School counselor reform
- General counseling skills

LEGAL AND ETHICAL ISSUES

School counselors are barraged daily with situations about what is the right or wrong thing to do. Even the most experienced counselors need to be kept current on changes in the laws and standards of the counseling profession. Answers to the dilemmas faced are often not found in a book. Proper training is even more challenging considering that each state may have different laws regulating what school counselors can do (for example, student record regulations).

SCHOOL VIOLENCE/BULLYING

School violence and bullying are issues that all schools (whether urban, suburban or rural) must face, and school counselors should be heavily involved with the services provided to address these issues (both preventative and reactive). Often, these are community issues that extend beyond the school walls, with school counselors providing the first line of defense.

Appropriate training is essential to provide counselors with the tools necessary to tackle the complexities of school violence and bullying.

TECHNOLOGY

Technology is constantly evolving, and school counselors must keep up with those changes to meet the needs of their constituents. Whether it be computer or audio-visual technology, counselors must be trained how to use it. Creating electronic presentations, using administrative software and designing Web pages are just some of the skills that all school counselors need. Although some have resisted technology, not integrating it into our work is no longer an option.

SCHOOL COUNSELOR REFORM

With the creation of the ASCA National Model®, many states, regions and school districts are looking at how to change the way school counselors provide services. Disseminating information that will be necessary to implement all or parts of the ASCA National Model and state models will have to take place at all levels and in many forms.

Unfortunately, this will be particularly difficult in communities where:

- Administration is not open to the idea of change.
- Re-prioritizing counselor duties is considered unnecessary.

GENERAL COUNSELING SKILLS

Individuals who have obtained a job as a school counselor most likely have a master's degree in counseling. While it may be safe to assume that some of these skills will stay current throughout their career, school counselors simply must continue to develop and review counseling skills for a variety of reasons:

- New counseling techniques or theories may have emerged since the completion of training.
- Continuing training provides an opportunity to practice techniques not recently used.
- Ongoing exposure to counseling methods improves overall counseling skills.

CONCLUSION

Professional development in these five areas can take many forms such as workshops, conferences and coursework. The bottom line is that if school counselors are not provided with these opportunities, they must seek them out on their own. Professional development is essential to the success of a school counselor; without it, a school counselor will become stagnate, ineffective and obsolete.

REFERENCES AND RESOURCES

American School Counselor Association
www.schoolcounselor.org

Association for Supervision and Curriculum Development
www.ascd.org

The Education Trust
www.edtrust.org

Hatch, T. (2001). *The power of professional development.* ASCA School Counselor, 39, 8–12.

What can I do to best prepare for an interview as a school counselor? What kinds of things is an employer looking for in the school counselor candidate?

Jim Bergin, Counselor Educator
Georgia Southern University
Statesboro, Ga.
jim_bergin@gsvms2.cc.GaSoU.edu

The following recommendations are directed toward the prospective employee's interview with the school principal, but also apply to interviews with a faculty search committee or central office personnel:

- Do your homework
- Use your counseling skills
- Focus on issues/needs of the school and students
- Bring resources to the interview

DO YOUR HOMEWORK

First, do your homework, including the following:

- Learn as much about the school (and district) as possible before the interview
- Check school and district Web sites for their philosophy, vision and mission statements
- Review student demographic data to determine achievement levels among various student groups by grade level, gender, race and special needs
- Appraise the school as an educational institution as if it were your client
- Tour the school grounds and neighborhood after school hours and look for evidence of school pride in terms of cleanliness, landscaping, display of student products and participation in school maintenance
- Observe the daily procedures for student arrival and dismissal

What does this accumulate data tell you about the character of the school?

USE YOUR COUNSELING SKILLS

Second, use your counseling skills to take the best advantage of the interview process:

- Present yourself as a counselor—warm, caring, understanding and trustworthy
- Focus on making the principal (interviewer) feel accepted and respected. (Remember, your relationship with this person is the most important one you will have as an employee. Moreover, it will make or break your school counseling program.)
- Interview the principal (e.g., What are the strengths and weaknesses of his/her leadership style? What is it like to work with this person? How does this leader's personality/values shape the character of the school?)

FOCUS ON ISSUES/NEEDS OF THE SCHOOL AND STUDENTS

Third, focus the interview on the students rather than on you:

- Make it abundantly clear to the principal that this interview is not about you and your achievements; rather, it's about the school counseling program and how it will address the needs of students and promote their achievement

- Emphasize the comprehensive and developmental nature of the program, assisting all students to attain academic, career and personal/social success
- Present executive summaries of the ASCA National Model and ASCA National Standards, and use them as talking points during the interview when asked about your goals as a prospective employee
- Be prepared to respond to the question, "What is your philosophy of counseling?" and articulate how that philosophy complements your philosophy of education, emphasizing how the role of counselor supports that of the teacher in the learning process
- Stress advocacy for student achievement and collaboration with the principal, teachers and parents in meeting student needs

BRING RESOURCES TO THE INTERVIEW

Finally, have the following documents available at the interview to supplement your discussion. They should be used as resources for responding to the interviewer's requests for information, not as presentation materials focusing on your achievements and/or qualifications:

- Executive summaries of ASCA publications
- Personal philosophy of counseling and education
- Personal philosophy of education (and/or teaching)
- Counselor disclosure statement (for high school position candidates)
- Copy of state certification credentials and master's degree diploma
- Portfolio, including school counseling publications, research and work samples
- One page vita and full resume

REFERENCES AND RESOURCES

American School Counselor Association. (2005). *The ASCA national model: A framework for school counseling programs, second edition.* Alexandria, VA: Author.

Campbell, C. A., & Dahir, C. A. (1997). *Sharing the vision: The national standards for school counseling programs.* Alexandria, VA: American School Counselor Association Press.

Dahir, C. A, Sheldon, C. B., & Valiga, M. J. (1998). *Vision into action: Implementing the national standards for school counseling programs.* Alexandria, VA: American School Counselor Association.

Myrick, R. D. (2003). *Developmental guidance and counseling: A practical approach.* (4th ed.). Minneapolis, MN: Educational Medial.

Possible interview questions for school counselors
www.schoolcounselor.com/resources/interview.htm

What is the nature of the CACREP standards by which many school counseling programs design their training? That is, how are they developed and updated?

Mary Alice Bruce, CACREP Chair
University of Wyoming
Laramie, Wyo.
mabruce@uwyo.edu

Input from stakeholders is the top priority in developing and updating the Council for Accreditation of Counseling and Related Education Programs (CACREP) standards every eight years. As an independent accrediting body since its inception in 1981, CACREP has provided leadership in determining the global direction of our counseling profession, and the CACREP standards are the foundation of that direction. CACREP accreditation:

- Assures program quality
- Encourages continual improvement of programs through self-assessment
- Advances the profession of counseling
- Provides consumer protection

To start the formal revision process of existing standards, CACREP puts out a far-reaching call for applications for membership in the standards revision committee (SRC). This committee usually has five members and one alternate. As soon as the members are appointed by CACREP, they begin developing an action plan to:

- Request initial input and feedback from all possible stakeholders related to needs, structural considerations, and visions for developing and updating the standards
- Personally invite specific organizations (for example, ASCA, state licensure boards and international bodies) to give their views regarding revisions

- Acknowledge that the counseling profession emphasizes a developmental, prevention-oriented approach and honors traditional remediation, all within a caring relationship
- Take into account the influence of a variety of historical, social, institutional and political forces by means of reflective discussions
- Learn about trends and possible issues by asking for experts to join them in critical conversations
- Consider the research results of the perceived benefit of the standards and areas cited for improvement
- Widely distribute drafts of revised standards for further comment and change.
- Develop a final draft of the standards

As a result of several years of intense work, the SRC recommends a final draft of the newly developed and updated standards for formal consideration, approval and distribution by CACREP after final editing by a writing consultant.

In addition to this cyclical process, CACREP has a procedure in place to change or update a given standard at any time as approved by the council.

REFERENCES AND RESOURCES

CACREP Standards Revision
    www.cacrep.org/StandardsRevisionText.html

Council for Accreditation of Counseling and Related Education Programs. (2001). *Accreditation standards and procedures manual.* Alexandria, VA: Author.

McGlothlin, J. M., & Davis, T. E. (2004). Perceived benefit of CACREP (2001) core curriculum standards. *Counselor Education and Supervision, 43,* 274–285.

Schmidt, J. J. (1999). Two decades of CACREP and what do we know? *Counselor Education and Supervision, 39,* 34-45.

What should I look for when choosing a quality graduate program in school counseling?

Richard Hazler, Counselor Educator
Penn State University
State College, Pa.
hazler@PSU.EDU

The best programs will match your interests, emphasize the essentials recognized by professional school counselors, focus on current issues, and have experienced, committed faculty. Quality programs want to develop your self-understanding, which will make a huge difference in how well you do in the program, the satisfaction you feel and your effectiveness as a counselor.

In addition, quality programs seek to prepare you for the real world of school counseling with a combination of theory, skills and practical application. The theory and basic skills provide the foundation you'll need, while the practicality emphasizes flexibility in meeting the ever-changing needs and responsibilities of the school counselor.

When choosing for a quality graduate program, look for the following specifics.

THE PROGRAM SHOULD EMPHASIZE THE EXPANSION OF YOUR SELF-UNDERSTANDING.

Quality programs go beyond knowledge and skills to emphasize who you are in terms of interests, motivations, and beliefs about yourself, others and life. They ask you to discuss these topics from the first interaction, seeking to know such things as why you want to be a school counselor, how you view people, how well you understand yourself and how you deal with change. You should recognize this interest in printed materials, application procedures and conversations with faculty.

THE PROGRAM SHOULD INCLUDE CORE INFORMATION, SKILLS AND EXPERIENCES.

Most states now recognize the general requirements outlined by CACREP that emphasize the necessary skills, knowledge base and personal development for counselors. They also are giving increasing attention to the ASCA National Model, which emphasizes how counselors need to develop and manage a school program, deliver it and demonstrate accountability for results. You will be receiving a solid foundation in running a modern program when these concepts are mentioned prominently in training program materials. Quality programs include:

- Helping skills
- Human growth and development
- Group work
- Career development
- Appraisal
- Research
- Orientation to, and organization and administration of, school counseling services

You will also spend 100 hours of counseling practicum and another 600 hours doing an internship in the schools with the best programs.

COURSES AND FACULTY SHOULD EMPHASIZE CURRENT ISSUES AND RESPONSIBILITIES.

How current programs and faculty are should be visible in their professional publications, conversations and use of technology. Are faculty members talking about the old days, or are they discussing how to meet the current changes in schools and counseling? The more current they are, the better prepared you will be.

FACULTY SHOULD HAVE EXPERIENCE IN SCHOOLS.

The best faculty will be able to tell you about their school experiences as well as how schools and counselors in the area deal with the unique challenges. You want a program where faculty members know and are involved in modern schools and current issues.

COURSES AND FACULTY SHOULD EMPHASIZE A DIVERSITY OF ISSUES AND PEOPLE.

The best programs seek a faculty that reflects this country's growing diversity of race, cultural heritage and gender preference. While no faculty is fully able to reach that goal, the more diversity you see, the more likely faculty is to be committed to dealing with the issues.

No matter how diverse the faculty, however, you should recognize in program information and faculty conversations how much they emphasize the need to identify, understand and appreciate diverse views of the world. The profession no longer has for the simplistic belief that one person's view of the world must be the right one that others need to accept.

REFERENCES AND RESOURCES

American School Counselor Association. (2005). *The ASCA national model: A framework for school counseling programs, second edition.* Alexandria, VA: Author.

American School Counselor Association. (2004a). *Careers/roles.* Alexandria, VA: Author. Available online at *www.schoolcounselor.org/*

American School Counselor Association. (2004b). *Recognized ASCA model program.* Alexandria, VA: Author. Available online at *www.schoolcounselor.org*

Counsel for Accreditation of Counseling and Related Educational Programs (CACREP) *www.counseling.org/*

Hazler, R. J., & Kottler, J. A. (2004). *The emerging professional counselor: Student dreams to professional realities* (2nd ed.). Alexandria, VA: American Counseling Association.

Biographies

Jennifer Baggerly is an assistant professor in the University of South Florida's counselor education program. She is also a licensed mental health counselor supervisor and a registered play therapist supervisor. Her research studies include school counselor trends, play therapy, trauma resiliency in children and homelessness.

Deryl Bailey is an assistant professor in the counseling department at the University of Georgia in Athens, Georgia. Prior to earning his education specialist and doctorate degrees from the University of Virginia, he worked as a secondary school counselor for 10 years. His areas of specialization include group work, multicultural and diversity issues in schools, bridging the achievement gap for students of color, issues related to professional development for school counselors, adolescent African American male development, and the development and implementation of enrichment and empowerment initiatives for children and adolescents. He is the founder and director of Empowered Youth Programs. Bailey is the president-elect of the Southern Association for Counselor Education and Supervision, and a member of the American Counseling Association and ASCA.

Stanley Baker is a professor of counselor education at North Carolina State University. He has been a teacher and school counselor in Wisconsin for 12 years. Previously, he was a counselor educator at Penn State University and North Carolina State University. Baker has supervised master's and doctoral counseling practicas and field-based internships for school counselors. His doctoral and master's level teaching experience includes guidance and counseling in schools, use of tests in counseling, prepracticum, career development theory and research, professional issues in counseling, and research in counselor education. Baker has authored books and journal articles covering topics such as preparing school counselors, effects of primary prevention programming, enhancing acquisition of counseling skills, evaluation and accountability in school counseling, developing professional counselors and clinical supervision of counselors.

Maryann Baldwin is a middle school guidance counselor in Hillsborough County, Fla. and an adjunct professor at the University of South Florida. Her guidance career began when she was chosen as one of the first 15 elementary guidance counselors in Hillsborough County in 1972. Baldwin continued to work as a guidance counselor at the senior and junior high levels and remained at her school when it became a middle school. She received her doctorate in education from the University of South Florida.

Robert Bardwell is the guidance director for the Monson Public Schools in Monson, Massachusetts, where he supervises counselors, a career counselor and a school social worker. He is also an adjunct professor of school counseling at Westfield State College and Springfield College, teaching career development and college counseling courses. Bardwell chairs the Professional Development Committee for the Western Massachusetts Counselors Association. He also chairs the Ad Hoc Committee on Graduate Coursework for the National Association for College Admission Counseling.

Nancy Beale is a school counselor and is working on her doctorate in school psychology from Walden University. She has worked in schools in North Carolina, Virginia and Hawaii. Beale has presented at local and national ASCA conferences, and looks forward to continuing to contribute to the field through writing and speaking engagements. She volunteers with the local Red Cross chapter by assisting the disaster relief services mental health team.

Jim Bergin is a professor of counselor education at Georgia Southern University in Statesboro, Georgia. He spent 11 years as an elementary school counselor and teacher, during which time he initiated developmental school counseling programs in four different states. In addition, Bergin spent 20 years teaching and supervising graduate students who were preparing to become professional school counselors. He serves as a national trainer for the ASCA National Standards and has presented many workshops on how to implement the standards. Both ASCA and the Georgia School Counselor Association have honored him as the post-secondary counselor of the year. Bergin also has received the Carl Perkins Government Relations Award from the American Counseling Association for his work in promoting school counseling.

Barbara Brady Blackburn, LPC, is ASCA's 2004-2005 president-elect. She has been a practicing high school counselor for 20 years in West Virginia. Blackburn has held various leadership positions in the West Virginia School Counselor Association including president. She was named West Virginia Counselor of the Year in 2002. Blackburn continues as WVSCA Government Relations chair. Her leadership resulted in passing state code and policy that redefined the role of the school counselor in West Virginia, requiring every school counseling program to use the ASCA National Model as a foundation. This policy mandates that school counseling only perform duties related to designing and delivering their school counseling program. She is co-author of a state resource manual that supports these programs. She is a state model trainer for the state department of education. Blackburn serves on various advisory/leadership teams and presents nationally on legislative advocacy and organizational leadership.

Mark Boggie is the lead counselor at Buena High School in Sierra Vista, Arizona. He has been a high school counselor for the past eight years. Prior to that, he was an elementary school counselor for four years. He received his master's degree in education counseling from the University of Arizona following an 11-year career teaching high school and middle school science. Boggie is an active member of the Arizona School Counselor Association's Governing Board and ASCA. He also serves on the ACT Advisory Board and on the Leadership Cadre of the Arizona Counselor Academy.

Judy Bowers, Ed.D., supervises the 170 school counselors K-12 who serve 61,000 students in the Tucson Unified School District (TUSD) in Tucson, Arizona. Bowers has been a counselor supervisor for 11 years. Prior to that, she was a teacher for six years and a high school counselor for 16 years. She has worked with the state of Arizona and TUSD since 1990 to restructure school counseling programs. Under her leadership, the TUSD school counseling department has been awarded four federal elementary demonstration grants, and the number of school counselors has increased from 95 counselors in 1994 to 170 counselors in 2004. Active in professional associations, Bowers is the 2004-2005 Governing Board president of ASCA. Other leadership activities include president of the Arizona School Counselor Association and western region vice president for ASCA. She is a national and international consultant to school districts, state departments and university counseling departments. Bowers is the co-author of the ASCA National Model (ASCA, 2003) and the ASCA National Model Workbook (ASCA, 2004). Bowers received her doctorate degree in educational leadership from the University of Arizona.

Bob Bowman is president of Developmental Resources, Inc. and YouthLight, Inc. He taught in the educational psychology department at the University of South Carolina for more than 20 years. He has presented motivational workshops and conference keynote addresses in 42 states and nine countries, including 14 keynotes at ASCA state and national conferences. He is an innovator and collector of creative, research-proven techniques and strategies for helping youth, and is known as a relentless cheerleader for professionals working with chronically difficult young people. He has authored more than 25 professional books and programs and was the first editor of the National Peer Helpers Association's professional journal. Interviews with Bowman have appeared in numerous publications. His awards include induction into the inaugural Illinois State University College of Education Hall of Fame. He also received the President-Elect Lifetime Professional Achievement Award from the South Carolina Counseling Association.

Kay Brawley is director of Achieving New Directions and consults with organizations, institutions and individuals. She is a master trainer with the Rutgers University Heldrich Center for Workforce Development's Working Ahead Global Career Development Facilitator (GCDF) curriculum, teaching graduate courses at Loyola and George Mason Universities, among others. She helped create the initial GCDF training model and has presented numerous workshops. Brawley has served in a variety leadership and board positions for numerous counseling organizations such as ASCA, the Maryland Association for Counseling and Development, and the National Career Development Association. She serves on the board of the International Association for Educational and Vocational Guidance. Brawley holds a doctor of arts degree from George Mason University and a master's of education counseling from the University of North Carolina.

Greg Brigman is a professor in the counselor education department at Florida Atlantic University in Boca Raton, Fla., where he coordinates the school counseling program. Among his honors are two national awards as a school counselor from ASCA, Teacher of the Year for the College of Education, and Researcher of the Year, Associate Professor level, for the College of Education and for Florida Atlantic University. Brigman regularly works with school districts to develop comprehensive school counseling and to evaluate the impact of school counseling programs. He presents training workshops related to school counseling nationally and internationally, and is a regular presenter at professional conferences.

Mary Alice Bruce is an associate professor and the coordinator of the CACREP-accredited school counseling program at the University of Wyoming. Bruce has served as chair of the CACREP board and has recently been appointed to the 2008 Standards Revision Committee. As a former teacher, school counselor, and now counselor educator, she enjoys teaching practicum, supervision, group work and ethics. Her research interests include collaborative relationships in the schools, counseling children and adolescents, adolescent spirituality and the internationalization of counseling.

Rachel Campbell is a graduate student and graduate assistant in the department of counseling at Indiana University of Pennsylvania. She will be completing her M.Ed. in school counseling in 2005, and her area of concentration is elementary school counseling.

Cindi Carlisle is a counselor at Chief Joseph Middle School in Richland, Wash., and a current member of ASCA's Governing Board.

Jay Carey is the director of the National Center for School Counseling Outcome Research and the director of school counseling program at the University of Massachusetts. His research interests include school counseling outcome measurement, school counseling program evaluation, standards-based models of school counseling and academic interventions to eliminate the achievement gap.

Jill Cook is the program director for ASCA. She spent 11 years in public education in North Carolina as a music teacher, school counselor and assistant principal. Cook is the content specialist for ASCA and coordinates the resource center, bookstore, Professional Interest Network Specialist Program and Recognized ASCA Model Program.

Edward Coyle is the technology chair and president-elect for the Wisconsin School Counselor Association, as well as a past elementary vice president. He also sits on the board of the Wisconsin Counselor Association. He holds licenses as a K-12 counselor, licensed professional counselor, and independent clinical social worker in Wisconsin. He has been employed as a middle school counselor, K-8 counselor and, most recently, a K-5 counselor in Wisconsin.

Vicki Crawford is a counselor at Vinton Middle School in Vinton, Louisiana. She received her bachelor's and master's degrees in elementary education from Southeastern Louisiana University and her master's +30 from McNeese State University. Crawford is certified in elementary grades one through eight, academically gifted education for grades one through eight, and as a guidance counselor and counselor in elementary schools. She is a member of the Calcasieu School Counselor's Association, Louisiana Counselor's Association, Louisiana School Counselor's Association, Louisiana Middle School Association and Associated Professional Educators of Louisiana.

Tammy Davis is an associate professor of psychology at Marymount University in Arlington, Virginia. With almost 20 years of experience in education, she teaches primarily graduate school counseling courses in Marymount's CACREP-accredited program. Previously, she was an elementary and high school counselor for nine years in Manassas, Virginia. Her professional positions include being past president of the Virginia Association for Counselor Education and Supervision and president-elect of the Virginia School Counselor Association. She has presented locally, regionally and nationally on a number of topics in school counseling, including developing resilience and handling perfectionism. Her publication topics include professional practices, counseling suicidal children and small group counseling in schools.

Carey Dimmitt is the associate director of the National Center for School Counseling Outcome Research and the clinical coordinator of school counseling program at the University of Massachusetts. Dimmitt's research interests are in the development evidence-based school counseling interventions to enhance academic success.

Colette Dollarhide is an assistant professor of counselor education at the University of South Carolina. She has been involved with schools for 20 years as a volunteer, consultant and educator. She has published a textbook on counseling in the secondary schools and several articles, and she has presented at state and national conferences on topics such as school counseling leadership, supervision and mentoring.

Linda Eby is an LPC in Oregon and has been a child development specialist at Gordon Russell Middle School in Gresham, Oregon for 23 years. She received her master's degree in counseling from Lewis and Clark College. Eby was honored as Oregon School Counselor Association's Middle Level Counselor of the Year in 1994. She received the Oregon Counseling Association's Distinguished Service Award in 2002, and she was honored as the recipient of the Gresham-Barlow School District's Judy Daugherty Lewis Award for Excellence in Teaching in 2003. Active in her professional organizations, Eby is a past president of the Oregon School Counselor Association and past middle level vice president of ASCA.

Teesue Fields is a professor and program coordinator of counselor education at Indiana University Southeast. She is a past president of the Indiana Counseling Association and a nationally certified counselor. IU Southeast is a companion school in the Transforming School Counseling Initiative of The Education Trust. Fields' main areas of publication and presentation involve the school counselor's roles in school reform and in raising the academic achievement of students.

Cynthia Floyd is a school counseling and safe schools consultant for the North Carolina Department of Public Instruction. As a state consultant, she provides technical assistance and training across North Carolina to school counselors and other instructional support personnel. She also assists in the development of state documents, guidelines and policies related to safe schools and school counseling.

Cynthia Francis is a counselor at Chalmette Middle School. She has served on the board for the Louisianna School Counselor Association as treasurer and president. She has also served as ASCA's southern region vice president.

John Galassi is a professor and the coordinator of the school counseling program at the University of North Carolina at Chapel Hill. His work focuses on developmental advocacy, a strengths-based approach to school counseling that asserts a counselor's primary mission is to promote the optimal development of all students. While remediation of deficits and the removal of barriers play a role in the model, developmental advocates focus on proactive and preventive approaches to help students build skills and to enhance the asset-building capacity of the school environment.

Marie Geyer is an elementary school counselor at Cider Mill School in Wilton, Connecticut. After starting her professional life as a high school English teacher on Long Island and in Japan, she went on to the business world, where she was a configuration engineer, training specialist, magazine editor, proposal specialist, technical writer and consultant. Geyer returned to school and earned a master's degree in school counseling from Marymount University in Virginia. She was also a counselor at Belvedere Elementary School in Falls Church, Virginia.

Deborah Hardy chairs the school counseling services department for the Irvington School District in New York, where she oversees the high school and middle school counselors and assists her department with implementing a comprehensive school counseling program. Hardy has served as the president for the New York State School Counselor Association and coordinated the New York State Comprehensive School Counseling Program. She is a member of the Pupil Personnel Task Force for the New York State Education Department. As an adjunct professor at Mercy College, Hardy teaches in the graduate program for school counseling and has trained more than 30 school counseling interns.

Gisela Harkin is the career development program officer for the U.S. Department of Education's Office of Vocational and Adult Education. She is assigned to the Effective Practices and Dissemination Branch, charged with systemic education reform so that all students are prepared for the transition to the world of work and further education. She has been with the Department for more than 25 years, being involved in national initiatives to address issues related to career technical education, school-to-work, comprehensive career guidance and counseling, workforce development and tech prep education. She holds a bachelor's degree in sociology and a master's degree in education/guidance and counseling. Prior to coming to the Department, Harkin was a counselor and a sociologist.

Trish Hatch, Ph.D. is the director of school counseling programs at San Diego State University and the co-author of "The ASCA National Model: A Framework for School Counseling Programs" (ASCA, 2003). A former school counselor and administrator, she was awarded ASCA's administrator of the year. She has served as vice president for ASCA, an appointed member of the National Panel for Evidenced-Based School Counseling Practices and is a nationally recognized speaker, trainer and consultant.

Tim Hatfield is a professor at Winona State University. He has more than 30 years of experience as an educator and counselor with an interest in school counselor training, promoting professional wellness, and developmental education. Hatfield has a bachelor's and master's degree from Harvard University as well as a doctoral degree from the University of Minnesota. He is actively involved in state and national counselor organizations as well as with The Education Trust Initiative for Transforming School Counselor Training.

Theresa Hawkins is a teaching assistant in the University of Iowa's Educational Technology Center, where she teaches school counseling, rehabilitation counseling and student development and technology courses. She provides support to the ePortfolio project that has been implemented within the counseling, rehabilitation, and student development department. She also works as a middle school counselor for the Anamosa Community School District.

Stuart Chen-Hayes is an associate professor of counselor education/school and family counseling at Lehman College of the City University of New York and a consultant with The Education Trust's National Center for Transforming School Counseling. His research, writing, consulting and presentations focus on closing achievement, opportunity and attainment gaps through transforming school counseling. He also writes on sexuality and family counseling and advocacy with multiple cultural identities. Chey-Hayes has been published in numerous journals and book chapters, and is co-authoring on professional school counseling with Brooks/Cole-Thomson Learning. He is a past president of Counselors for Social Justice.

Richard Hazler is a counselor education faculty member and the coordinator of the elementary school counselor training program at Penn State University. He has become particularly well-known for his work in the areas of peer-on-peer abuse, youth violence, and humanistic approaches to school counseling and counselor development. His interests in youth and counseling began as a sixth grade school teacher and his direct involvement grew through work as a school counselor. Over the years, he has developed a wide variety of programs for at-risk students, general populations and the gifted for grade schools, high schools and universities. He is the author of two books in this area of counseling youth.

Mary Hermann is an assistant professor at Mississippi State University. She holds a law degree and a doctoral degree in counselor education. She teaches courses in school counseling, legal and ethical issues in counseling, school law, counseling theories, counseling skills, group counseling, gender issues in counseling, and she supervises school counseling students during their practicum and internship. She is the co-editor of "Ethical and Legal Issues in School Counseling," a book published by ASCA. She has written numerous articles and book chapters. She has also co-authored a law review article on school violence. Hermann is a licensed attorney, a licensed professional counselor, a national certified counselor and a certified school counselor.

Jackie Hoagland is a school counselor at St. James High School in Murrells Inlet, South Carolina. She has also been a counselor at Dorman High School in Spartanburg, a counselor at Sims Junior High School in

Union, and a teacher and counselor at Clinton High School in Clinton. She earned her bachelor's degree from Presbyterian College and her master's from Clemson University. She has 30+ hours of post-graduate study, including coursework from Furman University, Lander University, University of South Carolina, Citadel, Limestone and Winthrop. She has served on the boards of the South Carolina Counseling Association and the South Carolina School Counselor Association for the last eight years.

Cheryl Holcomb-McCoy is an assistant professor in the Department of Counseling and Personnel Services at the University of Maryland, College Park. She has written extensively on school counselors' multicultural counseling competence, urban school counseling and reforming school counselor preparation. She is a former elementary school counselor and teacher.

Reese House is director of the Transforming School Counseling Initiative of The Education Trust. He also taught at Oregon State University, where he focused on preparing school counselors to be proactive change agents and advocates for social, economic and political justice. He believes that school counselors can be critical players in school reform if they connect their work to the current mission of schools. He has been a school counselor, community activist and HIV/AIDS educator. He has worked to upgrade standards and accreditation guidelines for counselors at the state and national levels. He has served on several committees for the development and revision of CACREP standards.

Madelyn Isaacs, Ph.D is a professor and the program coordinator of the counseling program at Florida Gulf Coast University. She has worked in college student services and academic administration, and has consulted with mental health and school organizations on a variety of topics. Isaacs received her doctorate in educational research and counseling from Hofstra University, her master's degree in counseling from the University of Connecticut and her bachelor's degree in social studies/history education from the University of Albany. She is an LMHC in Florida as well as NCC and ACS. Isaacs is a member of ASCA, the American Counseling Association, American Mental Health Counselors Association, Association for Counselor Education and Supervision, National Career Development Association, Fla. Counseling Association (FCA), Fla. School Counselor Association (FSCA), Fla. Association for Counselor Education and Supervision, and has been an officer and executive board member of FCA and FSCA over the years.

Clarence "Curly" Johnson has been involved professionally in school counseling for more than 40 years. He has been a middle school and high school counselor, a district level and county level administrator of guidance programs, and a counselor educator. He has also been a consultant in planning, implementing and evaluating guidance programs. He has authored and co-authored books and articles in the areas of existential counseling, at-risk students, futures, identifying potential drop-outs, family and schools partnerships, group leadership, therapeutic techniques, career development, program evaluation and management for results.

Carol Kaffenberger is an assistant professor at George Mason University in Fairfax, Virginia, where she teaches counselor preparation courses and supervises interns. She was an elementary school counselor for 11 years and is a MetLife Fellow for The Education Trust Transformation of School Counseling Initiative. Her research interests include helping children with chronic illness, transforming school counselors and the effectiveness of school counseling preparation programs. Her publication topics include school reentry issues and diagnosing mental disorders in children. Kaffenberger developed a model for school reintegration and provided training to school counselors, social workers and public health nurses. Her presentations include coping with chronic illness for children and adolescents, transforming counselor education programs, implementing the ASCA National Model, providing narrative counseling in schools, and integrating counseling and technology.

Michael Karcher is an associate professor and the school counseling training program coordinator at the University of Texas at San Antonio. He conducts research on pair counseling, youth mentoring and adolescent connectedness. He is on the editorial board of Professional School Counseling.

Dawn Kay is the coordinator of student services and comprehensive counseling and guidance programs at the Utah State Office of Education. She received her master's degree in school counseling and her bachelor's degree in teaching English from Brigham Young University. In addition, Kay received her education administration license from the University of Utah. A certified school counselor, Kay is certified in education administration. She is a member of the following professional associations: Utah School Counselor Association, ASCA, Utah Association for Career and Technical Education, American Association of Colleges for Teacher Education, and Association for Counselor Education and Supervision.

Kathleen Kellum, a doctoral student at the University of Iowa, has interests in distance education, supervision, spirituality and group work. She teaches undergraduate counseling-related courses utilizing ecollege and WebCT. Her work history includes residence life administration, pastoral care and counseling, teaching and research. Practicum and internship experiences include both community mental health and high school counseling. Supervision experiences include residence life staff and graduate counseling students during basic skills, group counseling and internship classes.

Kenyon Knapp is an assistant professor of counselor education and school counseling program director at Troy University, Dothan Campus. He serves on the board of the Association for Spiritual, Ethical, and Religious Values in Counseling. A graduate of the Psychological Studies Institute, Knapp has worked in the areas of sexual addiction, school violence prevention and spirituality.

Mark Kuranz is an educator and professional school counselor for the Racine Unified School District, where he has been the lead high school counselor for the past 16 years. He served as a teacher of exceptional education students in high school for 13 years. He is an adjunct professor in the school counseling program at Marquette University. Kuranz has had several positions with the Wisconsin School Counselor Association and ASCA, serving as president in 2000-2001. He has been described as a quiet leader who knows volumes about getting groups to move forward toward a shared vision while maintaining composure and honoring everyone involved. Kuranz has presented numerous workshops and programs on transforming school counseling.

Nadene A. L'Amoreaux, Ph.D. is an assistant professor in the department of counseling at Indiana University of Pennsylvania. Her clinical experience includes counseling with children, adolescents, adults, couples and families. Her research and teaching interests include ethical, legal and professional issues.

Marcia Lathroum is a specialist in school guidance and counseling for the Maryland State Department of Education, leading school counseling programs, student records, suicide prevention, post-secondary planning and legislation. She also assists with emergency planning in schools and safe schools initiatives. She has a bachelor's degree in elementary and special education from Boston University and a master's degree in school counseling from Loyola College. She also has certification in supervision and administration from Loyola College. She spent 33 years in the Baltimore County public school system as a special education teacher, guidance counselor, guidance chairperson and assistant principal. She has worked extensively with peer programs, conflict resolution skills, college counseling, mental health issues in schools and multi-hazard emergency planning.

John Littrell is a professor and program coordinator of counseling and career development at Colorado State University, Fort Collins. On the topic of brief counseling, he has published extensively, produced five videotapes and presented numerous workshops. He recently coauthored with Jean Peterson a book about an exemplary school counselor, "Portrait and Model of a School Counselor" (Lahaska Press/Houghton Mifflin).

Beth McCann is an elementary counselor in Tallahassee, Fla.. She received her educational specialist degree from the University of Florida. She is a member of the National Board of Certified Counselors. She has served as president for the Florida School Counselor Association and a member of the ASCA Position Statement Committee.

Mary Pat McCartney is a counselor at Bristow Run Elementary School in Prince William County, Virginia. She has been an elementary counselor for 16 years and received her master's degree from George Mason University. McCartney has advocated for school counseling in the Commonwealth of Virginia through several years of leadership on the board of directors for the Virginia School Counselor Association. She also chaired the writing team for Virginia's standards for school counseling programs. She is the elementary vice president for ASCA.

Donna Mazyck is a specialist in school health services and teen pregnancy prevention for the Maryland State Department of Education. She graduated from the University of Pennsylvania with a bachelor's degree in nursing. She received a master's degree in counseling from Loyola College in Maryland and has national certifications as a school nurse and counselor. Mazyck has been a school nurse in high schools, including an alternative school, and has collaborated with school counselors in various capacities, both formal and informal. She and school counselor colleagues have co-led groups for parenting teens, students with recent losses and girls in an alternative school. Mazyck also provides consultation regarding school health services programs in Maryland. Her specific areas of interest are school-based mental health, adolescent health and leadership development.

Brenda Melton is a professional school counselor at Navarro Academy in the San Antonio Independent School District, where she has served since 1982. She received her master's degree in counseling and guidance, with a special education certification, from Trinity University. She also received her bachelor's degree in English, speech/drama and education from Trinity University. Melton has completed postgraduate work at the University of Incarnate Word, Southwest Texas State University and the University of Texas at San Antonio. She is a licensed professional counselor. In addition, Melton has completed 40 hours of training in alternate dispute resolution and 20 hours of training in child abuse and neglect mediation. She is a member of numerous professional organizations, including: ASCA, American Counseling Association, Texas Counseling Association, Texas School Counselor Association and STCA.

Paul Meyers is the principal of Ferndale Elementary School in Ferndale, California. He is the past president of the California Association of School Counselors and the former school counseling consultant for the California Department of Education. Meyers has accumulated more than 20 years of experience in public education as a teacher, school counselor and administrator.

Linda Miller has been a public school educator for 30 years, teaching both regular and special education and serving as a counselor, assistant principal and principal of a large urban middle school. Her last position was the director of school programs and services at the district office of Jefferson County Public Schools, where she supervised more 250 K-12 guidance counselors in Jefferson County Public Schools. Miller recently retired and works part time with the Wallace Leadership for Education Achievement in Districts grant in her district. The focus of her work is collaborating with the University of Louisville to redesign the counselor preparation program for the master's degree in school counseling, and develop and support programs for school counselors. Miller has served on committees at the state level to re-tool state standards and certifications for school counselors. She is a certified trainer for the National Transforming School Counselor Initiative with The Education Trust.

Lynne Miller serves as an assistant professor in the Counseling and Human Development Services Department at Kent State University. She is a certified school counselor in Louisiana and is seeking licensure as a school counselor and professional counselor in Ohio. She is a member of ASCA, the Ohio School Counselor Association, the American and Ohio Counselor Associations, the Association for Counselor Educators and

Supervisors, and the Southern and North Central Association for Counselor Educators and Supervisors. Miller serves on the government relations committee of the Ohio Counseling Association. Her research interests include legal and ethical issues, counselor preparation and supervision.

Amy Milsom is an assistant professor at the University of Iowa and chair of ASCA's Students with Special Needs professional interest network. She has experience as a middle and high school counselor. Milsom's research addresses students with disabilities, school counselor preparation and professional development, and group work in schools.

Bob Milstead is the lead secondary counselor for Orange County Public Schools in Orlando, Fla.. He helps school counselors interpret and implement local, state and national policies and programs. He also offers advice to parents and assists administrators in understanding the valuable role of school counselors. He also develops ways to encourage students to take more challenging courses commensurate with their ability level. A former teacher, Milstead has been a school counselor for more than 25 years. He is a past president of the Orange County Counseling Association and served as treasurer for both the Florida School Counselor Association and the Florida Counseling Association. He also contributed to "Critical Incidents in School Counseling" by Larry Tyson and Paul Pederson.

Patricia Neufeld is an associate professor and interim chair of the Department of Counselor Education and Rehabilitation Programs at Emporia State University. Neufeld is also the president of the Kansas School Counselor Association. She holds certification as a licensed professional clinical counselor, national certified counselor, K-12 school counselor, mediator approved by the State of Kansas and a K-12 vocal music teacher.

Suzan Nolan has been a school counselor for 20 years and has worked at every level from elementary to high school. She has also taught school counseling classes at the graduate level. Recently retired, she is serving her second term on the CACREP board as the ASCA liasion. She served on the ASCA board from 2000-2002. Nolan finds school counseling to be a very challenging and exciting field, especially as school counselors move into the age of accountability where data is so much a part of public school life.

Pam Paisley is a professor and the coordinator of the school counseling program at the University of Georgia. Previously, she lived in North Carolina and worked as a teacher and counselor in public schools and as a counselor educator at Appalachian State University. Paisley has won teaching awards at both Appalachian State University and the University of Georgia. In addition, she has been the principal investigator on a national grant to transform school counseling preparation and practice, and has been president of the Association for Counselor Education and Supervision. Her research interests are in school counseling program development, issues related to children and adolescents, and promoting development for the adults in children's lives. Paisley is committed to social justice and is active in related initiatives at the local, state and national levels.

Pat Partin is a counselor educator at Gardner-Webb University in North Carolina and a former school counselor. Previously, she spent eight years as counselor educator at North Dakota State University, 11 years as a middle and high school counselor in North Carolina and five years a public school teacher. She is a graduate of Wake Forest, the University of North Carolina at Chapel Hill and Duke University. She uses technology in her graduate classes, which can be "blamed" in part on Russ Sabella's "Boot Camp for School Counselors." Patin is a licensed school counselor in North Carolina and a member of numerous professional associations, including: ASCA, the American Counseling Association, AAMCCD, Association for Counselor Education and Supervision, National Career Development Association, North Carolina Counseling Association, North Carolina School Counselor Association, North Carolina Association for Counselor Education and Supervision, NCMCD and North Carolina Career Development Association.

Robert Pate is a professor of counselor education at the University of Virginia Curry. His area of professional practice is life and career planning. He teaches professional issues, and ethical and legal aspects of counseling. Recently Pate has published on the topic of the relationship between spirituality and counseling, and use of the Internet in counselor education. He is a past chair of the National Board for Certified Counselors. Pate has been honored as the 1993 outstanding professor in the Curry School and by election to the Raven Society and Omicron Delta Kappa at the University of Virginia. He has received both the William H. VanHoose and John R. Cook awards from the Virginia Counselors Association. He delivered the 1996 John R. Cook lecture at Virginia Commonwealth University.

Jennifer White-Peters is a school counselor and district test coordinator for Burlington City High School. She has presented at four state counseling conferences and two national ASCA conferences. She has a bachelor's degree in education, English, and gender studies from the College of New Jersey in Ewing, New Jersey, and a master's degree in school counseling from the University of Colorado at Colorado Springs. Her extracurricular challenge has been breaking into freelance writing for women's health publications.

Debra Ponec is a counselor educator at Creighton University. Her work focuses on the role and function of school counselors, relationships that support effective guidance and counseling programs, and curriculum development and assessment. She has made numerous presentations at regional and national conventions and has several publications in state and national journals detailing her research efforts.

Tarrell Portman is an assistant professor in the Department of Counseling, Rehabilitation and Student Development at the University of Iowa. Portman has 15 years of experience in K-12 public schools as a teacher and school counselor. She is a licensed school counselor and a licensed mental health counselor. As the technology coordinator for her department, she supervises the technology instruction required in the school counseling master's degree program. Portman serves on the editorial board for Professional School Counseling.

Marcia Price is a school counselor for approximately 400 students grades six through 12 in Mobridge, South Dakota. She has been a school counselor for 16 years. Her responsibilities include classroom guidance, small groups, individual counseling, and consulting with administrators, staff, parents, and agencies. As an employee of a small school district, Price finds herself wearing many hats, including some in the administrative domain.

Kevin Quinn has been in the educational field more than 27 years, including 14 years as a school counselor. He is a school counselor at South Kingstown High School in Wakefield, Rhode Island. Prior to counseling, Quinn was a business educator and received the Rhode Island Outstanding Business Educator of the Year Award in 1988. Quinn received his bachelor's and master's degrees in education from the University of Rhode Island. He also received a master's degree in counseling and educational psychology from Rhode Island College. He is a member of ASCA, currently serving as the secondary level vice president. He is a member of the Rhode Island School Counselor Association (RISCA) and the National Education Association. He is a past president of RISCA and has served on a number of professional committees. Quinn has diverse experience in the fields of counseling, education and business.

Linda Reynolds is a counselor at The Sanibel School on Sanibel Island, serving kindergarten through eighth grade. She has 23 years of experience, working in the high school setting as well as elementary and middle school. She is a state licensed mental health counselor with a part-time private practice at a local church. Linda is a member of the American Association of Christian Counselors and part of the Focus on the Family network of Christian family counselors. She finds herself discussing spiritual topics with students because they are familiar with her spiritual roots in the community and invite her opinion.

Martin Ritchie is a professor and the coordinator of school counseling at the University of Toledo. He received his master's and doctoral degrees in counselor education from the University of Virginia. After working as a school counselor in Virginia, Ritchie moved to Australia, where he trained school counselors and developed one of the country's first elementary school counselor training programs. He has written and presented on school counseling issues at the state, national and international levels, and has more than 50 publications. He was editor of Counselor Education and Supervision and a past president of the Ohio Counseling Association. He has received the Charles Weaver Award for Distinguished Service and the Herman J. Peters Award for exemplary leadership in the counseling profession. He is co-founder and past president of the International Association for Marriage and Family Counselors.

Joe Rotter is professor in the counselor education program at the University of South Carolina. He is a former school counselor, past editor of the *Elementary School Guidance and Counseling* journal, past president of the Association for Counselor Education and Supervision and former member of the ACA governing council and executive committee. He serves as associate editor of *The Family Journal*.

Russell A. Sabella, Ph.D. is an associate professor in the counseling program at Florida Gulf Coast University. His concentration of research, training and publication includes counseling technology, comprehensive school counseling programs, peer helper programs and training, sexual harassment risk reduction and solution-focused brief counseling. He has authored various articles in journals, magazines and newsletters, including the popular SchoolCounselor.com: A Friendly and Practical Guide to the World Wide Web (2nd edition; Educational Media; 2003). He is well-known for his workshops conducted throughout the country. He is a past president of ASCA.

Judith Sasser is an assistant professor of the counselor education and rehabilitation programs at Emporia State University. She is president-elect of the Kansas Association of Specialists in Group Work. She holds certifications as a school counselor, behavior disorder teacher, adapted physical education teacher and elementary education teacher. She worked in public education for 40 years.

Janna Scarborough is an assistant professor and school counseling program coordinator at Syracuse University. She earned a master's degree in school counseling from Western Carolina University and a doctorate in counselor education from the University of Virginia. She is a former elementary and middle school counselor. Her professional interests include the professional development and identity of school counselors, school counselor process and outcome research, and counseling students with disabilities.

John Schmidt is a professor in the counselor and adult education department at East Carolina University. He has been a teacher, school counselor (K-12), system director, state coordinator of school counseling and university department chair. He has authored many articles, manuals, chapters, reviews and books. He has also received numerous professional awards, including the Ella Stephens Barrett Award for leadership in counseling and the Ruth C. McSwain Award for service to the profession, both from the from the North Carolina School Counselor Association. A past president of the North Carolina Counseling Association and the North Carolina Association for Counselor Education and Supervision, he also served two terms on the North Carolina Board of Licensed Professional Counselors.

Chris Sink, Ph.D., is a professor of school counseling and psychology at Seattle Pacific University. He is the former editor of *Professional School Counseling* and continues to serve on the journal's editorial board. For many years, he was an associate editor for the *National Association for Laboratory Schools Journal*. Sink served for many years as a secondary and community college counselor. He has received distinguished service awards by state counseling organizations for his work on fostering comprehensive school counseling programs in the State of Washington. His research and teaching interests focus on the role of school counselors in preventing school violence, encouraging citizenship education, recognizing student spirituality and developing systemic approaches to educational restructuring. Sink works and consults with school districts around the country as a comprehensive school counseling program developer and evaluator.

Gerald Sklare is a professor at the University of Louisville. He has also served as a high school counselor in Michigan, a high school teacher in Japan, and a junior high school teacher and an elementary school teacher in Michigan. Gerald earned his bachelor's, master's and doctoral degrees from Wayne State University in Detroit. He is one of only three people selected to be in the Kentucky Counseling Association's Professional Development Hall of Fame for continued outstanding contributions to the professional development of counselors in Kentucky. Sklare has made more than 200 presentations at national, regional, state and local conferences, school districts and meetings on effective education, group work, counseling techniques and solution-focused brief counseling. He has authored or co-authored more than 20 publications.

Kenny Smith is the counseling department chair and crisis team leader for Thatcher Schools in Thatcher, Arizona. He is the vice president of the western region for ASCA and the outreach chair for the Arizona School Counselor Association (AzSCA). Previously, he was a professional school counselor at Thatcher Schools. Smith has served in many leadership positions with ASCA and AzSCA, including ASCA parliamentarian/bylaws chair and AzSCA president and treasurer. Smith received his master's degree in school guidance counseling from Northern Arizona University and his bachelor's degree in secondary education from Arizona State University. He has presented at numerous professional conferences and is an ASCA National Model trainer, and a True Colors consultant and certified trainer. He is a member of ASCA and AzSCA.

Emily Snyder is the founder of Know Your Options, an educational consulting services company located in Fairfax County, Virginia, that focuses on student advocacy, day and boarding school placements, and the college admission process. She has held numerous educational leadership positions within her community, including serving as her district's representative on the Fairfax County Board of Education. She has worked at the elementary, middle and high school levels in both public and private education and is frequently called upon to advise local, state and federal officials on educational policy issues. She is actively involved in a number of professional organizations. Snyder is an editorial board member of Professional School Counseling and is a frequent presenter at professional development workshops. She received her master's degree in school counseling psychology from Marymount University in Arlington, Virginia and a bachelor's degree in English from Washington and Jefferson College in Washington, Pennsylvania.

Ercell Somerville is a public school counselor in Toledo, Ohio. He received his master of education degree in guidance and counseling form Bowling Green State University, and his teaching certificate and bachelor's degree in communication from Purdue University. Somerville is the parliamentarian of the Ohio School Counseling Association and has been active on its board since 1998, serving in positions such as district representative and executive board secretary. He is past president of the Northwest Ohio Counseling Association and has active on its board since 1997. Somerville is a certified school guidance counselor and an LPC.

Angie Stansell is a school counselor and certified psychometrist at Hatton High School in Town Creek, Alabama. Previously, she was a secondary teacher and community college career/admissions counselor. She has also worked with victims of domestic violence, serving for two years as a counselor for children's program and teaching parenting skills to victims. Her work in these grant-funded programs led to experience writing grants and seeking resources. In addition, her work in a rural school district has underscored for her the value of networking with other school counselors.

Renee Staton is an associate professor in the counseling psychology program at James Madison University. She has worked as a public school teacher, school-based mental health practitioner, community counselor and counselor educator. In all of those roles, she relies on the benefits, challenges and joys of inter-professional collaboration.

Reid Stevens has been a counselor educator for 23 years and a practicing counselor for 31 years at the University of Southern Maine in Gorham.

Carolyn Stone, Ph.D., is an associate professor at the University of North Florida where she teaches and researches in the area of school counselors in the accountability climate of educational reform, and legal and ethical issues. Prior to becoming a counselor educator in 1995, she spent 22 years with the Duval County Public Schools in Jacksonville, Fla., where she served as guidance supervisor for 225 counselors, an elementary and high school counselor, and an elementary and secondary teacher. She serves as ASCA's ethics chair and is the immediate past president of the Florida Counseling Association. She has authored more than 30 publications and delivered more than 200 workshops on legal and ethical issues, and school counselors as leaders, advocates and systemic change agents.

Alice Cryer-Sumler works in accountability for the Louisiana Department of Education. Her primary responsibility is to assist schools with improving student achievement. Prior to that, she supervised counselors in the St. Charles Parish School System.

Warren Throckmorton is associate professor of psychology and director of counseling at Grove City College. He is past president of the American Mental Health Counselors Association (AMHCA) and current chair of the ethics committee for AMHCA.

Janice Tkaczyk is the guidance director for the Cape Cod Regional Technical High School in Harwich, Massachusetts. She supervises a staff of 10, including three school counselors, two secretaries, and five special program staff. The latter operate a program for 40 under motivated eighth graders who attend school from January to June each year. She has a caseload of about 175 students, working with one grade and following the students through to graduation. Her school uses the ASCA National Standards and the ASCA National Model to implement a program demonstrates increased effectiveness. She has been a school counselor for 28 years.

Toni Tollerud, Ph.D., is a professor of counseling in the Department of Counseling, Adult and Higher Education at Northern Illinois University. She is also the director of the Illinois School Counselors' Academy. As a consultant, she advocates for the role of the school counselor, including helping counselors redesign their programs around state and national standards, and promoting change with administrators. Tollerud has received numerous awards, including Illinois School Counselor's Association Advocate of the Year Award in 2000 and ASCA's Advocate of the Year in 2001. She holds numerous counseling certifications and is a graduate of the University of Iowa.

Deborah Trust is a school counselor at Paul Laurence Dunbar Middle School in Fort Myers, Fla.. She is a graduate of the University of Massachusetts and earned a master's degree in counseling and consultation from Keene State College. She was a national advisor for Future Homemakers of America-Home Economics Related Occupations and was chosen for Who's Who Among America's Teachers in 1996. She leads the middle school crisis response team for the Lee County school district and is a national certified trainer for crisis prevention institutes.

Bob Tyra works as a consultant in guidance and counseling for the Los Angeles County Office of Education. He is a former middle, high school and vocational counselor. He has also worked as an adjunct faculty member in the California State University system and administrator in alternative education settings.

Tom Valesky is a professor in the educational leadership program at Florida Gulf Coast University. He previously chaired the educational administration and supervision program at the University of Memphis. He has authored numerous publications on school-based decision-making and school finance. He has been a teacher, high school counselor, elementary principal, superintendent, researcher and professor. He served as superintendent of the American School of San Salvador, El Salvador, and the Anglo-American School in Sophia, Bulgaria for the U.S. and British embassies. He earned his doctorate degree in educational administration and supervision from Memphis State University (now University of Memphis). He has served as president of the Southern Regional Council on Educational Administration and as a member of the executive board of the National Council of Professors of Educational Administration.

Barbara Varenhorst works in peer helping/peer ministry private consulting. She has served as a teacher, counselor and psychologist in the Palo Alto School District. She started the first peer counseling program in the Palo Alto school district in 1970. She is a founder of the National Peer Helpers Association, serving as its second president, and is a past president of the California Peer Programs Association. An author of three curriculum guides related to peer counseling, she received her doctorate from Stanford University in counseling psychology.

Ann Vernon is professor and coordinator of counseling at the University of Northern Iowa in Cedar Falls, where she teaches courses on counseling children and adolescents. In addition, she has a private practice and specializes in working with children, adolescents and their parents. She has written numerous books on the subject of counseling children. She is the vice president of the Albert Ellis Board of Trustees and the director of the Midwest Center for Rational Emotive Behavior Therapy (REBT). She routinely presents workshops on applications of REBT in the U.S., Canada, South America and Holland. She has also held various leadership positions in professional associations.

José Villalba is an assistant professor in the Department of Counseling and Educational Development at the University of North Carolina at Greensboro. He received his doctorate degree in counselor education from the University of Florida. Previously, he was an assistant professor in the Department of Counseling at Indiana State University and a school counselor in suburban and urban settings throughout Florida. His teaching interests include multicultural counseling, career development and counseling, group counseling and school counseling internship supervision. His research interests include addressing the academic success of Latino students through school counseling interventions, as well as establishing relevant school counseling interventions specifically aimed at Latino school children living in rural and nonrural burgeoning Latino communities.

Colin Ward is an associate professor at Winona State University. He has more than 20 years of experience as an educator and counselor with an interest in school counselor training, strength-based approaches to counseling, and public policy for promoting the counseling profession and social mental health. Ward has a bachelor's degree from the University of Northern Colorado, a master's degree from Winona State University and a doctoral degree from Oregon State University. He also is actively involved in state and national counselor organizations as well as with The Education Trust Initiative for Transforming School Counselor Training.

Linda Webb is a counselor educator at Florida Atlantic University. She received her doctorate from the University of Florida after working as a teacher, school counselor and guidance director at the elementary and high school levels for 20 years. Webb works with "counselors in training" as well as those in the field to implement comprehensive guidance and counseling programs that help all students become more academically and socially successful. Embedded in this type of preparation is the critical role of data in maintaining effective programs over time.

Bill Weikel is professor emeritus at Morehead State University in Kentucky and former owner of Eastern Kentucky Counseling and Rehabilitation Services. He teaches as an adjunct professor at Florida Gulf Coast University and maintains a private consulting practice in Cape Coral, Fla.. Weikel is a graduate of the University of Florida and past president of the Kentucky Counseling Association and American Mental Health Counselors Association. He has chaired many committees for the American Counseling Association and is past chair of ACA's southern region. He was the founding editor of the Journal of Mental Health Counseling and author of numerous articles and books. Bill recently completed a three-year term on the editorial board of the Journal of Counseling and Development. He is an LPC, NCC, CCMHC and ACS.

Jim Whitledge is the counseling and guidance program consultant for Oakland Schools, an intermediate school district in Oakland County, Michigan. Previously, Whitledge was on the faculty and coordinated the school counseling program at the University of Detroit – Mercy. He served as a professional school counselor for public schools in Farmington, Michigan. Whitledge has been active in leadership with professional counselor associations at the local, state and national levels, having served as president of ASCA and the Oakland Counseling Association. He chairs the ethics committee of the Michigan School Counselor Association. Whitledge serves on the task force to revise the Michigan Comprehensive Guidance and Counseling Program to align with the ASCA National Model. He received his doctorate from Mississippi State University.

Rhonda Williams is an assistant professor in the counseling and human services department at the University of Colorado – Colorado Springs. She spent 25 years in public education as a school counselor, where she received state and national Middle School Counselor of the Year awards. Rhonda has been active in the professional school counseling organizations at the state and national levels. She focuses on connecting community with education programs and initiating, implementing and coordinating prevention and intervention programs for youth.

Laurie Williamson is an associate professor and the coordinator of the school counseling program at Appalachian State University in Boone, North Carolina. She is a licensed professional counselor, a nationally certified school counselor and an approved clinical supervisor. She has more than 25 years of counseling experience, with 10 years specific to school counseling. She has worked in schools on three continents and considers herself fortunate to have received quality supervision from a long list of psychiatrists, psychologists, therapists, professors and school counselors.

Sally Woodruff is the district special services director and behavior consultant for Hellgate School District in Missoula, Montana. At Hellgate, she supervises a support staff of 30 and oversees an on-site county school-based mental health program. She has a doctorate in education, is licensed as an LCPC with the state of Montana and is certified as a school counselor and a school psychologist. She is also an adjunct professor with the University of Montana, teaching in the graduate counseling program. She is a past president of the Montana School Counselor Association. She works extensively with students with challenging behaviors and in environments with challenging characteristics.

Carlos Zalaquett is an assistant professor in the counselor education program at the University of South Florida. He is an author and national and international presenter on the skills and abilities necessary to succeed in the 21st century, focusing on the importance of teaching technological competencies to counselors. He is a recognized author of both traditional publications and Web pages, including "Succeeding in the 21st Century: A Qualitative Analysis" and "The Successful Latino Student" Web pages.